D1099362

DESIGN FOR THE REAL WORLD

Human Ecology and Social Change

Second Edition Completely Revised
With 121 illustrations

VICTOR PAPANEK

 Thames & Hudson

First paperback edition published in the United Kingdom in 1985 by
Thames & Hudson Ltd, 181A High Holborn, London WC1V 7QX

www.thamesandhudson.com

Reprinted 2004

British Library Cataloguing-in-Publication Data
A catalogue record for this book is available from the British Library
ISBN 0-500-27358-8

Printed and bound in China

This volume is dedicated to my students, for what they have taught me.

Contents

Preface to the First Edition

There are professions more harmful than industrial design, but only a very few of them. And possibly only one profession is phonier. Advertising design, in persuading people to buy things they don't need, with money they don't have, in order to impress others who don't care, is probably the phoniest field in existence today. Industrial design, by concocting the tawdry idiocies hawked by advertisers, comes a close second. Never before in history have grown men sat down and seriously designed electric hairbrushes, rhinestone-covered shoe horns, and mink carpeting for bathrooms, and then drawn up elaborate plans to make and sell these gadgets to millions of people. Before (in the "good old days"), if a person liked killing people, he had to become a general, purchase a coal mine, or else study nuclear physics. Today, industrial design has put murder on a mass-production basis. By designing criminally unsafe automobiles that kill or maim nearly one million people around the world each year, by creating whole new species of permanent garbage to clutter up the landscape, and by choosing materials and processes that pollute the air we breath, designers have become a dangerous breed. And the skills needed in these activities are carefully taught to young people.

In this age of mass production when everything must be planned and designed, design has become the most powerful tool with which man shapes his tools and environments (and, by extension, society and himself). This demands high social and moral responsibility from the designer. It also demands greater understanding of the people by those who practice design and more insight into the design process by the public. Not a single volume on the responsibility of the designer, no book on design that considers the public in this way, has ever been published anywhere.

In February of 1968 *Fortune* magazine published an article that foretold the end of the industrial design profession. Predictably, designers reacted with scorn and alarm. But I feel that the main arguments of the *Fortune* article are valid. It is about time that industrial design, *as we have come to know it*, should cease to exist. As long as design concerns itself with confecting trivial "toys for adults," killing machines with gleaming tailfins, and "sexed-up" shrouds for typewriters, toasters, telephones, and computers, it has lost all reason to exist.

Design must become an innovative, highly creative, cross-disciplinary tool responsive to the true needs of men. It must be more research oriented, and we must stop defiling the earth itself with poorly designed objects and structures.

For the last ten years or so, I have worked with designers and student design teams in many parts of the world. Whether on an island in Finland, in a village school in Indonesia, an air-conditioned office overlooking Tokyo, a small fishing village in Norway, or where I teach in the United States, I have tried to give a clear picture of what it means to design within a social context. But there is only so much one can say and do, and, even in Marshall McLuhan's electronic era, sooner or later one must fall back on the printed word.

Included in the enormous amount of literature we have about design are hundreds of "how-to-do-it" books that address themselves exclusively to an audience of other designers or (with the gleam of textbook sales in the author's eye) to students. The social context of design, as well as the public and lay reader, is damned by omission.

Looking at the books on design in seven languages, covering the walls of my home, I realized that the one book I wanted to read, the one book I most wanted to hand to my fellow students and designers, was missing. Because our society makes it crucial for designers to understand clearly the social, economic, and political background of what they do, my problem was not just one of personal frustration. So I decided to write the kind of book that I'd like to read.

This book is also written from the viewpoint that there is something basically wrong with the whole concept of patents and copyrights. If I design a toy that provides therapeutic exercise for handicapped children, then I think it is unjust to delay the release of the design by a year and a half, going through a patent application. I feel that ideas are plentiful and cheap, and it is wrong to make money from the needs of others. I have been very lucky in persuading many of my students to accept this view. Much of what you will find as design examples throughout this book has never been patented. In fact, quite the opposite strategy prevails: in many cases students and I have made measured drawings of, say, a play environment for blind children, written a description of how to build it simply, and then mimeographed drawings and all. If any agency, anywhere, will write in, my students will send them all the instructions free of charge. I try to do the same myself. An actual case history may explain this principle better.

Shortly after leaving school nearly two decades ago, I designed the coffee table shown on page xii based on entirely new concepts of structure and assembly. I gave a photograph and drawings of the table to the magazine *Sunset*, which printed it as a do-it-yourself project in the February 1953 issue. Almost at once a Southern California furniture firm, Modern Color, Inc., "ripped-off" the design and went into production. Admittedly they sold about eight thousand tables in 1953. But now it is 1970. Modern Color has long since gone bankrupt, but *Sunset* recently reprinted the design in their book *Furniture You Can Build*, so people are still building the table for themselves.

Thomas Jefferson himself entertained grave doubts as to the philosophy inherent in a patent grant. At the time of his invention of the hemp-break, he took positive steps to prevent

"Transite Table," author's design. Courtesy: Sunset Magazine.

being granted a patent and wrote to a friend: "*Something of this kind has been so long wanted by cultivators of hemp that as soon as I can speak of its effect with certainty, I shall probably describe it anonymously in the public papers in order to forestall the prevention of its use by some interloping patentee.*"

I hope this book will bring new thinking to the design process and start an intelligent dialogue between designer and consumer. It is organized into two parts, each six chapters long. The first part, "How It Is," attempts to define and criticize design as it is practiced and taught today. The six chapters of "How It Could Be" give the reader at least *one* newer way of looking at things in each chapter.

I have received inspiration and help in many parts of the world, over many years, in forming the ideas and ideals that made the writing of this book so necessary. I have spent large chunks of time living among Navahos, Eskimos, and Balinese, as well as spending nearly one-third of each of the last seven years in Finland and Sweden, and I feel that this has shaped my thoughts.

In Chapter Four, "Do-It-Yourself Murder," I am indebted to the late Dr. Robert Lindner of Baltimore, with whom I corresponded for a number of years, for his concept of the "Triad of Limitations." The idea of *kymmenykset* was first formulated by me during a design conference on the island of Suomenlinna in Finland in 1968. The word *Ujamaa*, as a simple way of saying "we work together and help each other" (without colonialism or neocolonial exploitation), was supplied in Africa during my UNESCO work.

Mr. Harry M. Philo, an attorney from Detroit, is responsible for many of the examples of unsafe design cited in Chapter Five.

Much in Chapter Eleven, "The Neon Blackboard," reflects similar thinking by my two good friends Bob Malone, of Connecticut, and Bucky Fuller.

Four people are entitled to special thanks. Walter Muhonen of Costa Mesa, California, because the example set by his life has kept me going, even when my goals seemed unattainable. He taught me the real meaning of the Finnish word *sisu*. Patrick Decker of College Station, Texas, for persuading me to write this book. "Pelle" Olof Johansson of Halmstad and Stockholm, Sweden, for arguing the fine points of design with me, long into many nights, and for making the actual completion of this book's first Swedish edition possible. My wife, Harlanne, helped me to write what I wanted to say, instead of writing what seemed to sound good. Her searching questions, criticism, and encouragement often made all the difference.

The incisive thinking and the help of my editor, Verne Moberg, have made this book, revised from the Swedish original edition, sounder and more direct.

In an environment that is screwed up visually, physically, and chemically, the best and simplest thing that architects, industrial designers, planners, etc., could do for humanity would be *to stop working entirely*. In all pollution, designers are implicated at least partially. But in this book I take a more affirmative view: it seems to me that we can go beyond not working at all, and work positively. Design can and must become a way in which young people can participate in changing society.

As socially and morally involved designers, we must address ourselves to the needs of a world with its back to the wall, while the hands on the clock point perpetually to one minute before twelve.

Helsinki—Singaradja (Bali)—Stockholm
1963–1971

Preface to the Second Edition

Design For the Real World was written between 1963 and 1970. Originally published in Sweden, some updating readied the manuscript for publication in the United States in 1971. During the following two years it appeared in England and in translation in Germany, Denmark, Italy, Finland, Yugoslavia, Japan, France, Spain, and Latin America. Since then it has been translated into twelve more languages, making it the most widely read book on design in the world. After more than a decade it seemed a good time to add new material that reflects a dynamically changed world and the reaction of a profession that is still slow to respond to change, to revise old material, and to explain the social and ethical roles of design more fully.

It is difficult to think oneself back to the late 1960s and early 1970s, when *Design For the Real World* was rejected by several publishers for using such unfamiliar concepts as "ecology," "ethology," or "the Third World." Those were the days of *The Greening of America,* a book that falsely persuaded many that the average age of people in the United States was declining (the reverse is true), when the concept of unchecked growth was still advocated by the majority. Women's rights, pollution, the "graying of America," mass unemployment, extensive cutbacks in the automobile and steel industries in the United States, and the global race toward a thermonuclear Armageddon had still not been accepted as real by most people.

On its first American appearance, the ideas in this book were derided, made fun of, or savagely attacked by the design

establishment. One professional design magazine printed a review that classified some of my suggestions, such as greater
energy savings, the return to sailing ships and lighter-than-air
craft, and research into alternative power sources, as "idiosyncratic pipedreams" and dismissed the book as "an attack
on Detroit mixed with a utopian concern for minorities." I
was asked to resign from my professional organization in the
United States, and, when the Centre Georges Pompidou
planned an exhibition of American industrial design, my
professional society threatened to boycott it if any of my work
was included. The tin-can radio (see page 225) was especially
ridiculed and earned me the title of "the Garbage Can Designer."

Design for the Real World appeared in most European
bookstores together with two other books, Alvin Toffler's *Future Shock* and my good friend Fritz Schumacher's *Small Is
Beautiful*. There is an important communality among these
three volumes. Toffler lucidly describes an ever changing future and how we might make our peace with continuous
change. But the possiblity of reversing the increasing mechanization of mankind (". . . a variable environment demands
flexible behavior and reverses the trend to its mechanization,"
says Arthur Koestler) was not fully grasped by Toffler. Schumacher saw this more clearly and agreed with my own for-
mulation that *nothing big works*.

Maybe we learn best from disasters. Detroit is floundering
in high unemployment, and, with three oil crises, four unusually cold winters, two major droughts leading to water
shortages, extensive floods, a global energy shortage, and a
major recession behind us, this book has been slowly accepted
even in the United States over the last thirteen years. Besides
being bought by consumers, it has become a required text in
design and architectural schools and is now used in anthropology, behavioral science, English, and industrial-manage-
ment courses at many universities.

For the second edition several chapters of *Design for the
Real World* have been rewritten entirely. All chapters have

been updated and much new material has been added. I decided to retain many of the predictions I made in the first edition. Some of the things I stated in 1970 are by now embarrassingly wide of the mark. Others have become true in the intervening thirteen years, and both outcomes are discussed. Still other predictions I made in 1970 are just now on the point of becoming reality: simpler packaging, energy-saving devices and alternative power sources, ecological understanding, the return to sailing ships (although now with computer-steered rigging), the reemergence of lighter-than-air craft. Other forecasts still await fulfillment. What I wrote about U.S. automobiles has become all too true—with disastrous consequences for millions of workers and their arrogant bosses in Detroit—but the same rethinking in the field of housing is long overdue. We have learned to think of large cars as gas-guzzlers; similarly we must learn to see our homes as the space-guzzlers they are. With high energy costs for heating and air conditioning, large houses, enormous glass walls, or guest rooms that stand unused most of the time are no longer feasible.

Most of the original pictures and diagrams have been retained; in some cases new illustrations have been added to make a point more clear. I draw the reader's attention to a revision of my definition of design (see Chapter One). The Bibliography has been brought up to date and expanded.

In 1971 I moved to Northern Europe and have lived and worked there, with lengthy tours of duty to developing countries, for some years. Much of what I wrote about design for the Third World in this book's first edition now seems somewhat naive. Nonetheless I have decided to let some of my observations stand in the second edition because they illustrate the somewhat patronizing viewpoint many of us had about the poorer countries more than a decade ago. While we fought against colonialism and exploitation, I and others failed to appreciate how much we could *learn* in the places we had set out to teach. While mass housing designed and built by young Scandinavian designers in Nigeria stands unused and unusable, these same young people have learned important lessons about how housing patterns can serve extended families, develop neighborliness, or cement social ties into strong and lasting communities. The road between the rich nations of the North and the poor southern half of the globe is a two-way street. It is reassuring to understand that designers in the Third World can solve their own problems free from interference by "experts" imported for two weeks.

Still, some facts are devastating: more than three times as many people live in the Third World as in developed countries. They earn, on average, less than one-tenth of the income of the people of the rich nations; their life expectancy is only half that of those in the North. They can spend only three cents (per capita) on public health to every dollar spent in the developed world, and every dollar spent per capita in the North on education is matched by only six and one-half cents in the Third World. Even these bare statistics cannot begin to tell the story of disease, malnutrition, starvation, and despair that stalks the lives of 2.6 billion people in the poor nations.

Two classes of reason are usually advanced for why we in the technologically developed part of the world ought to help those in need. One of these classes relates to our own security, the other is ethical.

The primary security argument is fallacious: the fear that more than three billion people will attack us in our homes—a sort of apocalyptic reprise of the ghetto uprisings in the 1960s but on a global scale—is absurd. Even the most developed countries find modern warfare too expensive.

Some people—no doubt worried by recent immigration from Nicaragua, Haiti, Vietnam, and so forth—are actually afraid that millions of people from the poor countries will move North. This second "security" argument is as wrongheaded as the first. People in all countries (poor or rich) are tied to their culture and native soil in many ways and have no strong motivation to become exiles in a strange society.

There are valid ethical and moral reasons to help the poor

countries. On a pragmatic level, a world of shrinking distances, fast air travel, and instant global communication cannot afford to have three-fourths of its inhabitants diseased, starving, or dying from neglect. The ethics of the situation are clear: we are all citizens of one global village and we have an obligation to those in need. How to bring our philosophical and moral reasoning to bear on the widening economic distance between North and South is an issue simultaneously pressing and complex. We now know that throwing money, food, or supplies at an underdeveloped country doesn't work. Neither does the wholesale export of "turnkey factories" or "instant technical experts." The experiences of Soviet aid to China, U.S. developmental programs in Iran, Chinese help to Tanzania, and Cuban intervention in Angola—to name but a few examples—have made that clear.

Massive foreign financial intervention could not eliminate poverty in India—conversely the *lack* of such aid helped China. In 1956 Mao Tse-Tung established a policy of "regeneration through our own efforts" in the People's Republic of China. The results were far-reaching social changes and, most importantly, a change in the consciousness of the people, which led to education and the development of autonomous, decentralized solutions.

It is a curious paradox that those "poor" countries most emphatic in their call for aid are materially rich. Their wealth resides in natural resources and, in the southern half of the globe, enormous sources of alternative energy. It is south of the equator that solar power can be tapped most easily. It is there that geothermal power, biomass conversion, and alternative fuels (Brazil runs nearly eighty percent of its cars on alcohol derived from sugar cane) can be found. The desert regions present the greatest opportunities for heat-exchange-based energy, with temperatures varying by as much as forty degrees between night and day. Again it is the southern half of the globe where tropical rainfalls are predictable and where wind power is strongest.

Aid to developing countries engenders the hatred a cripple

feels toward his crutch. What is needed is cooperation that works both ways, a strong movement to restrict the financial and systems dependence of poor countries. A tough reappraisal by both sides is long overdue. Outsiders can make education and the pharmacology of birth control available, but population control must emerge from the will of the people themselves. Self-reliance is a basic-training course that each people must go through on its own.

There is much we in turn can learn from developing countries about living patterns, small-scale technology, reuse and recycling of materials, and a closer fit between man and nature. Nonwestern medicine and social organization are other fields we can explore cooperatively.

The Soviet Union, the United States, and Japan have this in common: they attempt to sell and impose their present state of development on the poor countries. It is a bad fit. The United States and Russia have reached their present stages of development through many years of identity building, education and self-reliance. The cliché "You don't hand a loaded gun to a baby" is apt in this circumstance. It makes no sense to hand a fully automated factory to a country with an untrained, labor-intensive economy or rock television stations and Star Wars video games to a preliterate society.

My experience over the last thirteen years has shown me that autonomy and self-reliance are being realized in the Third World. The "Establishment" together with its tame experts and a small power elite that has been trained abroad may still pray for salvation from the International Monetary Fund— but the people in the villages, farmers, workers, designers, and innovators in the Third World are increasingly coming to realize that poverty is not destiny but a challenge that can be faced successfully.

The original dedication in this book, "This volume is dedicated to my students, for what they have taught me," still stands. But I would like to dedicate this revised edition also to designers, architects, farmers, workers, young people, and students in Brazil, Cameroun, Chad, Colombia, Greenland,

Guatemala, Indonesia, Mexico, Niger, Nigeria, Papua New Guinea, Tanzania, Uganda, and Yugosalvia with whom I have worked and who demonstrated to me that poverty is the mother of innovation. Examples of this are given throughout this book.

The developing countries and all the rest of us must cooperate by combining simpler and small-scale approaches with new technologies, which for the first time make decentralized and human-size development feasible. The poor in the developing world, together with the poor and handicapped in the rich nations and with all those of us who must make wiser choices about the tools, systems, and artifacts we make and use, form one global constituency. The challenge lies in together exploring all functions appropriate to the last years of this century. Out of this exciting search for the interplay between beauty, cultures, and design alternatives will come a new and sensuous frugality.

Penang (Malaysia)—Dartington Hall, Devon—
Bogotá (Colombia)
1981–1984

Part One

HOW IT IS

1

What Is Design?

A Definition of the Function Complex

The wheel's hub holds thirty spokes
Utility depends on the hole through the hub.
The potter's clay forms a vessel
It is the space within that serves.
A house is built with solid walls
The nothingness of window and door alone renders it us-
  able,
That which exists may be transformed
What is nonexistent has boundless uses.

LAO-TSE

All men are designers. All that we do, almost all the time, is design, for design is basic to all human activity. The planning and patterning of any act toward a desired, foreseeable end constitutes the design process. Any attempt to separate design, to make it a thing-by-itself, works counter to the fact that design is the primary underlying matrix of life. Design is composing an epic poem, executing a mural, painting a masterpiece, writing a concerto. But design is also cleaning and reorganizing a desk drawer, pulling an impacted tooth, baking an apple pie, choosing sides for a backlot baseball game, and educating a child.

3

Design is the conscious and intuitive effort to impose meaningful order.

It is only in recent years that to add the phrase "and intuitive" seemed crucial to my definition of design. Consciousness implies intellectualization, cerebration, research, and analysis. The sensing/feeling part of the creative process was missing from my original definition. Unfortunately intuition itself is difficult to define as a process or ability. Nonetheless it affects design in a profound way. For through intuitive insight we bring into play impressions, ideas, and thoughts we have unknowingly collected on a subconscious, unconscious, or preconscious level. The "how" of intuitive reasoning in design doesn't readily yield to analysis but can be explained through example. Watson and Crick intuitively felt that the underlying structure of the DNA chain would express itself most elegantly through a spiral. Beginning with this intuition, they began their research. Their instinctive precognition paid off: a spiral it is!

Our delight in the order we find in frost flowers on a window pane, in the hexagonal perfection of a honeycomb, in leaves, or in the architecture of a rose, reflects man's preoccupation with pattern. We constantly try to understand our ever-changing highly complex existence by seeking order in it. And what we seek we find. There are underlying biological systems to which we respond on levels that are often unconscious or subconscious. The reason we enjoy things in nature is that we see an economy of means, simplicity, elegance, and an essential rightness there. But all these natural templates, rich in pattern, order, and beauty, are not the result of decision making by mankind and therefore lie beyond our definition. We may call them "design," as if we were speaking of a tool or artifact created by humans. But this is to falsify the issue, since the beauty we see in nature is something we ascribe to processes we often don't understand. We enjoy the beautiful red and orange tones of maple leaves in the autumn, but our enchantment is caused by a process of dissolution, the death of the leaves. The streamlining of a trout's body may be aesthetically satisfying to us, but for the trout it is a means for swimming efficiency. The profound beauty of spiral growth patterns found in sunflowers, pineapples, pine cones, or the arrangement of leaves on a stem can be explained by the Fibonacci sequence (each number is the sum of the two previous members: 1, 1, 2, 3, 5, 8, 13, 21, 34 . . .), but for the plant the arrangement serves only to improve photosynthesis by exposing a maximum of its surface. Similarly, the beauty we find in the tail of a peacock, although no doubt even more attractive to a peahen, is the result of intraspecific selection (which, in the case cited, may ultimately prove fatal to the species).

Intent is also missing from the random-order system of a pile of coins. If, however, we move the coins around and arrange them according to size and shape, we impose our intent and may produce some sort of symmetrical alignment. A symmetrical-order system is a favorite of small children, unusually primitive peoples, and some of the insane, because it is so easy to understand. Further shifting of the coins will produce an infinite number of asymmetrical arrangements that require a higher level of sophistication and greater participation on the part of the viewer to be understood and appreciated. While the aesthetic values of the symmetrical and asymmetrical designs differ, both can give ready satisfaction since the underlying intent is clear. Only marginal patterns (those lying in the threshold area between symmetry and asymmetry) fail to make the designer's intent clear. The ambiguity of such "threshold cases" produces a feeling of unease in the viewer. There are an infinite number of possible satisfactory arrangements of the coins. Importantly, none of these is the one right design, though some may seem better than others.

Shoving coins around on a board is a design act in miniature because design as a problem-solving activity can never, by definition, yield the one right answer: it will always produce an infinite number of answers, some "righter" and some "wronger." The "rightness" of any design solution will depend on the meaning with which we invest the arrangement.

Design must be meaningful. And "meaningful" replaces such semantically loaded expressions as "beautiful," "ugly," "cute," "disgusting," "glamorous," "realistic," "obscure," "abstract," and "nice," labels convenient to a bankrupt mind when confronted by Picasso's "Guernica," Frank Lloyd Wright's *Fallingwater*, Beethoven's *Eroica*, Stravinsky's *Le Sacre du Printemps*, Joyce's *Finnegan's Wake*. In all of these we respond to that which has meaning.

The mode of action by which a design fulfils its purpose is its function.

The American sculptor Horatio Greenough first stated that "form follows function" in 1739. His phrase became a battle cry for the architect Louis Sullivan roughly 100 years ago and was restated as "form and function are one" by Frank Lloyd Wright. Both statements have contributed to a seeming divorce between that which works well and that which is beautiful. The implication in "form follows function" is that as long as the functional requirements are satisfied form will follow and seem pleasing. Others have put the cart before the horse and misread these statements to imply that "ideal" form will always work well.

The concept that what *works* well will of necessity *look* well has been the lame excuse for all the sterile, operating-room-like furniture and implements of the twenties and thirties. A dining table of the period might have a top, well proportioned in glistening white marble, the legs carefully nurtured for maximum strength with minimum materials in gleaming stainless steel. But the first reaction on encountering such a table is to lie down on it and have your appendix extracted. Nothing about the table says: "Dine off me." *Le style international* and *die neue Sachlichkeit* have let us down rather badly in terms of human value. Le Corbusier's house *la machine à habiter* and the packing-crate houses evolved by the

Dutch *de Stijl* movement reflect a perversion of aesthetics and
utility.

"Should I design it to be functional," the students say, "or
to be aesthetically pleasing?" This is the most often heard, the
most understandable, and yet the most mixed-up question in
design today. "Do you want it to look good or to work?" Bar-
ricades are erected between what are really just two of the
many aspects of function. A simple diagram shows the dynamic actions and relationships that make up the function
complex.

It is now possible to go through the six parts of the function
complex and to define each of its aspects.

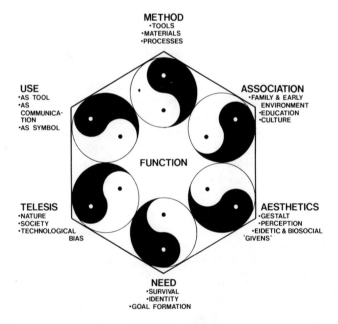

The function complex. The Yin-Yang monad appears at each of the
six aspects, indicating the soft-hard, feeling-thinking, intuitive-in-
tellectual mix, which determines each of these six evaluative criteria.

Method: The interaction of *tools, processes,* and *materials.* An honest use of materials, never making the material seem that which it is not, is good method. Materials and tools must be used optimally, never using one material where another can do the job less expensively, more efficiently, or both. The steel beam in a house, painted a fake wood grain; the molded plastic bottle designed to look like expensive blown glass; the 1967 New England cobbler's bench reproduction ("worm holes $1 extra") dragged into a twentieth-century living room to provide dubious footing for martini glass and ashtray—these are all perversions of materials, tools, and processes. And the discipline of using a suitable method extends naturally to the field of the fine arts as well. Alexander Calder's "The Horse," a compelling sculpture at the Museum of Modern Art in New York, was shaped by the particular material in which it was conceived. Calder decided that boxwood would give him the specific color and texture he desired in his sculpture. But box-wood comes only in rather narrow planks of small sizes. (It is for this reason that it traditionally has been used in the making of small boxes.) The only way he could make a fair-sized piece of sculpture out of a wood that only comes in small pieces was to interlock them somewhat in the manner of a child's toy. "The Horse," then, is a piece of sculpture, the aesthetic of which was largely determined by method. The final piece was done in walnut at the request of one of the museum's patrons.

Alexander Calder: "The Horse" (1982). Walnut, 15 1/2 × 34 3/4. Collection The Museum of Modern Art, New York. Acquired through the Lillie P. Bliss Bequest.

When early Finnish and Swedish settlers in what is now Delaware decided to build, they had at their disposal trees and axes. The *material* was a round tree trunk, the *tool* an axe, and the *process* a simple "kerf cut" into the log. The natural result of this combination of tools, materials, and processes was a log cabin.

Paolo Soleri's desert home in twentieth-century Arizona is as much the result of tools, materials, and processes as the log cabin. The peculiar viscosity of the desert sand where Soleri built his home made his unique method possible. Selecting a mound of desert sand, Soleri criss-crossed it with V-shaped channels cut into the sand, making a pattern somewhat like the ribs of a whale. Then he poured concrete in the channels, forming, when set, the roof-beams of the house-to-be. He added a concrete skin for the roof and bulldozed the sand out from underneath to create the living space itself. He com-

Paolo Soleri: Carved earth form for the original drafting room and interior of the ceramics workshop. Photos by Stuart Weiner.

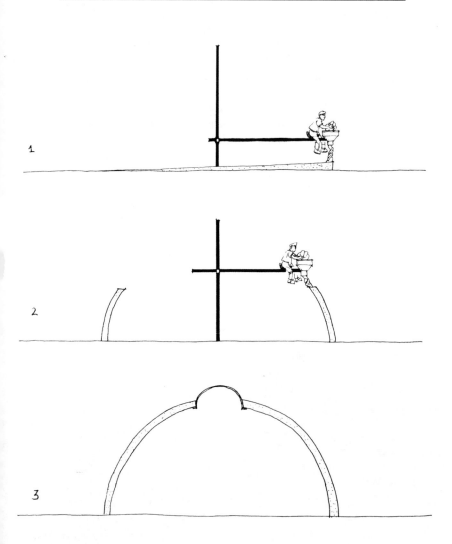

The self-generating styrofoam dome. Schematic drawing of three stages in the process. Drawing by Smit Vajaramant.

pleted the structure by setting in car windows garnered from automobile junkyards. Soleri's creative yet honest use of tools, materials, and processes was a *tour de force* that gave us a radically new building method.

Dow Chemical's "self-generating" styrofoam dome is the product of another radical approach to building methods. The foundation of the building can be a twelve-inch-high circular retaining wall. To this wall a four-inch-wide strip of styro-foam is attached, which raises as it goes around the wall from zero to four inches in height, forming the base for the spiral dome. On the ground in the center, motorized equipment operates a spinning boom, with an operator and a heat welding machine. The boom moves around, somewhat like a compass drawing a circle, and rises with a spiraling motion at about three feet a minute. Gradually it moves in towards the center. A man sitting in the saddle feeds an "endless" four-by-four-inch strip of styrofoam into the welding machine, which heat-welds it to the previously hand-laid styrofoam. As the feeding mechanism follows its circular, rising, and ever-diminishing diameter path, this spiral process creates the dome. Finally, a hole thirty-six inches in diameter is left in the top, through

Medical clinic designed using seven interlinked styrofoam domes, Lafayette, Indiana.

which man, mast, and movement arm can be removed. The hole is then closed with a clear plastic pop-in bubble or a vent. At this point the structure is translucent, soft, and entirely without doors or windows. The doors and windows are then cut (with a minimum of effort; in fact the structure is still so soft that openings could be cut with one's fingernail), and the structure is sprayed inside and out with latex-modified concrete. The dome is ultralightweight, is secured to withstand high wind speeds and great snow loads, is vermin-proof, and inexpensive. Several of these fifty-four-foot-diameter domes can be easily joined together into a cluster.

Under the leadership of the designer/mathematician Steve Baer, groups of young people built "Drop City," a commune near Trinidad, Colorado. In 1965, Steve Baer developed a new geometry called *Zomes*. Domelike forms are based on polyhedra and polygons; however, in a Zome, the polyhedra are pulled or "stretched"—a sort of topological rubber geometry. From 1965 to 1981 Zomes were built with foundations of fieldstone, concrete, or wood. The skeletal outline of the dome was then constructed of wooden two-by-fours. For the covering "skin" of the building, Steve Baer and his friends went to automobile graveyards and cut triangular segments out of

Car-top domes at Drop City, Colorado.

the tops of junked cars or station wagons with axes. These were then nailed in place and painted or enameled.

Drop City, which still exists as this is being written, provides a sort of postindustrial example of vernacular building. Its design authenticity is marred by dubious craftsmanship, rust, and some neglect. Nonetheless, it provides still another example of a new kind of building that is based on *method*: the interrelationship between material, tool, and process.

All these building methods demonstrate the elegance of solutions possible with a creative interaction of tools, materials, and processes.

Use: "Does it work?" A vitamin bottle should dispense pills singly. An ink bottle should not tip over. A plastic-film package covering sliced pastrami should withstand boiling water, yet open easily. Because in any reasonably conducted home, alarm-clocks seldom travel through the air at speeds approaching five hundred miles per hour, streamlining clocks is out of place. Will a cigarette lighter designed like the tailfin of an automobile (the design of which in turn was copied from a fighter aircraft of the Korean War) give more efficient service? A ballpoint pen shaped and colored like a pickle and made of a creepily yielding plastic is a tawdry perversion of design for use. On the other hand, look at some hammers: they differ in weight, material, and form according to use. The sculptor's mallet is fully round, permitting constant rotation in the hand. The jeweler's chasing hammer is a precision instrument used for fine work on metal. The prospector's pick is delicately balanced to add to the swing of his arm when cracking rocks.

The results of the introduction of a new device are never predictable. In the case of automobiles, a fine irony developed. One of the earliest criticisms of the car was that, unlike "old Dobbin," it didn't have the sense to find its way home whenever its owner was incapacitated by an evening of genteel drinking. No one foresaw that mass acceptance of the car would put the American bedroom on wheels, offering everyone a new place to copulate (and privacy from supervision by parents and spouses). Nobody expected the car to accelerate mobility, thereby creating the urban and exurban sprawl and the dormitory suburbs that strangle our larger cities; or to sanction the killing of 50,000 people per annum, brutalizing us and making it possible, as Philip Wylie says, "to see babies with their jaws ripped off on the corner of Maine and Maple"; or to dislocate our societal groupings, thus contributing to our alienation; or to put everyone from sixteen to sixty in permanent hock to the tune of $150 a month. In the middle forties, no one foresaw that, with the primary use function of the automobile solved, it would emerge as a combination status symbol and disposable, chrome-plated codpiece. But two greater ironies were to follow. In the early sixties, when people began to fly more and to rent standard cars at their destination, the businessman's clients no longer saw the car he owned and therefore could not judge his style of life by it. Much of Detroit's Baroque exuberance subsided, and the automobile again came closer to being a transportation device. Money earmarked for status demonstration was now spent on boats, color television sets, and other ephemera.

The last irony is now upon us: with carbon monoxide fumes poisoning our atmosphere, the electric car, driven at moderate speeds and with a cruising range of only 100 miles, reminiscent of the turn of the century, has made a comeback as a city transportation device in Sweden and Great Britain between 1978 and 1984. Since individual transportation devices still fulfill an important need in large rural sections without public transport, much experimentation is going on in 1984. This has resulted in fleets of post office vans, taxis, or delivery vehicles being fitted out with methane conversion systems; hydrogen powered cars; and vehicles powered by natural gas converters. The automobile provides an interesting case history: in nearly 100 years it has changed from useful tool to gas-guzzling status symbol and finally to a device the use of which pollutes the environment and destroys irreplaceable natural resources.

Detroit is in complete disarray. More than one million

workers in the automobile and automobile-connected industries have been laid off, and stockholder's dividends have dried
up. There are wild fluctuations in the world's available oil
supplies and consequently in gasoline prices. Although gasoline seems again to be more readily available in 1984, the new
escalations of the Iraqi-Iranian War may turn the tap off at
any time. Add to this mass unemployment, coupled with high
prices, and it is understandable that U.S. consumers are
choosing subcompact cars from Japan and other countries. Although carmakers in the United States have valiantly tried to
market their own small cars, as this is being written whole
new series of these automobiles have just been recalled for serious design faults, engineering errors, and manufacturing
mistakes. (According to the Associated Press in August 1983,
the Consumer Safety Division is attempting to get General
Motors and others to recall eight-and-a-half million *X*, *J*, and
K subcompacts manufactured between 1979 and 1983.) Since
the first edition of this book nearly one-third of Detroit's cars
have been recalled.

Need: Much recent design has satisfied only evanescent
wants and desires, while the genuine needs of man have often
been neglected. The economic, psychological, spiritual, social, technological, and intellectual needs of a human being
are usually more difficult and less profitable to satisfy than
the carefully engineered and manipulated "wants" inculcated
by fad and fashion.

People seem to prefer the ornate to the plain as they prefer
daydreaming to thinking and mysticism to rationalism. As
they seek crowd pleasures and choose widely traveled roads
rather than solitude and lonely paths, they seem to feel a sense
of security in crowds and crowdedness. *Horror vacui* is horror
of inner as well as outer vacuum.

In clothing the need for security-through-identity has been
perverted into role-playing. The consumer can now act out
various roles by appearing caparisoned in Naugahyde boots,
pseudomilitary uniforms, lumberjack's shirts, various types of
"survival gear," and all the other outward trappings of Davy

Crockett, a Foreign Legionnaire, Cossack Hetman, or John Wayne. All these furry parkas and elk-hide boots are obviously mere role-playing devices, since climate control makes their use redundant. In a society concerned with physical fitness, enormous design improvements have been made in jogging shoes (beginning with *Adidas* and *Puma* in Germany), and most athletic clothes have been improved or even newly invented. But fake-outdoorsy fashions have grown even more rapidly as people frantically try to tell others whom they would like to be.

Nearly twenty years ago the Scott Paper Company introduced disposable paper dresses for 99 cents. In 1970 I was disgusted by the fact that such paper party dresses were selling for between $20.00 and $149.50, whereas increased consumption might have dropped the price to less than 50 cents. But during the intervening years the functional *need* for paper clothing was discovered: we now accept paper gowns routinely in hospitals, clinics, and doctor's offices, and disposable paper clothing is used extensively in clean rooms for computer assembly and space hardware.

Greatly accelerated technological change has been used to create technological obsolescence. The enormous proliferation of electronically improved telephones during the last two years makes that case clearly. A mail-order house in New England sends out four forty-two-page catalogs a year that list telephones only. Here are phones that will automatically dial by responding to your voice stating the name of the person you wish to call, phones with built-in automatic dialers, answering services, microrecorders and speakerphones, hand-held computers that can be preset to dial your seventy-two most favorite numbers anywhere in the world without your having to push buttons or turn dials, telephones that will automatically dial your local fire station (being plugged into smoke detectors) even when you're away from home, and much else. The economy of the marketplace, however, is still geared to a static philosophy of "purchasing-owning" rather than a dynamic one of "leasing-using," and pricing policy has not resulted in lowered consumer cost. If a television set, for instance, shows enough technological improvements to make it worthwhile to replace it from time to time, then routine leasing arrangements (as in England) or much lower purchase prices should reflect this. Instead important values of real things have been driven out by phony values of false things, a sort of Gresham's Law of Design.

Telesis: "The deliberate, purposeful utilization of the processes of nature and society to obtain particular goals" (*Random House Dictionary*, 1978). The telesic content of a design must reflect the times and conditions that have given rise to it and must fit in with the general human socioeconomic order in which it is to operate.

The uncertainties and the new and complex pressures in our society make many people feel that the most logical way to regain lost values is to go out and buy Early American furniture, put a hooked rug on the floor, buy ready-made phony ancestor portraits, and hang a flintlock rifle over the fireplace. The gas-light so popular in our tract housing areas is a dangerous and senseless anachronism that only reflects an insecure striving for the good old days by consumer and designer alike.

Our thirty-five-year love affair with things Japanese—Zen Buddhism, the architecture of the Ise Shrine and Katsura Imperial Palace, haiku poetry, Hiroshige and Hokusai blockprints, and music of koto and samisen, lanterns and sake sets, green tea liqueur, and sushi and tempura—has been used to sell imported artifacts to consumers who disregard telesic aptness.

By now it is obvious that our interest in things Japanese is not just a passing fad or fashion but rather the result of a major cultural exchange. As Japan was shut off for nearly 200 years from the Western world under the Tokugawa Shogunate, its cultural expressions flourished in a pure (although somewhat inbred) form in the imperial cities of Kyoto and Edo (now Tokyo). The Western world's response to an in-depth knowledge of things Japanese is comparable only to the

European reaction to things classical, which we are now pleased to call the Renaissance.

It is not possible to just move objects, tools, or artifacts from one culture to another and then expect them to work. Exotic decorative accessories or art-objects can be translated in this way, but their value seems to lie precisely in the fact that they are *exotic*—in other words, seen in an unfamiliar context. When cultures truly intermingle, then *both* cultures are enriched and continue to benefit one another.

But it is not possible to just take everyday objects and without regard to context expect them to work in a different society. The floors of traditional Japanese homes are covered by floor mats called *tatami*. These mats are three by six feet in size and consist of rice straw closely packed inside a cover of woven rush. The long sides are bound with black linen tape. While tatami mats impose a module (homes are spoken of as six-, eight-, or twelve-mat homes), their primary purposes are to absorb sounds and to act as a sort of wall-to-wall vacuum cleaner that filters particles of dirt through the woven surface and retains them in the inner core of rice straw. Periodically these mats (and the dirt within them) are discarded, and new ones are installed. Japanese feet encased in clean, socklike *tabi* (the sandallike street shoe, or *geta*, having been left at the door) are also designed to fit in with this system. Western-style leather-soled shoes and spike heels destroy the surface of the mats and also carry much more dirt into the house. The increasing use of regular shoes and industrial precipitation make the use of tatami, difficult enough in Japan, absolutely ridiculous in the United States, where high cost makes periodic disposal and reinstallation ruinously expensive.

Beginning around 1980 a number of importers of tatami mats have sprung up in Oregon, California, and New England and sold tatami through advertisements in *Sunset* magazine. *A Japanese Touch For Your Home*, by Koji Yagi, published for the American Society of Interior Designers by Kodansha International of Tokyo, New York, and San Francisco, became a modest best-seller in bookshops during Christmas 1982 and has been selling well and steadily ever since. It is illustrated with diagrams and beautiful color photographs, instructing Americans how to make their homes more Japanese! But although there are apparently enough Americans to spend their money on such transformations, tatami are still wrong for our culture.

A tatami-covered floor is only part of the larger design system of the Japanese house. Fragile, sliding paper walls and tatami give the house definite and significant acoustical properties that have influenced the design and development of musical instruments and even the melodic structure of Japanese speech, poetry, and drama. A piano, designed for the reverberating insulated walls and floors of Western homes and concert halls, cannot be introduced into a Japanese home without reducing the brilliance of a Rachmaninoff concerto to a shrill cacophony. Similarly, the fragile quality of Japanese *samisen* music cannot be fully appreciated in the reverberating box that constitutes the American house. Americans who try to couple a Japanese interior with an American living experience in their search for exotica find that elements cannot be ripped out of their telesic context with impunity.

Association: Our psychological conditioning, often going back to earliest childhood memories, comes into play and predisposes us to, or provides us with antipathy against, a given value.

Increased consumer resistance in many product areas testifies to design neglect of the associational aspect of the function complex. After two decades, the television industry for instance, has not yet resolved the question of whether a television set should carry the associational values of a piece of furniture (a lacquered mah-jongg chest of the Ming Dynasty) or of technical equipment (a portable tube tester). Television receivers that carry new associations (sets for children's rooms in bright colors and materials, enhanced by tactilely pleasant but nonworking controls and preset for given times and channels, clip-on swivel sets for hospital beds) might not only clear up the astoundingly large back inventory of sets in warehouses, but also *create* new markets.

To television as furniture or equipment we must add television as jewelry. Dick Tracy's wristwatch television from the comic strip of the forties and fifties was turned into reality by Panasonic late in 1983. Sony has designed their Watchman: a flat minitelevision roughly the size of four checkbooks stacked on top of one another. Listening is done through headphones, as with Sony's Walkman minicassette player. And Sinclair Electronics in England has unveiled its portable television set with a picture the size of a postage stamp. Thus we see television moving into a new associational area. With consumer electronics becoming smaller, miniaturized, and finally microminiaturized, we can expect many objects to reclassify themselves as they shrink in size. But while the manufacturers and their designers may manipulate associational values, we have to look at the objective results: a television set with a stamp-sized screen has an image that is too small to see. While listening to wrist-television on earphones or to a Sony Walkman may carry associations of portability, lightness, or personal adornment, the net result is impaired hearing. And with a bathroom scale that announces one's weight in *an alluring contralto* or *a pleasing baritone* voice (synthesized, of course), the associational value pushed is sexiness and gadgetry rather than anything that has to do with health, fitness, weight, or bathrooms.

At a time of economic insecurity, the misassociation most heavily pushed by manufacturers and sales departments is status combined with gimmickry. The best example from the 1983/1984 Christmas Catalog by Diners Club is a solid gold telephone, selling for a mere thirty thousand dollars.

The influence of media advertising has become so powerful as to act as a great equalizer, turning the public into passive consumers, unwilling to assert their taste or discrimination. A picture emerges of a moral weakling with an IQ of about 70, ready to accept whatever specious values the unholy trinity of

Motivation Research, Market Analysis, and Sales has decided to inculcate in him. In short, the associational values of design have degenerated to the lowest common denominator, determined more by inspired guesswork and piebald graphic sales charts than by the genuinely felt wants of the consumer.

Some associations are shared by everyone, and this can be simply demonstrated. If the reader is asked to choose which one of the figures below he would rather call *Takete* or *Maluma* (both are words devoid of all meaning), he will easily call the one on the right *Takete* (W. Koehler, *Gestalt Psychology*).

Most associational values are universal *within a culture* and frequently are based on the traditions of that culture. These values come from unconscious, deep-seated drives and compulsions. The totally meaningless sounds and shapes shown above can mean the same thing to most of us. There is an unconscious relationship between the expectations of the spectator and the configuration of the object. The designer can manipulate this relationship. This can enhance the "chairness" of the chair and at the same time load it with associational values: elegance, formality, portability, the sense of fine woods crafted well, or what-have-you.

Aesthetics: Here dwells the traditional bohemian artist. A mythological figure, equipped with sandals, lover, garret, and

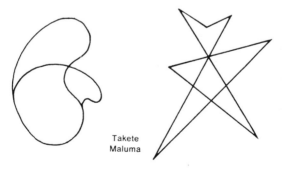

Takete
Maluma

Gestalt Comparison

easel, pursuing dream-shrouded designs. The cloud of mystery surrounding aesthetics can (and should) be dispelled. The dictionary definition, "*a theory of the beautiful, in taste and art,*" leaves us not much better off than before. Nonetheless we know that aesthetics is a tool, one of the most important ones in the repertory of the designer, a tool that helps in shaping his forms and colors into entities that move us, please us, and are beautiful, exciting, filled with delight, meaningful.

Because there is no ready yardstick for the analysis of aesthetics, it is simply considered to be a personal expression fraught with mystery.

We know what we like or dislike and let it go at that. Artists themselves begin to look at their productions as auto-therapeutic devices of self-expression, confuse license and liberty, and forsake all discipline. They are often unable to agree on the various elements and attributes of design aesthetics. If we contrast the "Last Supper" by Leonardo da Vinci with an ordinary piece of wallboard, we will understand how both operate aesthetically. As "pure" art, the painting was a source of inspiration, delight, beauty, catharsis . . . in short, a communication device for the Holy Church at a time when a largely preliterate population was exposed to few pictorial representations or graphic stimuli. But the "Last Supper" also had to fill the other requirements of function; aside from the spiritual, its *use* was to cover a wall. In terms of *method* it had to reflect the material (pigment and vehicle), tools (brushes and painting knives), and processes (individualistic brushwork) employed by Leonardo. It had to fulfil the human *need* for spiritual satisfaction. And it had to work on the *associational* and *telesic* planes, providing reference points from the Bible. Finally, it had to make identification through association easier for the beholder through such traditional symbols as the racial type, garb, and posture of the Savior.

Earlier versions of Christ's last supper, painted during the sixth and seventh centuries, depicted Christ *lying* or reclining in the place of honor. For nearly a thousand years, the well-mannered did not *sit* at table. Leonardo da Vinci disregarded

"The Last Supper" by Leonardo da Vinci.

the reclining position followed by earlier civilizations and painters for Jesus and his Disciples. To make the "Last Supper" acceptable to Italians of his time on an associational plane, Leonardo seated the crowd around the table on chairs or benches. Unfortunately the scriptural account of St. John resting his head on the Savior's bosom presented an unsolvable positioning problem to the artist, once everybody was seated according to the Renaissance custom.

On the other hand, the primary use of wallboard is to cover a wall. But an increased choice of textures and colors applied by the factory shows that it, too, must fulfil the *aesthetic* aspect of function. No one argues that in a great work of art such as the "Last Supper," prime functional emphasis is aesthetic, with *use* (to cover a wall) subsidiary. The main job of wallboard is its use in covering a wall, and the aesthetic assumes a highly subsidiary position. But both examples must operate in all *six* areas of the function complex.

The six parts of the function complex are informed by the past: experience and tradition. But Januslike the function complex also faces the future. The ongoing dimensions of what we design, make, and use lie in the *consequences*. All of our tools, objects, artifacts, transportation devices, or buildings have consequences that reach out into such diverse areas as politics, health, income, and the biosphere.

It has already been shown that the mere choice of *material* that is plastic and not biodegradable can have far-reaching consequences for the environment. The *process* of manufacturing may lead to immediate pollution problems, such as the acid rain denuding forests in Canada, New England, and the Scandinavian countries: this poisonous precipitation is caused by factory chimneys spewing pollutants in the Chicago-Gary area and the Ruhr and Saar valleys. Long-range pollution is making itself felt only now: the Environmental Protection Agency has so far identified 140,000 toxic waste sites in North America—the direct result of arbitrary dumping of chemicals, waste, and factory effluvia.

Falling property values in two of the worst dump-site areas, the Love Canal in New York and Times Beach in Missouri, demonstrate clearly the economic consequences when afterburners and postmanufacturing filtration systems are not designed—to say nothing of health problems and genetic damage caused by improperly designed storage barrels for toxic waste.

The design of gas-guzzlers has tied American consumers (and hence their government) to the whimsical foreign policies of oil exporting nations that are frequently unstable—a clear case of political consequences following the design act.

"Urban renewal" and "slum clearance" projects have verticalized ghettos into monolithic highrises that have had enormously damaging social consequences to people forced to live in them. Suicide, alienation, aggression, rape, murder, heavy drug use, and other departures from sexual norms have followed each urban renewal project. (Peter Blake, *Form Follows Fiasco*. Boston: Little Brown and Company, 1979; Victor Papanek, *Design for Human Scale*. New York: Van Nostrand Reinhold, 1983.)

The self-assertive greed of corporations has given us strips of quick-food restaurants in every town or sizable village in the United States. The societal and social consequences are clear: a destabilization of the family, new eating patterns that frequently result in obesity and dietary deficiencies, a debasement of the human palate forced to find the lowest common denominator, and finally a ready acceptance of horrendous garishness and visual pollution. In this connection it is interesting to note that the largest quick-food restaurant chain, proudly proclaiming on its signs, "31 billion hamburgers sold so far!," is also one of the worst chemical polluters in the world. Each hamburger, fish sandwich, egg burger, or what-have-you comes in its own styrofoam sarcophagus, is further wrapped in plastic foil and accompanied by numerous condiments (catsup, mustard, French dressing, salt, nondairy creamer) each in its own plastic or foil pouch. The beverages also come in styrofoam cups with styrene lids and plastic straws; this entire refection in turn comes in a larger foam box. It has been estimated that 600 tons of nondestructible, ecologically damaging, petroleum-based wrappings constitute the nonedible garbage this firm purveys annually (Granada Television, 22 November 1981). All of these plastic wraps are carefully designed and manufactured, as are the pseudofood served therein and the fake redwood structures that sell these quick meals. The consequences are disastrous.

How these wrappings pollute the environment has been shown. The fact is that the junk food itself provides too many empty calories and the enormous amounts of sugar and salt included in hamburger and bun can lead to devastating results to the health of millions who routinely consume these concoctions. Aesthetically and architecturally quick-food restaurants tend to group together. This has led to *the strip*, usually a road that cuts through many small towns and is entirely taken up by service stations, quick-food restaurants, and discount stores. (In Lawrence, Kansas, there are seventy-seven such restaurants along a three-and-a-half-mile street.)

More serious consequences may arise from the way we store atomic wastes. Less than one percent of the design and engineering skill used in atomics is given over to developing containers for this most destructive waste yet known to man, some of which has a half-life of 24,000 years. The various states are quarreling over where to dump atomic matter that comes from the relatively minor research and applications performed in hospitals and clinics. A whole series of science-fictional proposals are being seriously studied. This includes storing nuclear waste products in underground caves, dumping demonstrably imperfect barrels containing such wastes in the oceans, or even firing atomic garbage into space. In the ten years until 1983, newspapers and magazines were full of articles describing the complete inadequacy of *any* existing storage method—and meanwhile the nuclear waste pile rose. It is a fact that we have no present safe means of storing nuclear waste products.

Similar frightening statistics can be drawn from toxic waste storage; these are discussed at length in another chapter.

Designers often attempt to go beyond the primary functional requirements of *method, use, need, telesis, association,* and *aesthetics;* they strive for a more concise statement: precision, simplicity. In a statement so conceived, we find a degree of aesthetic satisfaction comparable to that found in the logarithmic spiral of a chambered nautilus, the ease of a seagull's flight, the strength of a gnarled tree trunk, the color of a sunset. The particular satisfaction derived from the simplicity of a thing can be called *elegance.* When we speak of an elegant solution, we refer to something that reduces the complex to the simple:

> Euclid's Proof that the number of primes is infinite will serve as an example. Primes are numbers that are not divisible, 3, 17, 23, and so forth. One would imagine as we get higher in the numerical series, primes would get rarer, crowded out by the ever-increasing products of small numbers, and that we would finally arrive at a very high number, which would be the highest prime, the last numerical virgin. Euclid's Proof demonstrates in a simple and elegant way that this is not true and that to whatever astronomical regions we ascend, we shall always find numbers that are not the product of smaller ones but are generated by immaculate conceptions, as it were. Here is the proof: Assume that P is the hypothetically highest prime;

then imagine a number equal to $1 \times 2 \times 3 \times 4 \ldots \times P$. This number is expressed by the numerical symbol (P!). Now add 1 (P! + 1). This number is obviously not divisible by P or any number less than P because they are all contained in (P!); hence (P! + 1) is either a prime higher than P or it contains a prime factor higher than P. . . . Q.E.D.

The deep satisfaction evoked by this proof is aesthetic as well as intellectual; it reveals our enchantment with the near perfect.

2

Phylogenocide:
A History of the Industrial Design Profession

We are all in the gutter, but some of us are looking at the stars.

OSCAR WILDE

The ultimate job of design is to transform man's environment and tools and, by extension, man himself. Man has always changed himself and his surroundings, but recently science, technology, and mass production have advanced so radically that changes are more rapid, more thorough, and often less predictable. We are beginning to be able to define and isolate problems, to determine possible goals and work meaningfully toward them. And an over-technologized, sterile, and inhuman environment has become one possible future; a world choking under a permanent, dun-colored pollution umbrella, another. In addition the various sciences and technologies have become woefully compartmentalized and specialized. Often, more complex problems can be attacked only by teams of specialists, speaking only their own professional jargon. Industrial designers, who are frequently members of such a team, find that, besides fulfilling their normal design function, they must act as a communication bridge between other team members. Many times the designer may be the only one able to speak the various technical jargons; because of his educational background, the role of team interpreter is forced upon him. So we find the industrial designer becoming the team synthesist, a position to which he has been elevated by the default of people from the other disciplines.

This has not always been true.

Many books on industrial design suggest that design began when man began making tools. While the difference between *Australopithecus africanus* and the modern designer may not be as great as one might think or hope, the idea of equating man the toolmaker with the start of the profession is just an attempt to gain status for the profession by evoking a specious historical precedent. "In the beginning was Design," obviously, but not industrial design. Henry Dreyfuss, one of the founders of the profession, says in *Designing for People* (probably the best and most characteristic book about industrial design):

> The Industrial Designer began by eliminating excess decoration, his real job began when he insisted on dissecting the product, seeing what made it tick, and devising means of making it tick better—then making it look better. He never forgets that beauty is only skin-deep. For years in our office we have kept before us the concept that *what we are working on is going to be ridden in, sat upon, looked at, talked into, activated, operated, or in some way used by people individually or en masse. If the point of contact between the product and the people becomes a point of friction, then the Industrial Designer has failed. If, on the other hand, people are made safer, more comfortable, more eager to purchase, more efficient— or just plain happier—the designer has succeeded.* He brings to this task a detached, analytical point of view. He consults closely with the manufacturer, the manufacturer's engineers, production men, and sales staff, keeping in mind whatever peculiar problems the firm may have in the business or industrial world. He will compromise up to a point but he refuses to budge on design principles he knows to be sound. Occasionally he may lose a client, but he rarely loses the client's respect.

Concern with the design of tools and machinery coincided almost exactly with the beginnings of the Industrial Revolution and, appropriately enough, made its first appearance in England. The first industrial design society was formed in Sweden in 1849, to be followed shortly by similar associations in Austria, Germany, Denmark, England, Norway, and Finland (in that order). The designers of the period were concerned with form-giving, an erratic search for "appropriate beauty" in machine tools and machine-made objects. Looking at the machine, they saw a new thing, a thing that seemed to cry out for decorative embellishments. These decorations were usually garnered from classical ornaments and from major raids into the animal and vegetable kingdoms. Thus, giant hydraulic presses dripped with acanthus leaves, pineapples, stylized wheat sheaves. Many of the "sane design" or "design reform" movements of the time, such as those engendered by the writings and teachings of William Morris in England and Elbert Hubbard in the United States, were rooted in a sort of Luddite antimachine philosophy. By contrast Frank Lloyd Wright said as early as 1894 that "the machine is here to stay" and that the designer should "use this normal tool of civilization to best advantage instead of prostituting it as he has hitherto done in reproducing with murderous ubiquity forms born of other times and other conditions which it can only serve to destroy." Yet designers of the last century were either perpetrators of voluptuous Victorian-Baroque or members of an artsy-craftsy clique who were dismayed by machine technology. The work of the *Kunstgewerbeschule* in Austria and the German *Werkbund* anticipated things to come, but it was not until Walter Gropius founded the German Bauhaus in 1919 that an uneasy marriage between art and machine was achieved.

No design school in history had greater influence in shaping taste and design than the Bauhaus. It was the first school to consider design a vital part of the production process rather than "applied art" or "industrial arts." It became the first international forum on design because it drew its faculty and students from all over the world, and its influence traveled as these people later founded design offices and schools in many countries. Almost every major design school in the United States today still uses the basic foundation design course developed by the Bauhaus. It made good sense in 1919 to let a German 19-year-old experiment with drill press and circular saw, welding torch and lathe, so that he might "experience the interaction between tool and material." Today the same method is an anachronism, for an American teenager has spent much of his life in a machine-dominated society (and cumulatively probably a great deal of time lying under various automobiles, souping them up). For a student whose American design school still slavishly imitates teaching patterns developed by the Bauhaus, computer sciences and electronics and plastics technology and cybernetics and bionics simply do not exist. The courses the Bauhaus developed were excellent for their time and place (telesis), but American schools following this pattern in the eighties are perpetuating design infantilism.

The Bauhaus was in a sense a nonadaptive mutation in design, for the genes contributing to its convergence characteristics were badly chosen. In boldface type, it announced its manifesto: "Architects, sculptors, painters, we must all turn to the crafts. . . . Let us create a *new guild of craftsmen!*" The heavy emphasis on interaction between crafts, art, and design turned out to be a blind alley. The inherent nihilism of the pictorial arts of the post-World War I period had little to contribute that would be useful to the average, or even to the discriminating, consumer. The paintings of Kandinsky, Klee, Feininger, *et al.*, on the other hand, had no connection whatsoever with the anemic elegance that some designers imposed on products.

In the United States, industrial design, like marathon dances, six-day bicycle races, the N.R.A. and the Blue Eagle, and free dishes at the movies, was a child of the Depression. At first glance the swollen belly of a child suffering from malnutrition gives it the appearance of being well fed; only later

do you notice the emaciated arms and legs. The products of
early American industrial design convey the same sleek obesity and have the same weaknesses.

For the Depression market, the manufacturer needed a new
sales gimmick, and the industrial designer reshaped his products for better appearance and lower manufacturing and sales
costs. Harold Van Doren's definition of that time in his book
Industrial Design was apt:

> Industrial Design is the practice of analyzing, creating, and
> developing products for mass-manufacture. Its goal is to
> achieve forms which are assured of acceptance before exten-
> sive capital investment has been made, and which can be man-
> ufactured at a price permitting wide distribution and
> reasonable profits.

Harold Van Doren, Norman Bel Geddes, Raymond Loewy,
Russel Wright, Henry Dreyfuss, Donald Deskey, and Walter
Dorwin Teague were the pioneering practitioners of design in
America. It is significant that all of them came from the field
of stage design and/or window display.

While the architects sold apples on street corners, the ex-
stage-designers and ex-window-dressers were creating "lem-
ons" in lush suites upstairs.

Raymond Loewy's redesign of the Gestetner duplicating
machine is probably the first and most famous case of industrial design development. But as Don Wallance was to remark
three decades later in *Shaping America's Products*:

> The "before and after" pictures showing mimeographs, lo-
> comotives, refrigerators, furniture and numerous other things
> transformed by industrial design were most impressive. Even
> more impressive were the differences in before and after sales
> figures. Oddly enough, when we look at these things now after
> a passage of more than twenty-five years, it is no longer so
> clear whether the "before" or the "after" version has best stood
> the test of time.

rged as a major reality of life. There *are*
in Mississippi and South Carolina. Ther
n sinks in the large city ghettos, and embit
from our rural areas, foiled in their atte
efully on $150 a month at age 65," haun
f Florida, southern Texas, and Orange Cou
aming paranoid dreams of a restoration t
."

scale the disparities between the haves
become even more terrifyingly vast. Since
widened, with the declining birthrate in
and Western Europe and the fantastic po
in the rest of the world.
of 1973, 1976, and 1979, combined with
policies to developing countries, have furt
ld. The increase in population in many of
is finally being brought down to more m
lthough the repressive means used in the P
China to penalize a couple having more th
ly a science fiction idea when this book w
e southern half of the globe still stands in a
ing that it has taken you twelve minutes
is chapter, 5,000 people have died of st
e in the developing world. (Paul Harriso
Tomorrow. London: Pelican Books, 1981
 to have a world cleft in two: total need
nspicuous consumption in the north. Coo
on many levels, such as exchange of healt
lternative energy research done in the sout
be but funded by the north, interchange c
echniques. With the growing interest in ap
 the technologically developed countries
nethods that can be brought north. Ther
ls for the redistribution of food supplies, i
emporary shortages caused by natural dis
ough food to go around. There is a problem
preservation in which designers can help.
s are demonstrated in a later chapter.

This sort of design for the manipulated visual excitement of the moment continued unabated until the beginning of World War II.

The automobile and other consumer industries had to turn their production facilities over to the creation of war supplies, and wartime demands forced a new (though temporary) sense of responsibility on industrial designers. "Ease-o-matic gear shifts" and "auto-magic shell feeding mechanisms" were out of place in a Sherman tank. Design staffs encountered real requirements of performance in the function complex, imposed by combat conditions. The necessity for honest design (design-in-use versus design-in-sales) imposed a healthier discipline than that of the marketplace. Critical material shortages forced those designers who remained in the consumer field to a much keener realization of performance, materials, and other war-imposed limitations. A three-quart casserole, made of plasticized cardboard able to sustain temperatures of 475 degrees for several hours, washable and infinitely reusable, *retailing* for 45 cents, is an excellent example and seems curiously to have disappeared from the market by 1945.

Shortly after the end of World War II the *New York Times* carried the first full-page ad for Gimbel's sale of the Reynolds ball-point pen at only $25 each. By Monday morning, Herald Square was so clogged with people waiting for Gimbel's to open that extra police had to be brought in to control the crowds. Places in the ball-point pen queue could be sold for $5 to $10, and, until Gimbel's slapped a one-pen-to-a-customer order on the sale Wednesday, pens could be readily sold for $50 to $60 each.

This zany state of affairs lasted for some five weeks: each day Hudson Lodestar monoplanes landed at LaGuardia airport with thousands of pens in their bellies. Even a three-day truckers' strike couldn't affect the sale, as the union promised to "deliver milk, critical food, and Reynolds pens." With a Reynolds pen you could write under water but practically nowhere else. They skipped, they blotted, they leaked in your pockets, and there were no replacement cartridges because the pens were one-shot affairs. You threw them away as soon as they ran dry, if not sooner. Still they sold. For the pen was a do-it-yourself Buck Rogers kit; you bought a pen and you were "post-war." Just as every "ruptured duck" insignia dully gleaming in the lapel of a service man's first civilian suit marked the end of one era, the Reynolds pen leaking in his breast pocket marked the beginning of a new. There were other consumer goods available, but this was the only totally new product on the market.

The science-fictional technology of the year 2000 seemed to have come to roost in 1945. Here was an apparently totally new, post-war product, and each man's miraculously light-weight Reynolds pen gleaming in aluminum was also his personal reassurance that "our side" had won the war. (Now it can be told: our pen was copied from German ball-points, found by Reynolds in a South American bar in 1943.)

Industry pandered to the public's ready acceptance of anything new, anything different. The miscegenation of technology and artificially accelerated consumer whims gave birth to the dark twins of styling and obsolescence. There are three types of obsolescence: technological (a better or more elegant way of doing things is discovered), material (the product wears out), and artificial (the death-rating of a product; either the materials are substandard and will wear out in a predictable time span, or else significant parts are not replaceable or repairable). Since World War II our major commitment has been to stylistic and artificial obsolescence. (Ironically enough, the accelerated pace of technological innovation frequently makes a product obsolete before artificial or stylistic obsolescence can be tacked on to it.)

Honest design striving for true simplicity has recently been frighteningly rare. Television specials (e.g., CBS *White Papers*) and articles in magazines and newspapers have pointed out that U.S. military hardware seems to have gone the way of consumer products during the late 1970s and early 1980s. There now *are* "ease-o-matic" firing mechanisms in armored

personnel carriers and
so cluttered with sop
puters and in-board vi
to whether this equipm
The abortive rescue a
five out of eight helic
engineered for testing
desert climate and e
pendent nations sho
assemble their "drea
made in Czechoslov
Israel. Only when gi
reluctantly choose ou
mentality seems to g

Technological ob
scale. Especially in
high-fidelity, came
changes have come
rection is making i
part of the public.
realize that by wa
tronic device, they
development and
greater production
niques lower cons
puter keyboard (f
a portable typew
would have cost
room.

In the seventie
which design ope
change, since the
laws have polariz
States the poor a
credibly richer.
Abject poverty (
mented maiden

attic) has em
dren starving
vast populati
senior citizen
to "retire gra
sleazy resorts
California, d
"good old da

On a glob
have-nots hav
this chasm ha
North Americ
lation explosic

The oil cris
responsible loa
divided the wo
poorer countri
ageable levels,
ple's Republic
one child was
first written. T
ject need. Assu
read so far in
vation in this t
The Third Wo

It is impossi
the south and
eration is need
services, funde
ern half of the
crafts, skills, an
propriate scale
there are many
have been loud
fact—except fo
asters—there is
of food storage
Some ideas for

But, looking at conflicts in the Middle East, Iran, Central Africa, Laos, and Central America, it is clear that the world's trouble spots, sites of violent upheavals and savage wars, are mainly poor countries. The designer can play an important role: it has been pointed out earlier that because of their training industrial and product designers frequently assume key positions as trained synthesists. They speak the languages of many disciplines and can frequently help both on a village level and with export markets. Examples of this are scattered throughout the book.

Unless nutrition specialists, doctors, designers, engineers, and many others from both sides of the equator can bring a two-way exchange into being, Paul Harrison's apocalyptic vision may yet come true: "The third world war will start in the Third World. It will be a war of desperation by peoples forced into a position where they have nothing to lose."

In *Never Leave Well Enough Alone*, Raymond Loewy amusingly reminisces about the early years of his crusade, a crusade to get clients. In the late twenties and thirties he, together with other designers, kept knocking on corporate doors, such as those of General Motors, General Electric, General Rubber, General Steel, General Dynamics. In all fairness it must be admitted that he and his coworkers served their corporate masters well and, in fact, still do. It is dismaying to find that all too many of today's graduating design students also eagerly join corporate design staffs, safely wrapped in the cocoon of corporate expense accounts, company-paid country club membership, deferred annuities, retirement benefits, dread-disease coverage, and a yearly revitalizing visit to one of the stomping grounds of the corporate Gauleiters in New England or Aspen, Colorado.

In 1970 I advocated the need for a new crusade. Just as Raymond Loewy and others had visited potential clients in the 1920s and 1930s to show them what industrial designers could do, I felt that this could be done again but on a global scale. I advocated that young designers could go to developing countries, clinics, and hospitals and show what they can do. I suggested that it was up to the designer to knock on doors

that had never opened before. Due to the civil rights movement in the United States, the ongoing concern for developing
countries in northern Europe, the women's movement for
equal rights, consumer associations, and the prescriptive writings of people like Fritz Schumacher, Rachael Carson, Ralph
Nader, and myself, this struggle has now been started in part.

But it is 1984 now, and, at least in the technological countries, the choices facing a young designer seem mainly economic. Financial security is understandably of enormous
importance to students and young designers. This brings a
whole new dimension to designing for the poor and needy.
The prime consideration now is a job. But to find too easy an
accommodation within the military-industrial establishment
is clearly not the answer. The designer is in a position where
difficult moral and ethical choices have to be made. And there
are many different ways of dealing with this ethical dilemma.
Having been in close touch with my students from many
countries during the last thirteen years, I have some rough
idea of how they—now that they are professionals—have dealt
with this problem. Some have sold out to an employer and
continue to design luxury items for a small privileged class.
One may fault this approach, nonetheless it is a legitimate
response to a difficult existential choice. Others have accepted
my suggestion (in a later chapter) and contribute one-tenth
of their time or one-tenth of their income to solving problems
of abject need, while continuing with their jobs. Others have
realized that the social changes of the last ten or so years are
providing new opportunities for designers. This is especially
true in the field of medical care and care for the handicapped
and the aged. Still others have chosen to teach architecture or
design and work as design consultants or free-lancers only on
those jobs they consider socially important. Others have created entirely new professions for themselves: product evalu-
ators for Ralph Nader or other consumer groups, design critics
for a national industrial export organization,* and so forth.

*In Norway and Japan.

There are a few who have dropped out of design entirely and found that living and working a farm or cooking decent meals for a restaurant are more acceptable to them than turning out objects for a wasteful society. Still others are seeing themselves as changing the system from within, in other words, trying to make their employer see that it is in his own interest to make better products. This last group tends to drift into small-scale enterprises, at least in the United States. This is not too surprising when we see an enormous amount of innovative talent in this country spent on paper deals and corporate mergers, rather than the making and selling of things that work. Finally there are a few who seem to find an answer to the dilemma between profit and social responsibility on a spiritual level only. They work either in or out of design and resolve any conflict between their work and their moral ideals through meditation or other spiritual activities.

Design for the sick and the handicapped has become a respectable activity now. In 1975 *Design* magazine wrote about me: "Papanek has been disliked, even loathed by his contemporaries; he has even been sneered at for his preoccupation with the non-profitable needs of Third World people; he has been accused of the single-minded subversion of design schools which previously had a reputation for industrial submissiveness." Eight years later I am delighted to see my former critics grown sleek on fat government and research grants, digging precisely into these areas.

This reassessment of the ethical dilemma faced by designers in 1984 is not to imply that the problems of the poor and needy have been solved. We have recognized more needs as genuine since we are more sensitive to voices raised in protest and despair. But in a few places and in many instances we have managed to swing the pendulum back the other way. In spite of a threatening economic situation, designers must contribute to real human and social needs. This will call for greater sacrifices and much more innovative work. The alternative is chaos.

3

The Myth of the Noble Slob:

Design, "Art," and the Crafts

Good taste is the most obvious resource of the insecure.
People of good taste eagerly buy the Emperor's old clothes.
Good taste is the first refuge of the non-creative.
It is the last-ditch stand of the artist.
Good taste is the anesthetic of the public.

HARLEY PARKER

The cancerous growth of the creative individual expressing himself egocentrically at the expense of spectator and/or consumer has spread from the arts, overrun most of the crafts, and finally reached into design. No longer does the artist, craftsman, or in some cases the designer operate with the good of the consumer in mind; rather, many creative statements have become highly individualistic, autotherapeutic little comments by the artist to himself. As early as the mid-twenties there appeared on the market chairs, tables, and stools designed in Holland by Wijdveldt, as a result of the *de Stijl* movement in painting. These square abstractions painted in shrill primaries were almost impossible to sit in; they were extremely uncomfortable. Sharp corners ripped clothing, and the entire zany construction bore no relation to the human body. These misguided attempts to transfer the two-dimen-

40

sional paintings of Piet Mondrian and Theo van Doesburg into "home furnishing" have parallels today. Profitable small industries have been started in Italy and Japan to make and market enormously expensive replicas of some of the most tortuous chairs and tables of the twenties and thirties. The thronelike Glasgow chairs designed by Charles Rennie MacIntosh in 1902—with six-and-one-half-foot ladderbacks and all the soft comforts of an orange crate—are manufactured in Italy. Some of the most hideous monstrosities designed by Gaudi in Spain or LeCorbusier in France are in production for the first time. A whole elitist nostalgia craze has elevated some of the most uncomfortable seating arrangements yet devised by man into trendy and expensive status symbols that lie halfway between refined torture racks and "art objects." The chairs are enormously expensive, unspeakably uncomfortable, and the movement affects only small bored cliques in New York, Milan, or Paris. Reassuringly, the genuinely innovative and comfortable bentwood chairs first designed by the Austrian firm of Thonet in 1840 are still produced and used all over the world.

Although specific objects inspired by particular fads may last only a short time, the trend, the attempt to translate fashionable daubs into three-dimensional objects for daily use, persists. Frequently such trends are even revived a decade or two later as part of some nostalgia wave. Salvador Dali's sofa constructed in the shape of Mae West's lips may have been a "disengaged" surrealist act (as was Meret Oppenheim's fur-lined cup and saucer of 1935), but this same sofa has just been revived in 1983 as a bit of kitschy nostalgia. In the late sixties inexpensive clear plastic pillows (ornamented with silk-screened polka dots) small enough to be folded and stored in one's pocket and blown up for use were sold by the scores of thousands to college students. These pillows too enjoyed a campus and home revival in mid-1983. There was little excuse for these transparent plastic horrors to begin with—being plastic they don't "breathe," and, when placed together in a cluster on a sofa, they have an unfortunate tendency to *squeak*

against one another like suckling pigs put to the knife. Their
use indicates that we have sacrificed all other aspects of function for shallow visual amusement. And then imagine the dismay of having some romantic interlude punctured by a sudden
pillow blow out.

With new processes and an endless list of new materials at
his disposal, the artist, craftsman, and designer now suffer
from the tyranny of absolute choice. When everything becomes possible, when all the limitations are gone, design and
art can easily become a never-ending search for novelty, until
newness-for-the-sake-of-newness becomes the only measure.

In the novel *Magister Ludi*, Hermann Hesse writes about
a community of intellectual élites who have perfected a mystical, symbolic language called the Bead Game, which has reduced all knowledge to a sort of unified field theory. The
world outside the community is convulsed by riots, wars, and
revolutions, but the players of the Bead Game have lost all
contact. They are engaged in exchanging their esoterica with
one another in the game. There is a disturbing parallel between Hesse's game and the aspirations of the contemporary
artist when he speaks of his goals in the exercise of his private
visions. He discourses on space, the transcendence of space,
the multiplication of space, the division and negation of space.
It is a space devoid of man, as though mankind did not exist.
It is, in fact, a version of the Bead Game.

Concerning the artist Ad Reinhardt, *Time* said:

> Among the new acquisitions currently on display at Man-
> hattan's Museum of Modern Art is a large square canvas called
> "Abstract Painting" that seems at first glance to be entirely
> black. Closer inspection shows that it is subtly divided into
> seven lesser areas. In a helpful gallery note at one side, Ab-
> stractionist Ad Reinhardt explains his painting. It is: "A square
> (neutral, shapeless) canvas, five feet wide, five feet high, as
> high as a man, as wide as a man's outstretched arms (not large,
> not small, sizeless), trisected (no composition), one horizontal
> form negating one vertical form (formless, no top, no bottom,

directionless), three (more or less) dark (lightless), non-contrasting, (colorless) colors, brushwork brushed out to remove brushwork, a mat, flat freehand painted surface (glossless, textureless, non-linear, no hard edge, no soft edge) which does not reflect its surroundings—a pure abstract, non-objective, timeless, spaceless, changeless, relationless, disinterested painting—an object that is self-conscious (not unconsciousness), ideal, transcendent, aware of nothing but art (absolutely no anti-art)."

This from one of America's "most eloquent artists."

Books by learned art historians make a great to-do over the influence of the camera and photography on the plastic arts. And it is certainly true that by placing an apparatus in peoples' hands that made "copying nature" possible for everyone with enough wit to push a button, one of the main objectives of painting—to produce a high-fidelity reproduction—seemed partially fulfilled. It is usually overlooked that even a photograph is a first-order abstraction. Thus in the Galician and Polish backwater sections of the old Austro-Hungarian Empire, village pharmacists did a brisk trade in male model photographs at the beginning of World War I. Each of these wily shopkeepers would stock four stacks of small identical photographs of a cabinet view of male models, five and one-half by four inches in size. One picture showed the face of a clean-shaven man. The second, that of a man with a moustache. The third picture showed a man with a full beard, while, in the fourth, the model's hirsute elegance encompassed both beard and moustache. A young man called up for military service bought the one of the four photographs that most nearly matched his own face and presented it to his wife or sweetheart to remember him by. And it worked! It worked because the picture of even a stranger with the right kind of moustache *was closer to the face of the departed husband than anything his wife had ever seen before except for his face itself.* (Only by glancing at several photographs could she have gained the sophistication to be able to differentiate among these various first-order abstractions.) But the role of photography and its influence on art is by now fairly well documented and established.

Hardly anyone, however, has considered the important impact made by the machine tool and machine perfection. The tolerances demanded of the case for a Zippo cigarette lighter and achieved by automatic handling machinery are far more exact than anything Benvenuto Cellini, possibly the greatest metalsmith of the Renaissance, could have achieved. In modern space hardware technology, plus-minus tolerances of 1/10,000 of an inch are a routine production achievement. This is not to make a value judgment of Cellini versus an automated turret lathe; it is merely to show that "perfection" can be routinely had on assembly lines and in factories, thus depriving the plastic arts of a second goal, the "search for perfection." Like it or not, the contemporary artist lives in contemporary society. Man lives today as much in the environment of the machine as the machine lives in the environment of man. It may be belaboring the obvious to say that there are more man-made objects in the landscape than landscape itself. Even an academic landscape painter living in, say, Cornwall, is bound to see more automobiles than cows on any given day.

Some artists, then, see the machine as a threat, some as a way of life, some as salvation. All of them have to find a way to live with it, and, unable personally to cope with this change in the environment, the modern artist has created a series of psychological escape mechanisms for himself. Seemingly, one simple way to get rid of a threat is to poke fun at it. (Freud would have called this displacement.) While, from its earliest days at the *Cabaret Voltaire* in 1916, the Dadaist movement attempted to show the general absurdity of twentieth-century man and his world, there was always a heavy dose of satirization of the machine involved. From Marcel Duchamp's "ready-mades" ("Why not sneeze," "Fountain") to many of Max Ernst's "collages" to the satirical conglomerations of mass-produced items in Kurt Schwitters's "*Merzbau*," the attempt has been to make fun of the machine through ridicule, satire, or burlesque. Jean Tinguely's "machines" are vast constructs of cogs, screws, umbrella guts, pinwheels, light bulbs, and deflowered sewing machines that shake, jiggle, and quake, sometimes exploding or (disappointingly) just smoldering a little. In 1960 one of these sculptures, composed of pieces of old machines, was erected in the garden of the Museum of Modern Art in New York and, with the setting sun, began to grind into motion. To the delight of an overflow audience, parts of the sculpture frenziedly came into action, catching fire and burning until they collapsed into puddles of kerosene and rust, a proceeding that was viewed with some dismay by those New York City fire companies that were called by frightened neighbors.

Overcompensation can be fun, too: Piet Mondrian, finding himself surrounded by machine-made precision in the middle twenties in Holland, decided to turn himself into a machine. His square white canvases divided by narrow black bands with only two or three primary-colored squares or rectangles dynamically balanced could well be the result of machine production. In fact, a computer in Basel, Switzerland, has created Mondrianlike pictures. This may raise the question of creativity: the computer versus Mondrian. Having visited him during his illness, I know that he would have preferred to sit calmly back in his chair and have two servants move the lines and color areas back and forth until he considered them to be in perfect balance. Had he lived to see graphic readout computers, he would have found them a delightful new toy. From the traces of tape on his white unfinished canvases we can see that Mondrian himself followed computerlike behavior patterns and that what creativity he brought to the process of painting was entirely in the area of aesthetic decision-making. Piet Mondrian's work has found a ready but debased acceptance in the facade design of contemporary buildings, Kleenex packages, and typographical layout.

A third way of dealing with the machine is to run away from it ("avoidance mechanism," in Freud's jargon). The Surrealist movement, inheritors of the irrational side of Dadaism, attempted to plumb that region, half cesspool and half garden, known as the unconscious or id. By basing their highly realistic canvases on subconscious symbols, they hoped to turn themselves into latter-day medicine men, witch doctors, shamans of the pigment. The trouble with this concept is that id-motivated emotions differ from person to person. Salvador Dali may experience a world of voluptuous sexuality from his painting of a burning giraffe (and in fact considers it his most potent painterly sexual stimulus), but it does not communicate sexuality to his spectators. Dorothea Tanning's jack-booted naked twelve-year-old girl wearing a Gay Nineties sailor hat and sensuously embracing the red-hot pipe of a stove also fails to elicit an appropriate response. In spite of a lot of loose talk about the "left hand being the dreamer," Jungian archetypes, poetic feeling tones, metaphysics, mysticism, etc., the totemistic and fetishistic emblems of the Surrealists failed to come across, being based on highly idiosyncratic and personal associations. The designer by contrast tries to use associational values that are accepted and understood more broadly in a culture or subculture. A reference point was missing from the surreal paintings. The Comte de Lautreamont definition of surrealism as "the chance encounter of a sewing machine and an umbrella upon a dissecting table" no longer works as thousands of those surreal chance encounters have taken place since then—and some are now one with the hot dust of Spain, of Europe, of Vietnam—and the concept is in itself no longer bizarre.

The human preoccupation of liking to play with dolls' houses has been used cleverly by Joseph Cornell. His little boxes, with strange and esoteric objects cunningly arranged therein, are manageable small universes, perfect within themselves, into which no hint of Dwight MacDonald's masscult or midcult can enter. (Jungians would call this hermeticism.)

Seeking refuge from the threatening surround by catering to a small coterie (as in the Bead Game) was carried to its highest level by Yves Klein, whose methods are described in the book *Collage*. When not busy glueing 426,000 sponges to the wall of a resort hotel, Mr. Klein was fond of painting watercolors and then placing them in his backyard during heavy rains in order to "obtain a dynamic interchange between nature and man-made images." He used the same rationale for doing oil paintings in a slow-drying vehicle and then strapping them to the roof of his Citroën and driving briskly around "to make the colors clarify." The height of his career was reached when the *Galerie Iris Clert* held his first nonpainting show in 1958. The gallery had been painted festively in white; the only objects in view were simple white frames hanging on the walls with descriptions of prices attached, such as "Nonpainting, 30 cm × 73 cm, Fr. 80,000." The show was a sellout. Hundreds of Parisians and American visitors solemnly paid for and carried empty white frames to their cars and, one supposes, then hung them triumphantly in their living rooms. It would be instructive to find out if Mr. Klein would have accepted nonchecks.

Andy Warhol, Roy Lichtenstein, and Robert Rauschenberg have surrounded their productions with much rationale. Their attempts to reduce the unusual to the commonplace and raise the commonplace to the stature of the unusual are losing propositions. Marilyn Monroe's face identically stenciled fifty times attempts to say that Miss Monroe was one of a herd, and interchangeably so, a charge that can be levelled at most Hollywood sex symbols but certainly not at the late Miss Monroe. The reduction of human emotions to the level of a comic strip episode is an attempt to shield oneself from involvement through banality. And Marcel Duchamp once said, "If a man takes fifty Campbell Soup cans and puts them on a canvas, it is not the retinal image which concerns us. What interests us is the kind of mind that wants to put fifty Campbell Soup cans on a canvas."

Art as self-gratification can, of course, also be an outlet for aggression and hostility. Niki de Saint-Phalle fires rounds of ammunition into her white plaster constructions from a gun, releasing little bags of paint that spurt out and dribble all over her pieces. When not engaged with plaster of Paris, fake blood, and her fowling-piece, Miss de Saint-Phalle got together with two "collaborators" and constructed a gigantic reclining nude in Stockholm that spectators entered through the vagina to view the interior constructions, a merry-go-round for the kiddies and a cocktail bar within her generously proportioned breasts.

Earlier we spoke about the artist suffering from the tyranny of absolute choice. But if he doesn't care to poke fun at the machine, become a machine, turn himself into a bogus witch doctor, construct tiny boxed universes, elevate the commonplace to a symbol of banality, or let out his aggressions on a middle class no longer capable of being shocked, the area of choice is narrowed abruptly. One thing remains—accidents—for a well-programmed computer makes no mistakes. A well-designed machine is free of error. What, then, is more logical than to glorify the mistakes and to venerate the accidents. Jean (Hans) Arp, one of the cofounders of the Dada movement in Zurich during World War I, tried it first in his "Forms Arranged According to the Laws of Chance."

Mr. Arp tore up one of his gouache paintings (without looking), then climbed up on top of a stepladder and let the pieces drop. Carefully, he glued them down where they had fallen. A few decades later, another Swiss named Spoerri invited his girlfriend for breakfast, then glued all the dishes, soiled paper napkins, bacon rinds, and cereal dregs down on the table, entitled the result "Breakfast with Marie," and hung it, table and all, in a museum. It was probably unavoidable that after Jackson Pollock's dribble-and-blob paintings of the forties and early fifties, other painters would whoop it up for mistake, accident, and the unplanned. One member of this group paints by strapping his brushes to his left forearm since, he says, he "can't breed the ability even out of his left hand." With other painters rolling naked models across their canvases or riding across their wet paintings on motorcycles, scooters, bicycles, roller-skates or trampling across them on snowshoes, the "desire for novelty" is getting full play.

Increasingly, many of us (especially the young) have come to reject the mere accumulation of material possessions. That this emotion is engendered largely by the fact that we live in a postindustrial society bursting with gadgets, knickknacks, and manufactured trivia is abundantly clear. So now we have "Conceptual Art." A 1971 production by a leading West Coast painter consisted of some fifteen pages of yellow paper. On each page he described with meticulous detail the sizes, colors, textures, and compositions that would have constituted nearly 400 paintings, *provided he had painted them*. Added to this were descriptions of the working conditions under which these canvases would have been painted, had they been painted at all. After a public reading of these descriptive passages, he then burned the papers and exhibited a pickle-jar containing the ashes.

George McKinnon, an exhibition-oriented photographer from the West Coast, rephotographs pictures appearing in old magazines and entitles the results "retrospective pieces."

Of course, even the self-indulgent salon drivel of New York, San Francisco, and Los Angeles could be justified in terms of the people who are doing it. But a recent encounter in New York can at least point to an alternative view: when a number of "painters" smashed two dozen violins and bass fiddles to glue the fragments to a wall and create a mural, some probing questions were asked about the young Puerto Ricans and blacks in the neighborhood who might wish to study music but who could never afford to buy instruments.

When museum patrons are invited to a formal opening and are advised *not* to come to the museum but to go instead to the Sixty-Third Street subway station and peer into the mirror of a gum-vending machine on the second level; while their friends at exactly the same time are advised to take the Staten Island Ferry and spend the entire trip in the toilet reading *Silence*, by John Cage; and still another party is told to rent a room at the Americana Hotel and spend the time shaving; and all these many activities, indulged in by all these many people simultaneously, constitute both the opening of the art show and the art show itself, we are in the presence of folks trying to play random games. And randomness, as has been stated earlier, is the one game the machine won't play, and, therefore, this too is a reaction against the machine.

Ever since the environment became an "in" thing, we have had Earthworks as an artistic trend. Now Earthworks can be many things: a 30-foot trench dug in the Mojave Desert, one leaf torn off every third oak tree in Tallahassee, Florida, or for that matter, snow lying on a meadow in Colorado, to which nothing has been done whatever.

I don't wish to make any judgments about others finding meaningful creative and artistic engagement by pissing into a snow bank, but surely the good people working in the arts can find more authentic ways of surprising us, delighting us, or reflecting their views. (Incidentally, all of this and what the future may bring in the arts was listed, described, and explained in a book written in 1948 in England by C. E. M. Joad. Its marvelously appropriate title is *Decadence*.)

The journalist George F. Will (*Newsweek*, 2 August 1981) has recently brought some more absurd examples of the Bead Game to our attention, as quoted below:

> Art-lovers are heartened by New York's decision not to prosecute the fellow who put what the police called a bomb atop the Brooklyn Bridge. The fellow, who calls himself an "environmental artist," says the bucket full of fireworks was a "kinetic sculpture." Well, it would have been if the "sculpture" had not had a defective fuse.
>
> A British gallery has a new work, "Room Temperature," featuring two dead flies and a bucket of water, in which float four apples and six uninflated balloons. A gallery official says the work left him "amazed by its completeness, its oneness, its apparent obviousness. Yet it had the ability to tease, to make me wonder, and question, to lead me in other directions."
>
> An American foundation paid $300,000 to finance "Vertical Kilometer," a brass rod one kilometer long buried in a hole one kilometer deep. The same artist also perpetrated "Light-

ning Field," a patch of New Mexico made into a pin cushion by metal rods. . . .

Robert Hughes, *Time* magazine's art critic and author of "The Shock of the New," says that every five years America's art schools graduate more people than lived in Florence in the last quarter of the 15th century, and that there probably are more galleries than bakeries in New York.

. . . college credit in "art" has been given for photographing 650 San Diego garages, and for spending a week in a gym locker (a work—or act—of art called "a duration-confinement body-piece").

The broadened definition of art to include doing anything, as well as making anything, is a triumph of democracy: Everyone can be—indeed, cannot help but be—an artist. Hughes notes that Richard Tuttle "was chosen to represent America at the 1976 Venice Biennale with a stick rather longer than a pencil and three-quarters of an inch thick, cut from a length of standard 1-inch lumber, unpainted, and placed in solitary magnificence on the wall of the U.S. Pavillion." Your tax dollars were at work in that display of purely democratic art: Having no content, Tuttle's "art" was immune to the charge of "elitism."

In the nineteenth century the avant-garde tried to challenge the banal standards of acceptable taste held by the bourgeoisie. The Dada movement of the early twenties attempted to shock the middle class through its all-out attack on art itself. But consider the plight of the artist today: all standards are gone. According to an *official* catalogue of the California Institute of the Arts "an artist is anyone who makes art" and "art is anything an artist makes." In other words: anything goes. If everyone is an artist, when everything is art, there can be no avant-garde.

What is the relevance of such "art games" to life? Without question, our time needs paintings, music, sculpture, and poetry. Seldom in fact have both delight and catharsis been needed more.

Even in 1984, there are far too few collections of design in art museums in the United States. There are special exhibits, like the Philadelphia Museum's *"Design since 1945"* (November 1983), but where are there permanent design collections? Besides the Museum of Modern Art in New York, there are vestigial collections in Minneapolis, San Francisco, Los Angeles, Philadelphia, Boston, and Buffalo. The rest of the country may sometimes see a travelling "good design" exhibition, but their exposure to well-designed objects ends with that.

For that matter, even the most prestigious exhibitions of "good design" can be disappointments. In New York the Museum of Modern Art held an exhibition of "well-designed" objects in 1971 that elevated the ugly, in fact *the consciously ugly*, to a new level. Thus we could see a small, high-intensity lamp that has been designed to look precarious and unstable no matter at what angle it is put down. An unruly gush of plastic, colored precisely the shade of frozen diarrhea, doubles as an easy chair. In short, in a society in which the "machine

"Armchair" (1964) by Gunnar Aagaard Anderson. Urethane foam, 30″ high. Executed at Dansk Polyether Industri, Denmark. Collection The Museum of Modern Art, New York. Gift of the designer. While the chair is ugly, it is incredibly comfortable and "grown" out of foam biomorphically.

perfect" or even the "fashionably pleasing" can be obtained with a minimum of effort, distorted repulsiveness and the beastly have become accepted as a new direction in furniture and furnishings by a small elite and their tame curators during the last twelve years. Other such exhibitions of objects are discussed in Chapter Six.

Much has been said about the decadence of Rome when the barbarians were outside the gate. There are no barbarians outside ours: we have become our own barbarians, and barbarism has become a do-it-yourself kit.

4

Do-it-Yourself Murder:

Social and Moral Responsibilities of Design

The truth is that engineers are not asked to design for safety. Further inaction will be criminal—for it will be with full knowledge that our action can make a difference, that auto deaths can be cut down, that the slaughter on our highways is needless waste . . . it is time to act.

ROBERT F. KENNEDY

One of my first jobs after leaving school was to design a table radio. This was shroud design: the design of the external covering of the mechanical and electrical guts. It was my first, and I hope my last, encounter with appearance design, styling, or design cosmetics. The radio was to be one of the first small and inexpensive table radios to compete on the postwar market. Still attending school part time, I felt insecure and frightened by the enormity of the job, especially since my radio was to be the only object manufactured by a new corporation. One evening Mr. G., my client, took me out on the balcony of his apartment overlooking Central Park. He asked me if I realized the responsibility I had in designing a radio for him.

With the glib ease of the chronically insecure, I launched into a spirited discussion of "beauty" at the market level and "consumer satisfaction." I was interrupted. "Yes, of course, there is all that," he conceded, "but your responsibility goes far deeper than that." With this he began a lengthy and cliché-ridden discussion of his own (and by extension his designer's) responsibility to his stockholders and especially his workers.

> Just think what making your radio entails in terms of our workers. In order to get it produced, we're building a plant in Long Island City. We're hiring about 600 new men. Workers from many states, Georgia, Kentucky, Alabama, Indiana, are going to be uprooted. They'll sell their homes and buy new ones here. They'll form a whole new community of their own. Their kids will be jerked out of school and go to different schools. In their new subdivision supermarkets, drugstores, and service stations will open up, just to fill their needs. And now, just suppose the radio doesn't sell. In a year we'll have to lay them all off. They'll be stuck for their monthly payments on homes and cars. Stores and service stations will go bankrupt when the money stops rolling in; homes will go into sacrifice sales. Their kids, unless daddy finds a new job, will have to change schools. There will be a lot of heartaches all around, and that's not even thinking of my stockholders. And all this because you have made a design mistake. *That's* where your responsibility really lies, and I bet that they never taught you this at school!

I was young and, frankly, impressed. Within the closed system of Mr. G.'s narrow market dialectics, it all made sense. Looking back at the scene from a vantage-point of a good number of years, I must agree that the designer bears a responsibility for the way the products he designs are received at the marketplace. But this view is still too narrow and parochial. The designer's responsibility must go far beyond these considerations. His social and moral judgment must be brought into play long *before* he begins to design, since he has to make a judgment, an *a priori* judgment at that, as to whether the products he is asked to design or redesign merit his attention at all. In other words, will his design be on the side of the social good or not.

Food, shelter, and clothing: that is the way we have always described mankind's basic needs. With increasing sophistication we have added tools and machines to our list because they enable us to produce the other three items. But man has more basic needs than food, shelter, and clothing. We have taken clean air and pure water for granted for the first ten million years or so, but now this picture has changed drastically. While the reasons for our poisoned air and polluted streams and lakes are fairly complex, industrial designers and industry in general are certainly coresponsible with others for this appalling state of affairs.

The American image abroad was frequently created by the movies. The make-believe, fairyland, Cinderellalike world of "Andy Hardy Goes To College" and "Singing in the Rain" communicated something that moved our foreign viewers more, directly and subliminally, than either plot or stars. It was the communication of an idealized environment, an environment upholstered and fitted out with all the latest gadgets available.

In the eighties we export the products and gadgets themselves. And with the increasing cultural and technological Coca-colonization of that part of the world we are pleased to think of as "free," we are also in the business of exporting environments and "lifestyles," as becomes plain to anyone who has watched reruns of "I Love Lucy" in Nigeria in 1982 or seen "Jaws 2" in Indonesia.

The designer-planner shares responsibility for nearly all of our products and tools and hence nearly all of our environmental mistakes. He is responsible either through bad design or by default: by having thrown away his responsible creative abilities, by "not getting involved," or by "muddling through."

Three diagrams will explain the lack of social engagement in design. If (in Figure 1) we equate the triangle with a *design problem*, we readily see that industry and its designers are concerned only with the tiny top portion, without addressing themselves to real needs.

Let's take microcomputers for example. Their introduction

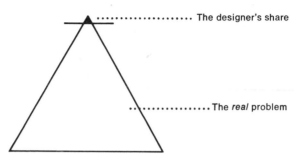

The designer's share

The *real* problem

FIGURE 1: THE DESIGN PROBLEM

into offices and homes has brought about many important changes in communication systems, the relationship between being at work and working at home, commercial and private links, data processing, information storage and retrieval: indeed they have changed the personal lives of many during the last three or four years. It is plain to see that designers really haven't done their job on most microcomputers, as well as the surrounding home or office landscape. Most computers sold for home use, as well as a startling large number of small computers in offices, have the capacity to be used for computer games or other electronic diversions. The rest, whether equipped with disk drives, diskettes, or cassette storage, tend to all look pretty much alike. *Some* attempts have been made by manufacturers and designers to deal with keyboard and display terminals, but these attempts are superficial at best. They have dealt with the exterior shell and frequently a superficial restyling of the buttons on the keyboard has also been performed. But to really examine the problem of minicomputers and word processors, both manufacturers and designers together must examine some of the deeper problems connected with the use of this tool:

1. Is the arrangement of letters, numerals, symbols, and commands on the keyboard in accordance with frequency of use and hand comfort? (We will see later in

This idiot gadget is made and successfully sold in one part of the world. . .

. . . while in another, this is a family's sole means of cooking. Mexican stove from Jalisco, made of used license plates and sold for about 8 cents. It is used as a charcoal brazier. When the soldering finally pops after some ten or fifteen years of use, it is repaired, if possible, or else the family has to invest another 8 cents for a "new" stove. (Anonymous design, collected by John Frost, author's collection. Photo by Roger Conrad.)

this book that typewriter keyboards are ergonomically badly designed.)

2. Is the relationship of green letters on a black screen comfortable, or does it produce eye strain, fatigue and unease

of recognition? Commodore and Osborne computers also offer amber on black with their visual terminals. It would add no more than $30 to $50 to a $3,000 microcomputer setup to give the user almost infinite choices and "at-will-variability" of both background and number or letter colors.

3. Is the *size* of characters appearing on the screen correct for the majority of people using microcomputers? Here again variability of size would be a very simple added option.

4. Can computer memories be routinely protected against erasure by power blackouts, electric storms, and so forth? Many people using word processors have lost an entire Ph.D. thesis, a bibliography, or part of a book due to a main transformer malfunction in their city. A simple clip-on device costing no more than $40 exists, but is not routinely installed.

5. Is the angle of the display screen correct for best vision? Could the screen be tilted (manually) to accommodate people wearing bifocals or trifocals?

6. Are the various command functions grouped in such a manner that some of them can be casually disregarded by two distinct user groups: those who do number-crunching, and those who use word processing?

7. Can the keyboard—or the surface on which the keyboard rests—be simply lowered or raised for people of differing stature, or people in wheelchairs? Here such adjustments should be mechanical, rather than electronic or hydraulic; they will cost less, and fewer things will go wrong.

8. Is the operator's chair easily adjustable upward or downward?

9. Is the operating manual that comes with the computer, as well as the instruction diskette, disk, or tape, clear and simple to understand?

10. To what extent is the operator forced to accommodate himself/herself to the machine, rather than the machine

being "user-friendly" or, as we call it in gliding planes or racing yachts, "forgiving"?

None of these questions is frivolous, and many others could be added. Dr. Robert Frank, in a three-year study performed for Mount Sinai Hospital, New York, found that severe eye strain, detached retinas, hallucinatory eye phenomena, headaches, back strain, and slipped disks occur with horrifying frequency among people working with video display terminals and home computers (*All Things Considered*, 18 October 1983).

The reason for this lack of forgiving and innovative design lies in the highly competitive market for small computers. Although *all* the improvements suggested in the above ten points at retail market prices might amount to only $400 (or roughly eight-and-a-half percent of the retail price of a personal word processor), and in true mass production could hardly amount to more than $200, savage market tactics, that peculiarly American contribution to free enterprise, a quarterly report to stockholders that must show increasing profits every ninety days, and marketing hoopla prevent design improvements. *

As a designer, my evaluation is that in terms of the office or home landscape, human factors, and ease of use, much needs to be done. Industry and its captive designers have not addressed themselves to the huge bottom area of our diagrammatic triangle.

Figure 2 is, of course, identical to Figure 1. Only the labels have changed. For "Design Problem" we have substituted "Country." In a way, this becomes immediately apparent when talking about some far-off, exotic place. If we let the entire triangle stand for nearly any South or Central American nation we can see its telesic aptness. Nearly all of these countries exist with wealth concentrated in the hands of a

---

*For an alternative view of computers that disputes all of our assumptions about our need for them, see Joseph Menosky's "Computer Worship" in *Science*, Vol. V, No. 4, May 1984.

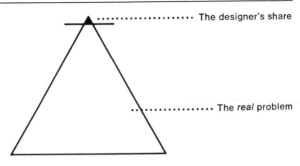

FIGURE 2: A COUNTRY

small group of "absentee landlords." Many of these people have never even seen the South American country that they so efficiently "administer" and exploit. Design is a luxury enjoyed by a small clique who form the technological, moneyed, and cultural "elite" of each nation. The ninety percent native Indian population that lives "up-country" has neither tools nor beds shelter nor schools nor hospitals that have ever been within breathing distance of a designer's board or workbench. It is this huge population of the needy and the dispossessed who are represented by the bottom area of our triangle. If I suggest that this holds equally true of most of Africa, Southeast Asia, and the Middle East, there will be little disagreement.

Unfortunately, this diagram applies just as easily to our own country. Our inner cities and rural areas, the educational tools we use in over ninety percent of our school systems, our hospitals, doctors' offices, diagnostic devices, farm tools, and so forth, suffer design neglect. New designs may sporadically occur in these areas but usually only as a result of a research breakthrough, not as a genuine response to a real need. Here at home we must assign those issues served by the designer to the minuscule upper part of the triangle.

The third triangle, shown on the next page, is identical to the first and the second. But again we have changed labels.

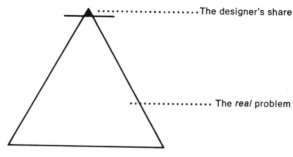

FIGURE 3: THE WORLD

For now we call it "The World." Can there be substantial doubt that the peoples of this world are not served by designers?

Where has our spirit of innovation gone? This is not an attempt to take all the fun out of life. After all, it is only right and proper that "toys for adults" should be available to those willing to pay for them in an abundant society. By 1983 there are virtually no radios for the home manufactured in the United States. Several are *assembled* in America from parts that come from Taiwan, Korea, and Hong Kong. Within two to five years at the most, they will come from mainland China, Indonesia, and whatever parts of Central America we have not vandalized. Sony, Hitachi, Panasonic, and Aiwa are highly innovative and carry lines of more than 120 table radios that are truly different from one another in terms of use, appearance, or specific application. This record could easily be duplicated with tape-recorders, television sets, or cameras. This is not to argue that every product a company sells must be a good one. After all, many book publishers, while pushing incredible trash on to best-seller lists, still manage to bring out a few worthwhile volumes each year.

All too often designers who try to operate within the entire triangle (problem, country, or world) find themselves accused of designing for the minority. This charge is completely false and reflects misconceptions and misperceptions under which the profession operates. The nature of these faulty perceptions must be examined.

Let us suppose that an industrial designer or an entire design office were to specialize exclusively within the areas of human needs outlined in this and other chapters. What would the work load consist of? There would be the design of teaching aids to be used in prenursery-school settings, nursery schools, kindergartens, primary and secondary schools, junior colleges, colleges and universities, graduate and postdoctoral research and study programs. There would be teaching devices for such specialized fields as adult education, the teaching of knowledge and skills to the retarded, the disadvantaged, and the handicapped, as well as special language studies, vocational re-education, the rehabilitation of prisoners, and the mentally ill. Add to this the education in totally new skills for people about to undergo radical transformation in their habitats: from slum, ghetto, or rural poverty pocket to the city; from the milieu of, say, a central Australian aborigine to life in a technocratic society; from Earth to space; from the tranquillity of the English countryside to life in the Arctic.

The design work done by our mythical office would include the design, invention, and development of medical diagnostic devices, hospital equipment, dental equipment, surgical tools and devices, equipment and furnishings for mental hospitals, obstetrician's equipment, diagnostic and training devices for ophthalmologists, and so forth. The range of things would go all the way from a better readout of a fever thermometer at home to such exotic devices as heart-lung machines, heart pacers, artificial organs, and cyborgian implants, and back again to humble reading mechanisms for the blind, improved stethoscopes and urinalysis devices, hearing aids, and improved calendrical dispensers for the pill.

The office would concern itself with safety devices for home, industry, transportation, and many other areas and with pollution, both chemical and thermal, of rivers, streams, lakes, and oceans, as well as air. The nearly seventy-five percent of the world's people who live in poverty, starvation, and need

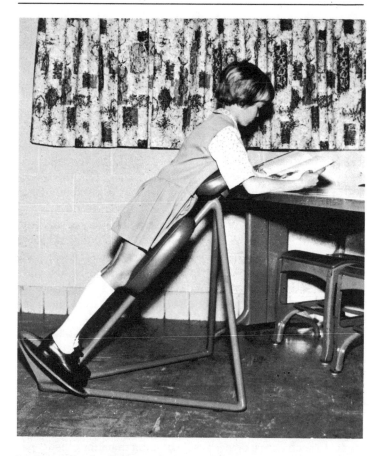

Perch or reclining structure to be used in classrooms *in addition* to regular chairs. This provides eight more positions for restless children. Designed by Steven Lynch, as a student at Purdue University.

would certainly occupy still more time in the already busy schedule of our theoretical office. But not only the underdeveloped and emergent countries of the world have special needs. These special needs abound at home as well. Black lung disease among the miners of Kentucky and West Virginia is

just one of a myriad of occupational ills, many of which can be abolished through redesign of equipment and/or processes.

Research tools are usually stuck-together, jury-rigged contraptions, and advanced research is suffering from an absence

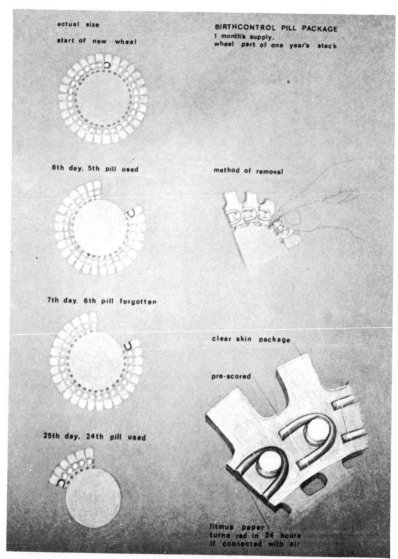

actual size

start of new wheel

BIRTHCONTROL PILL PACKAGE
1 month's supply,
wheel part of one year's stack

6th day, 5th pill used

method of removal

7th day, 6th pill forgotten

clear skin package

pre-scored

25th day, 24th pill used

litmus paper
turns red in 24 hours
if connected with air

Package for birth control pills for use by largely illiterate people. A run of placebos is included so that counting is unnecessary. If a user forgets to break off one day's pill from the styrene wafer, the U-shape tube turns red, as a reminder. Designed by Pirkko (Tintti) Sotamaa, Purdue University.

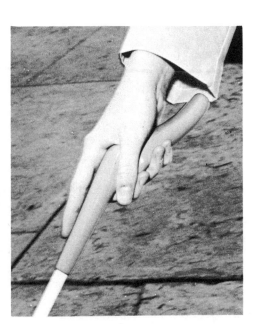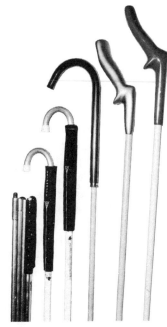

Canes for the blind, of hand-aligned fiber optics. They glow in the dark and also provide a more sensitive tactile feedback for the hand. Designed by Robert Senn, as a student at Purdue University.

of rationally designed equipment. From radar telescopes to simple chemical beakers, design has lagged behind. And what about the needs of the elderly and the senile? And of pregnant women and the obese? What about the alienation of young people all over the world? What about transportation? (Surely the fact that the American automobile is the most efficient killing device since the invention of the machine-gun doesn't permit us to rest on our laurels.)

Is this designing for minorities? The fact of the matter is that all of us are children at one point of our lives and that we need education throughout our lives. Almost all of us become adolescent, middle-aged, and old. We all need the services and help of teachers, doctors, dentists, and hospitals. We all belong to special need groups. We all need transportation, communication, products, tools, shelter, and clothing. We must have water and air that is clean. As a species we need the challenge of research, the promise of space, the fulfilment of knowledge.

If we then lump together all the seemingly little minorities of the last few pages, if we combine all these "special" needs, we find that we have designed for the majority after all. It is only the industrial designer, style-happy in the eighties of this century, who, by concocting trivia for the marketplaces of a few abundant societies, really designs for the minority.

In January 1982, I was asked to give the Keynote Speech when industrial designers, architects, medical people, other designers, and consumer/users met at the first international meeting of the *Coalition for a Barrier-Free Environment* at the United Nations building in New York. I was pleased to hear speaker after speaker address the concept that all people are handicapped in some minor or major way, throughout or for part of their lives. This concept has finally become acceptable to some designers and architects in this country. The idea of seeing the whole mosaic that forms society, instead of the individual pieces we called minorities, has finally caught on.

What is the answer? Not just for next year but for the future, and not just in one country but in the world? Nearly fifteen years ago I discovered a Finnish word dating back to medieval times. A word so obscure that some Finns have never even heard it. This word, *kymmenykset,* means the same thing as the medieval church word *tithe.* A tithe was something one paid: the peasant would set aside ten percent of his crop for the poor, the rich man would give up ten percent of his income at the end of the year to feed those in need. Being designers, we don't have to pay money in the form of *kymmenykset* or a tithe. Being designers, we can pay by giving ten percent of our crop of ideas and talents to the seventy-five percent of mankind in need. Since then I have been delighted as year after year designers from many countries accepted and practiced this social self-tithing.

There will always be people who spend all of their time designing for the needs of mankind. Most of the rest of us can't do that well, but I think even the most successful designer can afford to give one-tenth of his time. It is unimportant what the mechanics of the situation are: four hours out of every forty, one working day out of every ten, or ideally, every tenth year, to be spent as a sort of sabbatical, designing for many instead of designing for money.

In the 1970s, Björn Weckström, Finland's most famous designer of jewelery, left his international practice for one year to give his time to design survival shelters in East Africa, inspired by this tithing idea. Even if the corporate greed of many design offices makes this kind of design impossible, students should at least be encouraged to work in this manner. For in showing students new areas of engagement, we may set up alternative patterns of thinking about design problems. We may help them to develop the kind of social and moral responsibility that is needed.

One basic misunderstanding has come to haunt me during the thirteen years between the publication of this book and its revision: many design professionals found it difficult to accept my proposal that design for areas previously neglected was *one more direction for design*. Instead they felt that I proposed *substituting* concern for the vast human needs in the world *for all commercial design, as now practiced*. Nothing could be further from the truth: all I suggest is that we add some intelligently designed goods to a global marketplace now flooded with manufactured "bads." A discussion of a few such goods is given below.

There are many examples in commercial product design that show that the making of products can be done with sensitivity and skill. Examples from the United States seem to follow the interest of relatively small groups: many cooking utensils and gourmet-cooking utensils are innovatively conceived, well designed, and made to high-quality standards.

This also holds true in equipment and product design for backpacking, mountaineering, camping, and survival gear. Competition sports, fishing and hunting equipment, touring and racing bicycles, tents, and similar consumer products are of high quality. What all these things have in common is *performance*. Quality is essential to user satisfaction. This same excellence of design for need and use is true of hand tools, gardening tools, and craftsmen's equipment. Much of it is designed and made in the United States, with some excellent imports from Great Britain. In other areas of consumer products, the best designs come from Japan, Germany, Italy, and the Scandinavian countries. This is especially true of automobiles, cameras, television sets, furniture, and many other electronic or home furnishing products. The reason may be that United States' industries—and hence their designers—find themselves beset by problems of sheer scale: when designing for enormous potential markets, we seldom emphasize quality in design.

Radical groups used compelling rhetoric some years ago about "talking to the workers." But how about *working* for the workers? Hard hats are given their name because of the protective headgear they wear. But these hats are unsafe, not sufficiently tested for absorption of kinetic energy. I should like to quote from the pamphlet about the "safety" helmet made by Jackson Products of Warren, Michigan:

> CAUTION: This helmet provides limited protection. It reduces the effect of the force of a falling object striking the top of the shell.
>
> Contact of this helmet shell with energized electrical conductors (live wires) or equipment, should be avoided. NEVER ALTER or MODIFY the shell or suspension system.
>
> Inspect regularly and replace suspension system and shell at first sign of wear or damage.
>
> *The WARNING stated above applies to all industrial safety hats and caps regardless of manufacturer.* [My italics]

This last statement really seems to be true since all hard-hat pamphlets carry this warning, using almost identical words. (In 1970 I protested this state of affairs; unfortunately, nothing has changed.)

The nearly two million safety goggles manufactured annually in this country are unsafe—the lenses scratch easily, some may shatter, and most crack the bridge of the nose under a blow. So-called hard shoes, designed to protect the front of the foot against falling debris, do not absorb sufficient kinetic energy to be useful; the steel cap over the toes can be crushed by a small steel beam falling one yard. Most cabs in long-distance trucks vibrate so much they will materially destroy a man's kidneys in four to ten years. The list could go on. In spite of greater interest and more research during the past thirteen years, hard hats still await improvement, and working conditions for farmers, truckers, and laborers are still dangerous. I refer the reader to my book *Design For Human Scale* (New York: Van Nostrand Reinhold, 1983) for more design ideas for workers' safety devices.

Many interesting concepts for designs that would help improve social conditions emerge in discussions and meetings between designers. In the seventies I thought that a commune of designers, taking advantage of high technology together with the findings in the behavioral sciences, might lead to a sort of permanent designers' round-table. The economic realities of 1984 make this seem impractical today. The educational impact of designers engaging together in a stimulating environment are more fully discussed in Chapters Eleven and Twelve.

The impact of sensitive and intelligent design needs not to be limited to safety requirements of farmers or workers. The problems are global in scope. We are all together on this small spaceship called Earth, 9,700 miles in diameter and sailing through the vast oceans of space. It's a small spaceship, and fifty to sixty percent of the population cannot help to run it or even help themselves stay alive, through no fault of their own. Hunger and poverty lead small children to eat the paint off walls and die of lead poisoning in Chicago and New York ghettos; children in Los Angeles and Boston die of infected rat bites. To deprive ourselves of the brain and potential of any person on our spaceship is wrong and no longer acceptable.

All this raises the question of value. If we have seen that the designer is powerful enough (by affecting all of man's tools and environment) to put murder on a mass-production basis, we have also seen that this imposes great moral and social responsibilities. I have tried to demonstrate that by freely giving ten percent of his time, talents, and skills the designer can help. But help where? What is a need?

In the early fifties I had the good fortune to enjoy a lengthy correspondence with the late Dr. Robert Lindner of Baltimore. Together we worked on a book to be called *Creativity Versus Conformity*, a collaboration ending only with his untimely death. I should like to quote extensively from the Prologue of his book *Prescription for Rebellion* concerning his concept of value:

> The end to which man studies himself cannot be other than to realize the full potentiality of his being, and to conquer the *triad of limitations* fate or God, or destiny, or sheer accident, has imposed on him. Human beings are enclosed by an iron triangle that forms for their race a veritable prison cell. One side of this triangle is the medium in which they must live; the second is the equipment they have, or can fashion, with which to live; the third is the fact of their mortality. All effort, all being, is directed upon the elimination of the sides of this enclosure. If there is purpose to life, that purpose must be to break through the triangle that thus imprisons humanity into a new order of existence where such a triad of limitations no longer obtains. This is the end toward which both individual and species function; this is the end toward which the race strives; this is the end which gives meaning and substance to life.
>
> Behind and beyond the word-games philosophers play, and in the final analysis, all that man does—alone or in the organizations he erects—has as its design the overcoming of one

or more or all aspects of this basic triad of limitations. What we call progress is nothing more than the small victories every man or every age wins over any or all of the sides of the imprisoning triangle. Thus progress, in this one and only possible sense, is a measurable thing against which the sole existence of a person, the activities and aims of a group, even the achievements of a culture, can be estimated and assigned value.

The as yet uncalculated millennia during which man has tenanted Earth have been witness to his continued valiant efforts to escape from the triangle that interns him. Inexorably and against odds, over the centuries, he has fought against and conquered the medium of his habitat until now he stands poised on a springboard to the stars. Today, earthbound no longer, and loosening even the fetters of gravity, he can look backward to count his conquests. The elements have succumbed to him, and also the natural barriers of space and time. Once confined to a small area bounded by the height of the trees he could climb, the distance his legs could carry him, the view his eye could encompass, the length his voice could carry, the reach of his arms, and the acuity of his remaining senses— once a cowed victim of every hazard to existence vagrant Nature has in her catalogue—now he is lord over those containing powers that would have held him slave to them forever. So one iron wall of his cell has been worn thin, and, through the vents and cracks he has made in it, come far-travelled winds of freedom and the beckoning gleam of the universes outside.

Similarly, the second side of the triangle—the limitations imposed by the biologically given equipment of human

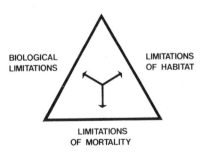

Triad of Limitations

beings—has yielded step by step to the ongoing, persistent struggle against it by men. In the main, this has been a process of extension. It has been marked by the fashioning of tools to improve the uses of the limbs, the sensitivities of the specialized end-organs and the efficiency of those other parts and organs that complete the body. Here the victories have been of an immense order of magnitude. They have culminated in what amounts to a total breakthrough of the envelope of skin that enwraps us, even to the point where the products of hand and brain—as in the giant computing machines and other physical miracles of our time—by far outdo many capacities of their creators. And, finally, in the matter of the last side of the triangle, while the days of our years still last but an eye-wink on the bland face of the eternal clock, longevity if not immortality is now more than a promise.

The uses of knowledge are clear despite the turgid morass through which a seeker must plough to find order and sense therein. The sciences and arts—like the individual lives men live—are all strivings and experiments. They are pointed toward the realization of human potentiality and ultimately contributory to that evolutionary breakthrough which will come when the walls of the containing triangle finally crash to earth. Thus the value of an item of knowledge, an entire discipline, or a deed of art can be placed upon a scale, and its measure also taken.

Much as we have established a six-sided "function complex" in order to evaluate design in the first chapter, we can now use the "triad of limitations" and see it as a primary filter to establish the social value of the design act. While the American automobile is examined in great detail in a later chapter, it can be used as a demonstration object now.

Early automobiles overcame one of the three prison walls of the triad. It was possible to go farther and faster in an automobile than a human being's legs would carry him and to carry a heavy load as well. But today the automobile has become so overloaded with false values that it has emerged as a fullblown status symbol, dangerous rather than convenient. It exhales a great amount of cancer-inducing fumes. It is overly fast, wastes raw materials, is clumsy, and kills 50,000 people in an average year. The time needed during rush hours to go from the East River to the Hudson River on Forty-second Street in New York is at least one hour: a man walking can easily do it in but a fraction of that time.* Considering these aspects, the automobile now shores up the wall of mortality in the triad; its contributions have grown negligible by comparison.

Safety in automobile design is a problem that has been addressed in two distinctly disparate ways:

1. U.S. car makers explain in painstaking detail to congressional committees why basic safety laws cannot be achieved within "reasonable" cost boundaries, although Japanese, German, and Swedish carmakers manage to anticipate and *exceed* U.S. guidelines for safety, and inexpensively at that. To strengthen their perjured testimony before congressional committees, they employ platoons of glib and well-dieted lobbyists to press their case with Congress.

2. European and Japanese car manufacturers, by contrast, allocate moneys to research rather than bribes. Thus Saab, Volvo, Mercedes Benz, and Porsche are eminently safe in collisions that would transmogrify many U.S. cars into concertinas—Honda *exceeded and surpassed* U.S. emission standards three years before such emission controls came into being. Honda announced that inflatable air bags will be standard equipment on all their cars by 1985, while the U.S. car makers have solemnly testified that the technology is still lacking. In April 1983, Honda's *Civic* (one of the smallest cars available in the U.S.) was

*Ivan Illich has amusingly demonstrated that traffic in excess of about six miles per hour is inordinately expensive and increasingly difficult to achieve without enormous losses of privacy, lowering of environmental and ecological standards, and vast energy losses. His statistical analyses of bicycle vis-à-vis automobile can be found in his booklets *Energy and Equity* and *Tools for Conviviality* (London: Calder Boyars Ltd., 1976, 1978).

tested in 28 mph collisions. It was among the top five saf-
est cars in the tests.

In 1971, the spokesmen of Detroit testified that a front-
bumper-collision proof at ten mph would add $500 to the price
of each car and, more dauntingly, would take three to five
years to develop. To show the falseness of that premise, I took
two wooden bookshelves twelve inches wide and seven feet
long. Between the two shelves I placed eighty or so empty beer
cans, thus constructing a sort of giant hero sandwich: the
shelves standing for the bread, the empty beer cans for the
pastrami. I lashed the shelves and beer cans together, tied the
whole zany mess to the front bumper of my car, and then
drove it at fifteen mph into a corner of the Senate office building.

Although it made for a minor news story on television, it
may have been the biggest nonevent of that year: it was ir-
ritating to hear the same automobile executives, who may have
seen my experiment on TV the night before, still testifying
under oath the next day that we might have a front bumper
one-half as effective as my homemade job in another five years

The beer-can automobile bumper. Drawing by Smit Vajaramant.

for around $500. I had invested $14 and approximately an hour for research, development, and installation. In the collision the beer cans collapsed (as they were intended to); both my car and the Senate office building remained splendidly unscathed.

The car, however, is only one example of lack of social responsibility and attention to value in design. Everything designed by man can be examined through the filter of the triad of limitations and evaluated in a similar manner.

K.G. Pontus Hultén's *The Machine as Seen at the End of the Mechanical Age* (1968) is an excellent book. A quote from it is relevant here. Hultén says:

> The production of articles that nobody really needs, but which occupy the ground floors of all big stores, is one of the many outward symptoms of something basically wrong in a world of overproduction and undernourishment. In order to control overproduction, without going through the intricacies of selling the product, it becomes necessary for a wilfully destructive war to be going on permanently somewhere. Today, the world is spending over $150 billion per annum on the actual or potential destruction of lives and property, as compared with the capital transfer from rich to poor countries of about $10 billion per year—including a large share for military aid.

What needs to be done? And how can we do it? A series of examples may serve as the best answer.

One of the world's few really great designs for emergent countries was developed in 1958 by a team of three designers from as many different countries and is used now—almost thirty years later—in many developing countries. It is a brick-making machine. This simple device is used as follows: Mud or earth is packed into a brick-shaped receptacle, a large lever is pulled down, and a perfect "rammed earth" brick results. This apparatus permits people to manufacture bricks at their own speed—500,000 a day or two a week. Out of these bricks schools, homes, and hospitals have been built all over South

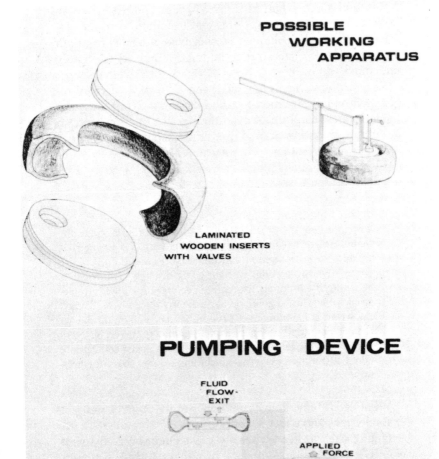

POSSIBLE
WORKING
APPARATUS

LAMINATED
WOODEN INSERTS
WITH VALVES

PUMPING DEVICE

FLUID
FLOW-
EXIT

APPLIED
FORCE

OPERATION

FLUID FLOW INTAKE

One of a series of twenty investigations into the use of old tires, which now abound in the Third World. Both of these irrigation pumps have since been built and verified. Designed by Robert Toering, as a student at Purdue University.

America and the rest of the Third World. Today schools, hospitals, and entire villages stand in Ecuador, Venezuela, Ghana, Nigeria, Tanzania, and many other parts of the world. The concept is a great one: it has kept the rain off the heads of people, and it has made instruction possible where schools themselves did not exist a few years ago. The brick machine has made it feasible to construct factories and install equipment in areas where this had never been attempted in the past. This is socially conscious design, relevant to the needs of people in the word today.

In African countries many problems still await solution. The circulatory systems of the Third World, and specifically Black Africa, are very bad. People get sick because waste products cannot be efficiently rinsed away; there is almost no sanitation. There is not enough water because water is polluted by precipitation, by flowing through open ditches, and by incredibly fast evaporation. Often water is uncontrolled and washes away precious topsoil. Irrigation is virtually nonexistent in many villages. The missing element is a *pipe* or rather a simple device that will make it possible to manufacture pipe segments in the village, by cottage industry, or by an individual. So the task is to design a pipe-making machine. A pipe-making machine that can be built in Africa by Africans and used for the common good. A machine (or tool) that will bypass private profit, corporate structures, exploitation, and neocolonialism.

A group of post-graduate students of mine in England began the design work on such a pipe system in 1973. Between 1973 and 1979 a way of making such pipe segments, using the brick-maker mentioned earlier, was built. About 600 miles of pipes have since been laid in Tanzania as a pilot project. This trial system is working well enough so that two other countries, Ghana and Niger, are now interested in working with this system.

On a seemingly more trivial plane, Roger Dalton found that unavoidably some pipe segments would be miscast or substandard. Realizing a different potential for these pieces, he

Playground sculpture. The author developed a pipe system for water in central Africa. These playground pieces were designed to use mis-cast pipe segment. Designed by Roger Dalton, as a post-graduate student at Manchester Polytechnic.

developed them into components for playrooms in schools and climbing frames in playgrounds. While many parts of Africa are becoming increasingly urbanized, adventure playgrounds and play equipment are still sadly lacking.

In 1969 Africans from seven nations told me that an inexpensive educational television set—distributed through UNESCO—would help enormously in their countries. When the East-African Confederation was dissolved by the defection of Uganda, the actual building of our low-cost educational television set came to an abrupt halt. By now East-Africa has been flooded by commercial television sets from Japan, Germany, and France. Nonetheless it is instructive to note in retrospect that we were able to develop three different television

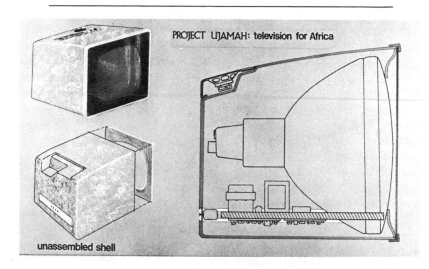

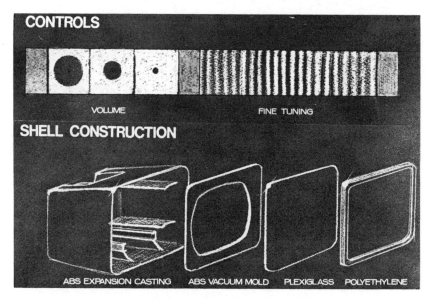

Low-cost educational TV set to be built by Africans in Africa. Designed by Richard Powers, as a student at Purdue University.

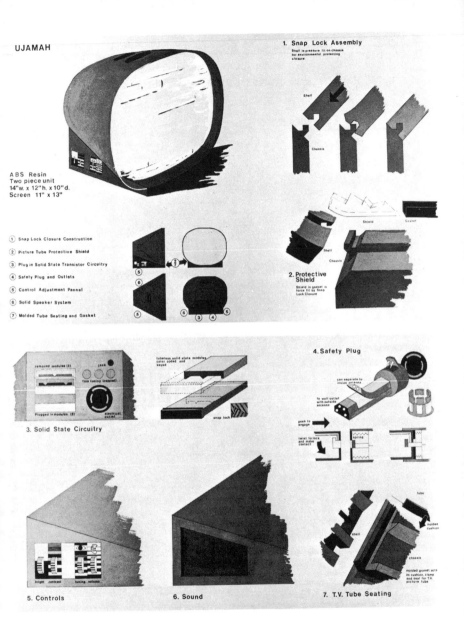

UJAMAH

ABS Resin
Two piece unit
14"w. x 12"h. x 10"d.
Screen 11" x 13"

1. Snap Lock Closure Construction
2. Picture Tube Protective Shield
3. Plug in Solid State Transistor Circuitry
4. Safety Plug and Outlets
5. Control Adjustment Pannel
6. Solid Speaker System
7. Molded Tube Seating and Gasket

1. Snap Lock Assembly

Shell is pressure fit on chassis
for environmental protecting
closure

2. Protective Shield

Shield in gasket is
force fit by Snap
Lock Closure

3. Solid State Circuitry

4. Safety Plug

5. Controls

6. Sound

7. T.V. Tube Seating

Another version of African TV proposal. Designed by Michael Crotty, as a student at Purdue University.

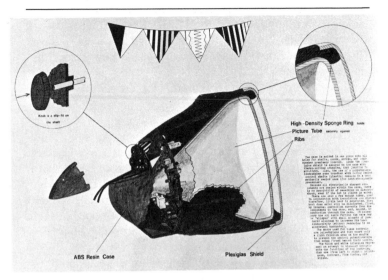

Another version of African TV proposal. Designed by Stanhope Adams, Jr., as a student at Purdue University.

sets that could have been manufactured for less than $10 in 1970 with use of local labor and with profit accruing to the African states only through the education of a trained work force and well-equipped factories. We discovered in our research that a highly sophisticated market-competitive television set (including thirty-six channels, internal fans, and acceptable appearance) retailed in the United States for under $120 in 1970, even though labor, manufacture, materials, and overhead cost the Japanese company less than $18 at that time.

Further attempts were made in 1970 to also make our set compatible with videotape cassettes and video disks, since there can be no doubt that prerecorded material would revolutionize education in the Third World.

From the vantage point of 1984 one can find case histories that were successful. One of these is the Indonesian tin-can radio described later in this book. The other is an educational tape cassette player developed for Tanzania and Nigeria, for

which the author received the ICSID/Kyoto Honors Award
1980/1981. (See "Papanek: *Design for Human Scale*" and my
"Project Batta Kōya," in *Industrial Design,* New York, July-
August 1978.)

There are many ways of working for the needs of underdeveloped and emergent countries:

1. The simplest, most often employed, and probably shab-
   biest is for the designer to sit in his New York, London,
   or Stockholm office and to design things to be made in,
   say, Tanzania. Souvenirlike objects are then manufactured, using native materials and skills, with the hope that
   they will sell in developed countries. They do, but for a
   short while only, for by designing "decorative objects for
   the home" and "fashion accessories," we merely tie the
   local economy to that of richer countries. Should the
   economy of the wealthy Western country fail, the emergent country's new economic independence fails with it.
   Should the economy of the wealthy Western country continue climbing, the fashion likes and dislikes of its population will be manipulated even more, and the emergent
   country's new economic independence will fail anyway.

2. A second and only slightly more effective way for the designer to participate would be to spend some time in the
   underdeveloped country developing design really suited
   to the needs of the people there. This still begs the question of meaningful engagement, since short-term experts
   can't become involved long enough or deeply enough to
   fully understand local customs and needs.

3. A somewhat better way is to move the designer to the
   underdeveloped country and have him train designers
   there, as well as designing and working out the logistics
   of design needs for that nation. Still far from ideal, this
   version tends to tie the country too closely to the particular design ideology—and design idiosyncracies—the
   particular designer represents.

4. Ideally (as things stand now), the designer would move
   to the country and do all the things indicated above. But

in addition, he would also train designers to train designers. In other words he would become a "seed project" helping to form a corps of able designers out of the indigenous population of the country. Thus within one generation at most, five years at the least, he would be able to create a group of designers firmly committed to their own cultural heritage, their own life-style, and their own needs.

Years of experience have convinced me that "instant experts" never work out. When foreign experts are brought to developing countries and faced with new problems, they frequently are able to provide answers that seem both sensible and workable. Their apparent ability to penetrate to the nub of the problem is illusory: unfamiliar as they are with the cultural background of the country, religious and social taboos, economic givens, and many other local considerations, they yet deliver an answer that appears convincing. Three weeks later when they have boarded their Silver Bird to return to their U.N. headquarters in Geneva, Paris, Vienna, or New York, the people on the ground realize quickly that, although they have solved the problem as stated, their "solution" has resulted in twenty or thirty new problems.

Since 1970 I have worked in six developing countries for a combined total of eight years. These experiences in Latin America, Africa, and Asia make me realize that the people of the Third World are more capable in solving their own design problems than they were when the first edition of this book was written. The people native to developing countries have an enormous amount of design and technological expertise. Increasingly the work of foreign experts (instant or otherwise) constitutes an unnecessary intrusion. Problems can now be solved in a better way by local designers and architects whose familiarity with local ways of living yields better and more appropriate solutions, rather than a quick fix leading to eventual disappointments. (See my "Proposal: For the Southern Half of the Globe," in *Design Studies*, London, January 1983.)

5

Our Kleenex Culture:

Obsolescence and Value

You have to make up your mind either to make sense or to make money, if you want to be a designer.

R. BUCKMINSTER FULLER

In all likelihood it started with automobiles. Dies, tools, and molds that are used in manufacturing cars wear out after about three years of usage. This provided the Detroit automobile makers with a timetable for their "styling cycle." Minor cosmetic changes are performed once a year; because of the need for rebuilt and redesigned dies, a major style change is plugged in about every three years. From the end of World War II until 1978 car manufacturers sold the American public on the concept that it is stylish to change cars every three years. Today economic stress has forced us into somewhat more frugal attitudes and we try to keep cars somewhat longer. With continuous change came sloppy workmanship and virtually nonexistent quality control. For a quarter of a century American national administrations have exhibited tacit approval or proclaimed enthusiastic support of this system. Some of the economic and waste-making results of this policy have been documented in other chapters. But the risk is the expansion

People don't care about → long lasting quality

of this attitude; from changing automobiles every few years, we may move to considering everything a throwaway item, and considering *all* consumer goods, and indeed, most human values, to be disposable.

When people are persuaded, advertised, propagandized, and victimized into throwing away their cars long before they wear out, their clothes with the latest demands of fashion, their high-fidelity sets whenever a new electronic gimmick comes along, and so forth, then we may begin to consider everything obsolete. Throwing away furniture, transportation vehicles, clothing, and appliances may soon lead us to feel that marriages (and other personal relationships) are throwaway items as well, and that on a global scale, countries and, indeed, entire subcontinents are disposable like Kleenex. That which we throw away, we fail to value. When we design and plan things to be discarded, we exercise insufficient care in design, in considering safety factors, or thinking about worker/user alienation from ephemeral trivia.

Some examples taken from such differing fields as automobile design, buildings, toys, and other areas will emphasize my point: when we deal with possessions as disposable trash, the objects or tools turn against us in the enormous numbers made possible by mass production like an updated version of the sorcerer's apprentice.

During 1977 the American automobile industry recalled more cars than it sold. Some 10.4 million passenger cars of various model years had to be recalled for design and engineering errors, whereas only 9.3 million new cars were sold. During the preceding three years (1974–1976) 7.1 million cars were recalled for similar design or engineering faults. Since then the pace has accelerated: General Motors is presently fighting court orders and injunctions that would lead to the recall of a further 9 million vehicles. With subcompacts design for safety has been even worse: during the week of 10 October 1983, GM alone was ordered to recall one-half million of the 1983 front-wheel drive *X*, *J*, and *A* cars (ABC News, 20 October 1983). (The above statistics were assembled from the

National Highway Safety Administration and the Detroit Bureau of the *New York Times*.)

In the first edition of this book I reported that General Motors recalled one out of seven automobiles and trucks for "remedial repairs" as these vehicles proved themselves clearly unsafe in operation (as of 1 April 1969). We have seen that things have become a good deal worse.

For nearly fifteen years several designers, Ralph Nader and I have advocated the installation of a third rear stoplight near the top of the automobile. This would cut down on the number of collisions in heavy traffic and during traffic jams. The National Highway Safety Association has placed them experimentally on a total of nearly 12,000 taxis in New York City, Philadelphia, Boston, and San Francisco. After three months it was found that there were fifty-four percent fewer collisions. The Highway Safety Administration has determined that the installation of such an extra back stoplight, located at eye level of other drivers, would add between $4 and $6 to the cost of the car. Predictably, the spokesmen of Detroit have called this "an unsightly and unnecessary design accessory that would add hundreds of dollars to the cost of each automobile" (ABC News, 13 October 1983).

According to the National Safety Council we killed nearly 26,000 Americans during 1982; we maim 300,000 more each year in traffic accidents. These figures are down by nearly fifty-five percent since the imposition of a fifty-five miles per hour speed limit. The cost to the country in human lives, hospital care, psychological trauma, and insurance is impossible to estimate.

But it's not just cars. The misdesign of railroad tank cars, the lack of regular inspections of such cars, and an antiquated rail network have combined to yield nearly one thousand tank car explosions or derailments every year. Many times each month we read about or hear about communities being evacuated because of dangerous chemicals being transported with badly designed equipment.

The collapse of the skywalks at the Hyatt-Regency Hotel in Kansas City on 17 July 1981 killed more than 100 people and injured more than 200 others. In retrospect it is easy to accurately identify the design mistakes by architects and engineers. But leaving aside human error, insufficient supervision, and lack of controls, one still more horrifying fact emerges:

Five days after the collapse of the skywalks on 22 July, the American Institute of Architects (AIA) published its two-year study on the design of skywalks. *The release date of 22 July had been known to the architectural profession for more than a year.* The AIA study determined that "skywalks longer than forty-five feet would need a redundant support system," that is, pylons, pillars, or columns supporting the walkway from below. The Hyatt-Regency skywalks were more than 100 feet in length. It is amazing that the architects designed so hazardous a structure (quite aside from later engineering errors) and caused it to be built *before the first study determining safety was released.* (Three years later, on 27 July 1984, Daniel M. Duncan, the engineer who worked on the skywalks, testified in court that the design of the critical part of the skywalk support was a substitute for one considered to be a "dust catcher." The change was made "since the hotel architects wanted a clean design that would be better looking.")

But consumers are beginning to fight back. A Consumers Affairs Committee was formed in Philadelphia three years ago that advises parents in the United States on toy safety and examines thousands of toys annually. Hundreds of these toys are condemned annually for posing safety and health threats for children, for being too complicated, or for being just plain silly.

The F-15 Eagle by Tootsie Toy was condemned by the Consumers Affairs Committee as "potentially dangerous because of its design, weight, its sharp edges, and its construction." Of Rodan by Mattel they said, "There are twelve instruction steps and it took our eleven-year-old testers forty-five minutes of straight concentration to put it together. It was not worth the effort." The panel commented that My Puppy Puddles, by Hasbro, was "a toy whose sole purpose is to make a dog go to the bathroom. The kids quickly caught on to the fact that you don't need all of the paraphernalia to make him go." (The above examples are from the Associated Press, 4 December 1980.) Understandably, the spokesmen of the Toy Manufacturers Association self-servingly explained that the only thing that matters is whether a toy has "fun value" or not.

This same Consumers Affairs Committee has also singled out toys of unusual merit for their approval. These toys share a sort of open-endedness, that is they give free play to the imagination of a child. The playthings so honored over the last few years include *Lego*, a plastic snap-together building block toy from Denmark, *Lincoln Logs* from the United States, and *Meccano*, a metal building toy from West Germany. During 1982–1983 a number of learning toys from Fischer Technik in Germany, retailed in this country by Sears Roebuck, were singled out. These construction toys permit the child to explore resistors, transistors, diodes, and circuit construction and to build simple loudspeakers, amplifiers, and so forth. *Capsela* has also been highly recommended. It is a Japanese construction toy, the plastic nodules of which contain small battery driven electric motors. A child can construct simple waterwheels, windmills, paddleboats, locomotives, cranes, and so forth. In Chapter Six of this book I will discuss wooden toys from Finland and Denmark, which through their good design and the sensuous feeling of fine woods make delightful playthings for smaller children.

Toys are marketed before they are fully evaluated. It will be remembered that during the 1982 Christmas season a talking doll, designed and manufactured in North Carolina, uttered the charming phrase: "Kill Mommy! Kill Mommy!" This was due to insufficient quality control and a badly designed circuit that garbled the toy's speech. Simple ethics and simple common sense would establish enough design supervision, inspection, and quality control to avoid such errors (NBC News, 13 December 1982).

Nearly fifteen years ago the Health Department of Suffolk County, New York, reported that many color television sets emitted harmful rays that might cause genetic damage to children watching. Only recently (1 November 1983) the Consumer Safety Commission has found that older color television sets are still unsafe when viewed from a distance of less than nine feet. "Older" is here defined as a set produced prior to 1977. Since millions of such sets are still in use and watched by children three to four feet from the screen on Saturday mornings, a continuing health hazard exists.

In Chapter Four, I mentioned that hard hats and safety helmets have not been tested sufficiently to absorb kinetic energy. In some accidents this may lead to a depression of the subcortical layers of the brain. This holds true of football helmets as well and leads to many severe injuries during the football season.

According to the National Heart Association, the lives of approximately fifty percent of all industrial workers are shortened by five years or more through heart stress caused by noisy equipment. Unsafe home appliances account for 250,000 injuries and deaths annually. Even the design of so-called "safety equipment" imposes further hazards: "approved" fire escapes tend to fry people trying to use them. Since the fire escape was introduced, eight thousand people have died when they were trapped by the escape mechanism.

A couple of years ago, I appeared in court as an expert witness in a tractor case. I appeared for the plaintiff, a Missouri farmer whose left foot was ripped off by a badly designed tractor when he was trying to apply the brakes. (In early 1983 the plaintiff won his case.) It is impossible to estimate how many thousands of people die or are severely hurt each year because of badly designed farm machinery and farming tools. Some work is inherently hazardous, such as working on cranes on a construction site. But there is no question that hundreds of thousands of injuries occur yearly at so-called safe work places, factories, offices, mines, and so forth.

Even white-collar jobs can be hazardous to your health. In

research that examined the effect of video display terminals on their operators, severe eye strain, back problems, periodic near-hallucinatory images, and misalignment of jaw and teeth caused by tension were among the effects found (Associated Press, 23 October 1983).

In the first edition of this book I reported that a young woman was literally cut to ribbons when leaving a drug store, since the plate glass door failed to pivot properly after a pebble got caught in its track. Twelve years later I had an identical accident when leaving Barclays Bank in Hong Kong—I was fortunate in being cut only slightly.

Over the last fifteen years or so the control panel on stoves (gas or electric) has been bounced backward and forward by household appliance designers like a yo-yo. These style changes always have plausible explanations and engineering rationales. When all switches were moved to the back of the unit in the early seventies, the manufacturers' explanation was that it would be more difficult for small children to reach control knobs. In reality it was a merchandising gimmick: running wires straight up the back of the stove is cheaper, yet the new design could be sold for more money. Predictably children climbed to the top of chairs to play with all the neat switches and knobs; some fell and burned arms or faces. Now, in the early eighties, most control panels are up front again. The cause of children's safety is forgotten in order to give women the illusion that they control the vast destinies of the galaxy by fiddling with knobs, idiot lights, and the like. A design solution would be simple: a double-security switch requiring *both* hands to engage "on" (similar to "Record" switches on tape-recorders). Instead appliance manufacturers woo the public with such felicitous confections as a 1978 Hotpoint Range, the oven of which played "Tenderly" whenever the roast was ready!

Since I collect examples of the idiocies dreamt up by some of my fellow designers, I found myself enchanted by some offerings for Christmas 1983. We are offered a number of robots that do remarkably little. "My Hero!" offered by Diners Club for a mere $2,499 incorporates a telephone and will talk and play records or tape cassettes. (This last function is described as "he will sing to you.") We are promised that the robot has "an astonishing ability to distinguish between 256 levels of light or sound." According to the advertisement he will also hand you a newspaper or magazine (Diners Club, 1983 Catalog). A similar robot is available from "The Sharper Image" for $1,795 with two extra options: a robot arm that will "lift and carry objects up to twelve ounces" for $595 and a clip-on vacuum cleaner for $604.50 (including shipping) (The Sharper Image Catalog, Holiday 1983). Those of us who have seen the excellent film *Harold and Maude* are astonished that one of the black jokes from the film has now been turned into reality by some unsung electronic genius. Among the other glittering gifts, we are offered *The Remington Aroma Disc Player* for roughly $20. For the same price we can also buy either a "Romantic Scents Assortment" or, should we prefer, a "Natural Scents Assortment." Essentially it is a machine that plays a long-playing disk that smells (Markline, Holiday Gift Guide, 1983). For the practical among us the Dazey Stripper will electrically peel an apple, orange, or even tangerine—one at a time. For a mere $29.95 we have the pleasure of cleaning this electronic model for ten minutes after it has peeled our orange, instead of merely rinsing off our hands (Aztech, Winter 1983–1984).

Children are also persuaded to become addicted to tawdry idiocies. In October 1983 Amurol Products began mass marketing Tubble Gum throughout drug stores and grocery stores. Tubble Gum is, according to the information appearing on the package, a "super-soft bubble gum" that comes in a tube, like toothpaste. This raises the question of whether small children should be trained to squeeze things into their mouths, whether Tubble Gum, toothpaste, or superglue! A secondary consideration is that Tubble Gum (a confection that stinks like a rotting geranium) poses other serious health hazards: this zany mixture is indeed "super-soft," in fact it has to be "chewed up" to attain the firmness of chewing gum. A very small child, squeezing this material into his mouth full tilt, might glue up his throat.

In spite of a major recession in the United States and the rest of the world, useless trivia seem to have become a permanent part of our product environment. *Life* (January 1983) lists a baker's dozen of these idiot delights in an article headlined "Cute Means Cash!" To continue the listing of totally useless but extraordinarily expensive gadgets is a dismal task indeed. It is enough to say that North Americans spent more on "toys for adults" than on the education of their young or public health for the poor. A list of the latest of these moron's delights includes an electric carrot peeler, an electronic fish scaler, heated shoe-trees, electric-hydraulic log-splitters, quarter-scale 1906 fire-engines for children (at a cool $9,000 each), electric dish-towels, and a bag full of "two-penny" nails made of 18-karat gold and selling for $8,500. These trivia items, even if sturdily made, have obsolescence built in because the owner soon tires of a product that is essentially useless.

In specific situations the concept of obsolescence can be a sound one. Disposable hospital syringes, for instance, eliminate some of the need for costly autoclaves and other sterilizing equipment. In developing countries, or climatic situations where sterilization becomes difficult or impossible, a whole line of disposable surgical and dental instruments has become useful. Throw-away tissues, diapers, and so forth are certainly welcome.

But when a new category of objects is consciously designed for disposability, two new parameters must enter the design process. For one thing, does the price of the object reflect its ephemeral character? Disposable surgical gloves that come on a roll, like toilet paper, or temporary protective clothing for laboratories reflect their transitory use in pricing.

The second consideration concerns what happens to the disposable article after it has been disposed of. Automobile junk-yards follow our highways from coast to coast. And even these appalling smears on the landscape at least have a (painfully slow) rusting process in their favor, so that five or twenty years hence the cars will have turned to dust. The new plastics and aluminum will not disintegrate, and the concept of being up to our armpits in discarded beer cans is not a pleasant prospect. "Bottle-laws" have been enacted in many states in the United States, as well as in several other countries, and aluminum cans are now accepted for recycling.

Biodegradable materials (i.e., plastics that become absorbed into the soil, water runoff, or air) will have to be used more and more in the future. The Tetra-Pak Company in Sweden, responsible for the distribution of seven billion milk, cream, and other packages a year, is now working on an ideal self-destructive package. A new process, developed in 1970 in collaboration with the Institute for Polymer Technology in Stockholm, accelerates the decomposition rate of polyethylene plastics. Thus, packages decompose much more rapidly after they have been discarded without affecting their strength and other properties while still in use. A new disposable, self-destructive beer bottle called Rigello has been on the market since 1977. Much more than these few early Swedish solutions will need to be introduced to save us from product pollution.

Fortunately, it has now become possible to use *the actual process of pollution* to bring about positive results. The result of a design research problem conducted with two graduate students in 1968 is a good example.

We began by studying cockleburs, burdocks, and other botanical seeds that possess "hook mechanisms." (This bionic investigation of seeds is more fully discussed in Chapter Nine.) Out of this we developed an artificial hooking seed, approximately forty centimeters in length, made out of biodegradable plastic. The particular plastic chosen has a half-life of about six to eight years. All plastic surfaces of these constructs are dipped in plant seeds and encapsulated in a hydrotropic nutrient solution. These "macroseeds" are furnished folded flat, 144 to a package. The concept is extraordinarily simple. It is possible to drop thousands of these seeds from airplanes into dry-wash areas of arid, desertlike country. Once dropped, the

Artificial burrs, 15½ inches long, made of biodegradable plastic and coated with plant seeds and a growth-boosting solution. To reverse erosion cycles in arid regions. Designed by James Herold and John Truan, as students at Purdue University.

seeds spring open and interlink (see illustration on page 96). With the first rain or even a substantial increase in moisture content of the air, the plant seeds on the surface of the artificial seeds begin to sprout (helped along by the nutrient solution encapsulating them). The macroseeds themselves, aided by these newly sprouted organic seedlings, now form a low but continuous dam. (Such a dam can be theoretically infinite in length and would be around twenty to thirty centimeters in height. The experimental dam we constructed at a dry-wash area is seventeen meters long.)

The dam, consisting by now of macroseeds that are hooked together and further augmented by true organic growth, begins to catch the first spring runoffs. Seeds, mulch, topsoil, and other organic particles are captured by it; the dam grows both literally and figuratively. Within three to six seasons it has grown into a compact area of vegetation and a permanent trap for capturing topsoil. Toward the end of this period the biodegradable plastic core begins to be absorbed by the surrounding vegetation and soil and turns into a fertilizing agent.

Experimentally at least, the erosion cycle has been halted and in fact reversed. The component factors of obsolescence, disposability, and self-destruction have been used for a positive ecological alteration.

An interesting use has been found for these artificial burrs. Magdy Tewfik, an architectural student at the Royal Academy of Architecture in Copenhagen, has had scores of thousands of burrs made in the Sudan. Made of cardboard and old newspapers and approximately forty centimeters in length, they lack only the biological booster solution and seeds. They can be used as "sand anchors" in the Sudanese desert to keep more sand anchored on the ground during dust storms. The idea sounds stupidly simple, but it works. (Magdy Tewfik. *Abatement of Dust Storms Afflicting the Tropics.* Copenhagen: Department of Urban and Regional Planning, 1972.)

To return to the discussion of a disposable society: With increasing technological obsolescence, the exchange of products for new, radically improved versions makes sense. Unfortunately, as yet there has been no reaction to this new factor on the market level. If we are to trade in yesterday's products and appliances for today's, and today's for tomorrow's at an ever-accelerating rate, then unit cost must reflect this tendency. Slowly, two methods of dealing with this problem are beginning to emerge.

Leasing rather than owning is beginning to make headway. There are a number of states in which it is less expensive to lease an automobile on a three-year contract than to own one. This concept has the added motivation built in that the man who leases his automobile is no longer bothered by maintenance cost, insurance, and fluctuating trade-in values. In some of our larger cities it has become possible to lease such large appliances as refrigerators, freezers, stoves, dishwashers, washers and dryers, air-conditioning units, and television sets. This trend has grown even more pronounced in manufacturing and office situations. Maintenance and service problems surrounding computer hardware, research lab, and office-filing fields make the leasing of equipment more and more rational. Property tax laws in many states are also helping to make the concept of temporary use rather than permanent ownership more palatable to the consuming public.

It now becomes necessary only to convince the consumer that, in point of fact, he *owns* very little even now. The homes that make up our suburbs are purchased on twenty- or thirty-year mortgages but (as we have seen above), with the average family moving every fifty-six months, are sold and resold many times over. Most automobiles are purchased on an installment plan lasting forty-eight to fifty-two months. They are usually traded in some months before the contract is completed, and the still partially unpaid-for car is used as a trade-in. The concept of ownership, as it applies to cars, homes, and large appliances in a highly mobile society, becomes a fiction.

This is indeed a major about-face regarding possessions. It is a change of attitude often condemned out of hand by the older generation (who are sublimely unaware of how little they themselves, in fact, ever own). But moral condemnation is not really relevant here and never has been. The "curse of possessions" has been viewed with alarm by religious leaders, philosophers, and social thinkers throughout human history. Our greatest hope in turning away from a gadget-happy, goods-oriented, consumption-motivated society based on private, capitalist, acquisitive philosophies lies in a recognition of these facts.

A second way of dealing with the technological obsolescing of products lies in restructuring prices for the consumer market. On 6 April 1969, the *New York Times* carried an advertisement for an inflatable easy chair (imported from England) at a retail price of less than $10 (including shipping, taxes, and import duties). Within five days mail and telephone orders were received for 60,000 chairs. In the early seventies hassocks and occasional chairs made of plastic-reinforced cardboard were available inexpensively at such national discount outlets as Pier One and Cost Plus. Such items, combining usefulness, bright color, modish design, comfort, extremely low cost, light weight, and easy "knock-down factors" with eventual disposability, naturally appeal to young people and college students. But the appeal of low-cost, lightweight furniture is filtering down to larger and more "settled" segments of the population, now that economic factors influence more people.

In 1970 I thought that mass production and automation would make an increasing number of inexpensive semidisposable products available to the public. I applauded this since, *if it did not lead to waste making and pollution*, it would be a healthy trend. With the great renaissance in crafts, I thought that with inexpensive recyclable goods, disposable income might be freed to bring more handmade and well-designed products into the lives of more people. It was easy to predict then that homes using inexpensive plastic dinnerware would also contain some pieces of fine craftsmen-produced ceramics. A near-disposable dress might be dramatized with a custom-designed, custom-made ring created specifically for the wearer by a silversmith. The inexpensive rattan sofas and easy chairs, bought at some national chain store like Pier One, might well contain hand-woven cushions bought at prestigious craft shops or galleries.

But hard times have changed this picture somewhat. Crafts are still bought by those who can afford to do so. Those who need to be more careful with their expenditures, as well as the new poor, have made two exciting new discoveries.

Because money is tight, there is a consumers' rebellion against artificial obsolescence, as well as shoddy goods. For the first time in several decades consumers are looking for quality, lasting value, and simple no-frills products. Moreover the public seems willing, when able, to pay a little extra for a cooking pot that will last twenty or thirty years, a well-made bicycle, well-crafted furniture, or decent tools.

The second discovery concerns good design of the past. Increasing numbers of people are forced to buy *used* products from such retail outlets as Goodwill, the Salvation Army, the Society of St. Vincent de Paul, or the Society for Crippled Civilians. They frequently find that a thirty-year-old toaster works better than the latest cheaply made equivalent—that a cherry wood bookshelf (after being stripped of its hideous paint) looks and works better than some expensive shelving unit made of chipboard.

The trend to move frequently has remained at nearly the same levels described thirteen years ago. Although on one hand people try to stay put because high mortgage rates and the cost of moving accelerate constantly, the search for work has also driven hundreds of thousands back to frequent moves.

If the trend towards disposability continues without jeopardizing the environment, we may well see a great sorting out of the objects, tools, and artifacts we own. Some will continue to be valued as permanent because they are family heirlooms, for sentimental reasons, for the love and craftsmanship that has been lavished on them, or for their intrinsic beauty.

A second category will consist of those things we unthinkingly throw away: Kleenex, disposable medicine containers, and returnable bottles and recyclable cans, both of which we will *return* rather than toss. A third group will be those things we accept as semipermanent: cameras, high fidelity equipment, or transportation equipment, and so forth. Such tools we will own, realizing that they will be used for a limited time only and that true technological improvements will continuously appear. The objects in this category must ultimately reflect such temporary "owning" patterns either through low prices or through leasing arrangements.

It is to be hoped that such changes will occur, and that those changes will in turn make us think more deeply and profoundly about that which we truly value.

In summary, we see readily that certain aspects of our Kleenex culture are unavoidable and, in fact, beneficial. However, the dominance of the marketplace has so far delayed the emergence of a rational design strategy. Neither users nor industry have done anything to decide what should be thrown away and what should not. It is also much pleasanter (for share-owners and vice-presidents in charge of marketing) to sell throw-away things that are priced as if they were to be kept permanently. The two alternatives to the present price system, leasing and lower prices combined with the customers' investment recovery through meaningful trade-in or "model-swapping," have not been explored. Technological innovation is progressing at an ever-accelerating pace while raw materials disappear.

The question of whether design and marketing strategies are possible under a system of private capitalism remains. But it is obvious that in a world of need, innovative answers to the question of obsolescence and value must be found.

6

Snake Oil and Thalidomide:

Mass Leisure and Phony Fads

*Moral indignation did and still does affect
me in a direct physical manner.
I can feel, during an attack, the
infusion of adrenaline into the
bloodstream, the craving of the
muscles for violent action.*

ARTHUR KOESTLER

All right—the designer must be conscious of his social and moral responsibility. For design is the most powerful tool yet given man with which to shape his products, his environments, and, by extension, himself. The designer must analyse the past as well as the foreseeable future consequences of his acts.

This is difficult since often the designer's life has been conditioned by a market-oriented, profit-directed system. A radical departure from such manipulated values is difficult to achieve.

It is the more fortunate nations, those favored by their geographical position and historical circumstances, that today show a grosser spirit and a weaker hold on moral principles.

Nor would I call these nations happy in spite of all the outward signs of their prosperity.

But if even the rich feel burdened by the lack of an ideal, to those who suffer real deprivation an ideal is a first necessity of life. Where there is plenty of bread and a shortage of ideals, bread is no substitute for an ideal. But where bread is short, ideals are bread. (Yevgeny Yevtushenko, *Precocious Autobiography*)

All design is education of sorts. The designer attempts to educate his manufacturer-client and the people at the marketplace. Because in most cases the designer has been relegated (or, more often, has relegated himself) to the production of "toys for adults" and a whole potpourri of gleaming, glistening, useless gadgets, the question of responsibility is a difficult one. Young people, teenagers, and prepubescents have been propagandized into buying, collecting, and soon discarding useless, expensive trash. It is only rarely that young people overcome this indoctrination.

One notable rebellion against it occurred in Sweden fifteen years ago when a ten-day "Teenagers' Fair" attempting to promote products for a teenage market was boycotted so thoroughly it nearly got put out of business. According to a report in *Sweden NOW* (Vol. 2, No. 12, 1968), a good number of youths resisted what they considered over-consumption by holding their own Anti-Fair, where the slogan of the day was "Hell, no, we won't buy!" On the big day, buses collected teens from all over Stockholm and drove them to experimental theaters where special programs of politically engaged films and plays were scheduled and such subjects as world hunger, pollution, and drugs were discussed in workshop sessions. In the kids' opinion, the official "Teenagers' Fair" had just been the beginning of a systematic plan to exploit young Europeans by enticing them to want more clothes, cars, and "status junk."

There still is strong resistance among Swedish youth in 1984 to becoming product junkies or even to letting themselves become passive consumers. "In many parts of western Europe what was once considered an alternative life-style has now become the dominant style of life for hundreds of thousands of German, Dutch, and Scandinavian young people. They empathize with the Third World. They bear a burden of guilt for their own prosperity" (*Newsweek*, 24 October 1983).

But Sweden is still the exception rather than the rule. The ideas of "pure" design and the moral neutrality of the designer always come up when designers achieve official status or become salaried or subsidized. It seems like an attempt to affirm the identity of the designer and to protect him against officious interference by managerial groups; unfortunately, it is also self-deception and a hoax perpetrated against the public.

Just what would happen if *all* social and moral obligations were to be removed, if the advertising-design-manufacturing-market research-profiteering complex were really to be given free rein? Assisted by their tame "scientists" in psychology, engineering, anthropology, sociology, and the media, how would they change, or distort, the face of the world?

I wrote a brief satirical piece that tried to show how the combination of irresponsible design, male chauvinism, and sexual exploitation might be turned to destructive profiteering. Entitled "The Lolita Project," it appeared in the April 1970 issue of *The Futurist*. My satire concerned itself with the proposition that, in a society that largely still views women as sex objects, an enterprising manufacturer might well begin tooling up for the production and marketing of artificial women. These plastic women were to be animated, thermally heated, response-programmed units, retailing at around $400, in a vast choice of hair colors, skin shadings, and racial types. My mythical designer-manufacturer also suggested various "improvements upon nature," offered by a Special Products Division that would fill orders for, say, a 19-foot tall, lizard-skin-covered woman equipped with twelve breasts and three heads and programmed to be aggressive.

To my surprise, I began receiving much correspondence as a result of my article. A teacher of social psychology at Harvard wrote me four times regarding a licence to begin man-

Advertisement from *Argosy*, February, 1969. A result of irresponsible design.

ufacturing. Designers and manufacturers are still writing, offering me money to go into partnership and begin turning out Lolita units. A full-size plastic doll was available in three hair colors for $9.95; the advertisement is reproduced here. And the December 1970 issue of *Esquire* magazine featured the construction of such women, with a cleverly faked color photograph.

Unfortunately reality surpassed my dourest predictions: since the time of *The Futurist* article a wide range of artificial women have become available, priced from $19.95 to $89.95 (the latter contain electronic orifices and movable fingers). Porn magazines like *Hustler* and *Screw* carry full-page ads. I feel somewhat reassured that the state-of-the-art of design has not yet quite reached the levels of decadence I advocated in my satirical essay.

My satirical piece on artificial women that are electronically-hydraulically controlled was written for two reasons. It exposed the way in which industry and its designers will cater to sexist male prejudices (the ensuing correspondence from people willing to put money into this idiocy for the last thirteen years strengthens my point). I also wanted to demonstrate the design development of a fairly complex product: the Lolita unit.

This satire combined sex with industrial design. Politics has also used industrial design to further its ends: One early use of project design to support political aspirations is recorded in Jay Doblin's *One Hundred Great Product Designs*. In 1937, aware of its fantastic propaganda value, Adolf Hitler placed high on his list of Nazi priorities the design of a car for everyone. He ordered the creation of a new automobile firm, the Volkswagen (People's Car) development company. In early 1939 the VW plant began in an area that later became the town of Wolfsburg:

> Hitler was convinced that large automobiles—the only type produced in Germany during the early thirties—were designed for the privileged classes and are therefore opposed to

National Socialist interests. In the spring of 1933, he met with Ferdinand Porsche to plan such a car for the masses—the *Klein-auto*. Porsche, who had experimented with smaller cars for many years, saw in Hitler's enthusiasm the opportunity to realize a dream. Porsche was one of the most highly regarded automotive engineers in Germany at the time. As chief engineer for a number of automobile companies, including Lohner, Austo-Daimler, Daimler-Benz, and Steyr, Porsche was ideally suited to the task. He and the Fuhrer agreed that the "people's car" should be a four-passenger vehicle with an air-cooled engine, average between 35 and 40 miles per gallon, and a top speed of 70 mph. In addition, Hitler stipulated it should cost the German worker approximately $600 to purchase. A sum of $65,000 was appropriated to underwrite preliminary development costs; Porsche completed the first prototype car about two years later in his Stuttgart workshop.

In the United States, design is not overtly used in a political manner: rather it operates mainly as a marketing tool of big business.

Turning away from both sex and politics to a consumer product, we can observe its development over a period of nearly twenty-five years, and, more important, we can see how the same problem has been handled by an American parent company and its German subsidiary. The Kodak Carousel slide projector was first introduced to the U.S. market in 1961. Using a gravity-feed method for handling slides, it represented a major conceptual and design breakthrough, virtually obsolescing all other ways of projecting color slides. But, as one of the pioneers of the American industrial design profession, Raymond Loewy, is so fond of saying, "Never leave well enough alone." Soon a new Kodak 600 Carousel came off the drawing board, the "slim-line," more compact, with push-button slide changing and a choice of lenses. At increasingly higher prices Kodak offered the model 650, which accepts several thicknesses of slides and has remote forward control; the 750, with remote forward and reverse and a high-low lamp-saver switch; the 800, with remote control focus and built-in

Two Kodak Carousel Projectors with remote focusing and control chords. The German Kodak Carousel "S" with variable voltage costing approximately $75 and equipped with extra heavy-duty wiring. The American Kodak Carousel Ektagraphic "VA," quite similar but heavier and without the voltage adjustments, awkardly designed and heavier, $279.50.

timer; the 850, with automatic focusing rather than remote, a tungsten-halogen lamp, and two lenses; the 860QZ, with zoom lens; and several other intermediate models with varying combinations of accessories. The line even included the RA960, with random access to slides, at ten times the price of the simplest model and, at twenty times the base price, a model with an arc-light. Finally the Carousel arc-light, random slide access model with built-in dissolve was the top of the special new line.

During these first twenty years Kodak also sold point-by-point copies of most of these projectors under the name Ektagraphic to schools and audiovisual departments. Ektagraphic projectors cost more, were painted gray instead of black, and had what Kodak archly called "sturdier wiring." (This meant that Ektagraphic projectors, generally not available to the public, have an earthed three-point plug, heavily insulated wiring, and are less liable to short circuits.) In other words the regular consumer's models were unsafe but cost less, even though the safety features were fairly inexpensive.

In 1983 U.S. Kodak unveiled their latest "improvements": their Carousel 5200 and 5600 projectors. These latest offerings feature a pull-out slide viewer (but the lens must be removed to use it) and a built-on carrying handle!

Meanwhile, back in Stuttgart, German Kodak quietly built and sold their continental version, called the Carousel-S. This model *is* safely wired, had its own remote focusing and slide-selection cables, and, to top it all, includes a built-in step-down and step-up transformer that made it usable anywhere in the world, regardless of local voltage. It sold (in Germany) at a very low price. Kodak of Rochester, New York, actively attempted to discourage Americans from buying it by refusing to answer inquiries about it and hinting that parts might be difficult to obtain or that it was somehow unsafe or unsuitable. This was, of course, untrue.

The German model communicated simple, safe, and accident-free function both through performance and looks. Automatic timing and other features were simple plug-in components that could be bought separately. Accessories that went with the German version, such as slide trays and extra lenses, were better designed, more solidly built, aesthetically pleasing, and far less expensive. The Germans used that good old American know-how: true mass production. They made just *one* projector with different plug-in options, whereas in the United States more than a dozen projectors (counting the Ektagraphic line) were made all slightly different, neatly trapping the buyer. Our system is designed for consumer dissatisfaction and forced obsolescence. That it is also expensive and not as safe has been demonstrated. By 1984 things have changed radically once more. The German Kodak projector (now named 2000 S-AV) has become fairly expensive and is machined from a solid cast-aluminum block. But even the earliest German version holds up amazingly well: both Jim Hennessey and I have used ours professionally (in our design offices and at our university) for seventeen years without malfunction.

American consumer resistance in 1984 seems to show that

you can't trick a new dog in old ways. Instead of any of the flimsy U.S. Kodak Carousels, serious photographers are buying the new German Leitz Pradolux 300 projector. Leitz decided to combine their well known optical excellence with Kodak's one real contribution: the round gravity-feed slide tray. A logical synthesis without sales gimmickry, the Pradolux sells in New York camera stores for less than U.S. Kodak projectors.

In order to work more directly for people, the whole field of design has to emphasize the role of the designer as an advocate. A new secretarial chair, for instance, is designed because a furniture manufacturer feels that there may be a profit in putting a new chair on the market. The design staff is then told that a new chair is needed and what particular price structure it should fit into.

At this stage, ergonomics (or human factors design) is used, and designers consult their libraries of vital measurements in the field. Most secretaries in the United States are female, and most human factors design data are unfortunately based on white males between the ages of eighteen and twenty-five. As the few books in the Bibliography that deal with ergonomics show, the data have been gathered almost entirely from draftees inducted into the Army (McCormick), Navy personnel (Tufts University), or Dutch Air Force personnel (Butterworth). Aside from some interesting charts in Henry Dreyfuss's *Designing For People*, until recently there existed no data concerning vital measurements and statistics of women, children, the elderly, babies, and the handicapped.

I am delighted that this situation has changed in the last ten years. Niels Diffrient, Alvin Tilley, and David Harman—all from the Henry Dreyfuss office—and others have developed superb books that deal with children, men, women, and the handicapped. Through a series of charts hundreds of critical dimensions, unavailable to designers before, are supplied in clear form: *Humanscale 1/2/3*, *Humanscale 4/5/6*, *Humanscale 7/8/9* (Cambridge. M.I.T. Press, 1974–1981).

A former student and coworker of mine, Harald Kubelka,

of Vienna, has worked with vital measurements of school-age children in Austria. This excellent workbook, heavily illustrated with pictures and graphs, has formed a precious data base for manufacturers of school furniture, clothes, school bags, etc., in Austria.

To return to our discussion of the secretarial chair, based on a manufacturer's hunch that a new secretarial chair might sell, substantiated by extrapolating and intrapolating the measurements of Dutch pilots during World War II, and fleshed out by whatever stylistic extravaganzas the designer performs, the prototype chair is ready. Now begins consumer testing and market research. Stripping this research of all the mystical clap-trap supplied to it by the snake-oil brigade from Madison Avenue, this means that a few chairs are either tested or sold under highly controlled circumstances in five test cities. (These are cities of medium population and average income, towns in which money is usually alleged to be ready for new ideas. San Francisco; Los Angeles; Phoenix, Arizona; Madison, Wisconsin; and Cambridge, Massachusetts, are five out of a long list.) So much for market research. If it sells, swell.

When designing a better typist's chair, the secretaries them-

Secretarial posture chair, designed by "Team Design," Bohl, Kunze, Scheel, and Grünschloss of Stuttgart. Courtesy: *Infordesign* magazine, Brussels.

selves must be part of the team. Too often an "average" typist is asked to sit in the completed new chair (sometimes even for five minutes) and then asked: "Well, what do you think?" When she replies, "Gee, the red upholstery is real different!" we take this for a significant evaluation and go into mass production. But typing involves eight hours a day, long stretches of work. And even if secretaries were intelligently tested on these chairs, how can we see to it that it is *the secretaries themselves who make the decision as to which chair is bought?* Usually *that* decision is made by the boss, the architect, or (God save us) the interior decorator.

A typist's chair has been designed in which secretaries formed part of the planning team and tested it thoroughly. The chair was designed by a team called *Umweltgestaltung*, of Stuttgart. Ergonomics was handled by Ulrich Burandt and the Institute for Hygiene and Worker's Physiology in Zurich, Switzerland, and the chair is manufactured by Drabert and Sons of Minden, Germany. It is thoroughly documented in *Infordesign* (No. 34, 1970, Brussels). But, as I feared in 1970, when it reached the U.S. marketplace it was greatly outsold by what American designers like to call "sexed-up" chairs. And remember again: secretaries have little say in their employers' purchase of chairs.

The Herman Miller Furniture Company of Zeeland, Michigan, has developed a series of excellent secretarial and working chairs during the early and mid-seventies and is still continuing to do so. Other ergonomically sound secretarial seating has been designed by Knoll International and Ettore Sottsass in Italy. However, all this seating is fairly expensive (in the case of European imports, middlemen sometimes arbitrarily raise prices by as much as 300 percent for "designer" chairs in New York), and, in any case, the secretary still has no say in the matter.

Another example shows that design and judgments about it still have far to go: during 1970–1971, an all-European design competition of table settings was held in West Germany under the name *"Tisch 80-Bord 80."* The most ecologically respon-

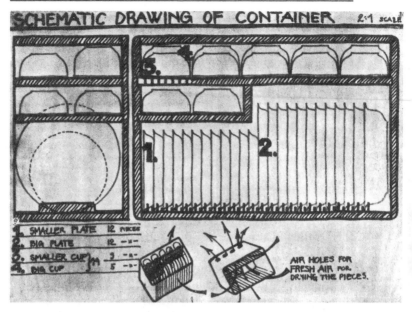

Drawing of aerated washing, drying, and storage container for recyclable dishes designed by Barbro Kulvik-Siltavuori of Finland. Courtesy: Barbro Kulvik-Siltavuori and Gruppe 21.

sible entry was submitted by Mrs. Barbro Kulvik-Siltavuori of Finland. Where all other entries attempted to pander to style-consciousness and consumerism, her submission concerned itself with recycling.

Her proposal (ironically for an entry from Finland) opposed the collection of pretty dishes and handsome glasses and storing them until they become damaged or are replaced for reasons of manipulated taste. She proposed to restrict dishes (at least initially) to a large plate, a small plate, and a mug for liquids. Mrs. Kulvik-Siltavuori suggesed salt-glazed red clay as a possible material; plastic was an alternative suggestion. These seasonal dishes would come in an aerated plastic container designed to make washing, drying, and storage of the dishes possible in the same container. More importantly, broken dishes and mugs can be returned (like empty beer bottles or recyclable milk bottles) in a garbage sack that is part of the system. The manufacturer uses the recycled dishes as raw material; new dishes can be made out of the returned plastic, bricks out of the fired clay, and so forth.

What is important is how the design establishment reacted to her entry. The entry was awarded the fifteenth prize (out of fifteen), and the jury remarked: "This concept has considerable originality . . . At any rate, *we know how to appraise the humor of this solution. It is an amusing* provocation against existing conditions." (Italics added.)

Although the design establishment may not encourage innovation, the consumer appears to disagree. In 1972–1973 the International Design Center in West Berlin held their annual exhibition of new furniture under the title "Good Form." Their director, Francois Burkhardt, invited me to hold a simultaneous exhibition of do-it-yourself and Nomadic furniture. My instruction pages on building do-it-yourself furniture were given away free, larger pieces had been prebuilt for exhibition purposes, and the people of West Berlin were also asked to bring in pieces of furniture they had invented and built for themselves. Attendance broke all previous records at the International Design Center. Francois Burkhardt told me delightedly; "There were thousands of people who have never come to our exhibitions before, the elderly, young environmentalists, and the poor!"

During the spring of 1973–1974 a similar exhibition was held at the gallery Grada Zagreba in Yugoslavia. Here again all previous attendance records were broken. The gallery had expected sixty to eighty people to come for my opening remarks—when over 6,000 people arrived, loudspeakers had to be mounted in the streets. The do-it-yourself diagrams—to be given away free, as in Berlin—ran out after 15 minutes, even though a two-month supply had been printed. When people are allowed to *participate*, museums, exhibition centers, and galleries are simply not large enough to hold them.

A curious note of paternalism still dominates design thinking. As the head of one of the largest Chicago design offices said to me at a meeting; "We've got to do something for the migrant workers that is good for them—but not too good, or they'll never get off their ass!" When the residents of a low-income area in Lafayette, Indiana, were designing a playground with help from architectural students, a solution v, as presented in the neighborhood council that better suited the community's desires. "They can't do that, those are *my* blacks!" was the reaction of one of the students.

I should now like to turn to some specific examples dealing with a child's first book, as well as some case histories that deal with seating, to show how design can respond to specific need areas.

Ten years ago, when my daughter Jenni Satu was three, there seemed to be no decent picture books available for very small children. The Hampton publishing company of Chicago had a total of only eight books, each consisting of a cover and back, and *three* leaves, a total of *six pages per book*. These volumes were printed in nontoxic colors on cloth. Each page had one illustration, done in 1935. Under each of the six pictures that made up a book, a helpful descriptive phrase such as "ball" was printed. Since most three-year-olds don't read and, if read, demand greater verbalization than that, these fairly expensive booklets were nearly useless. Their single redeeming value was that the pages were made of cloth and didn't cut tiny exploring fingers. In the intervening years a number of publishers have issued books for small children. In my opinion none of them goes far enough, since small children are turned on to more than pictures; they also respond with delight to texture, color contrast, optical effects, and things that make noise.

So one of my students designed a book: it has ten leaves, or twenty pages. One of them is a small pocket with teddy-bear-textured cloth on the inside. Another page is a mirrored-cloth surface. Still other pages present simple color spots, optical saturation patterns, textures that feel good, and things that go

Shown is a commercially available baby book that costs 2 dollars. Below it is a redesigned book more suited for a child's needs and estimated to sell for 60 cents. Designed and developed from an idea of the author's by Arlene Klasky, California Institute of the Arts.

squeak. In addition, the pages are split horizontally so that the child can combine the ten pages into more than forty patterns. It is still made of cloth. The colors are still nontoxic, and it can sell for less than $1. But that is not the end of the design process: my student also set up a jig, so that these books can be made by blind people, either in hospitals or as a sort of "cottage industry." Through this design it was possible to combine an advocacy for two groups—to give delight to small children and also to supply the need for meaningful work for the blind.

As indicated throughout this book, design excludes major sections of the population. Just by comparing the controls, switches, knobs, and general design of those tools and appliances which in our society seem to be in the province of women ("homemakers") with those that seem to be "male-oriented," we can see vast differences.

In spite of the new ergonomic data now available, as mentioned above, most design offices in 1984 still view their ideal client as between eighteen and twenty-five, middle-income, active, exactly six feet tall, and weighing exactly 175 pounds. This even though we have more older people in the United States today than ever before.*

While I was still in school, *Interiors* magazine coined the phrase, "The Chair as Signature Piece of the Designer." Good or bad, the phrase has stayed. Today the consumer who wishes to buy a chair is faced by a bewildering array of more than 20,000 different models. Many of these are American, but we also import from Denmark, Finland, Sweden, Italy, Japan, and many other countries. There are chairs in production that were carefully copied from predynastic Egypt; other chairs are inflatable and (incorporating the most recent bits of plastics and electronics) owe their aesthetic debts to the latest space

*Looking at the curricula of some fifty schools that teach design, I find that those courses offered to students in psychology and the social sciences nearly always bear such titles as *Buying Preferences of Consumer Groups*, *The Psychology of the Market Place*, *Consumer Testing*, and *Market Analysis for Export*. There are decent psychology and social science courses taught to nascent designers at some schools. However, when a mix between social psychology and other behavioral sciences and design is firmly established, a new danger arises: some designers and their students play with pop sociology instead of designing. It is obvious that better solutions to the design problems of the real world will come from young people *skilled in the discipline of design*.

shuttle. In between there are faithful reproductions of Hepplewhite, Early American, Duncan Phyfe, and much else, including such newly created styles as "Japanese Colonial," "Plastic Baroque," and the "Navajo Look." Prices vary: it is possible to get an inflatable chair for as little as $9.98; another easy chair, which is part Swedish but features Japanese electronics in its stereo headsets and a German impeller motor for a rippling motion in the back rest, now sells for a cool $16,500. Aesthetically, as well as for functions of use or telesic aptness, there are probably at least 500 well-conceived chairs. But I would like to talk about three chairs I consider great, two of which have stood the test of time so well that most people are astounded when they find out when these chairs first came into being.

The director's chair in its most current version is a scissor-legged wooden construction with slip-on seats and back, made of No. 8 duck, with a 300-pound test strength. It is extremely comfortable to sit in for long periods of time, which is odd in a chair without cushions or pads. For storage or ease of shipping, it folds up into a compact package, weighing less than 15 pounds. Its best feature is that it can serve equally well as an easy chair, desk chair, lounge, or dining chair. We use eight of them in our home, their unobstrusive good looks, compactness, and ease of maintenance together with great comfort and low price making them especially attractive chairs for today's greater mobility. The chair can still be bought from Sears Roebuck for a ridiculously low price. Jay Doblin, in his book *One Hundred Great Product Designs*, calls it ". . . a tremendous buy, probably the best dollar's-worth of furniture available." Most people, when asked to put a date to it, assume that it was designed during the late forties. They are mistaken by one century. The chair can be seen in early French and American photographs and reappears most frequently in pictures made during the Civil War. In its present form it is produced by a number of firms: the Telescope Folding Furniture Company of Granville, New York, and the Gold Medal Company of Racine, Wisconsin, now make at least

Director chair, manufactured by the Telescope Folding Furniture Co., Inc., Granville, New York.

"Lounge Chair" (1938) by Durchan Bonet and Ferrari-Hardoy. Metal rod and leather. Manufactured by Artek-Pascoe, Inc. Collection The Museum of Modern Art, New York, Edgar Kaufmann Fund.

75,000 chairs annually. Estimates made by current producers of the chair put the quantity produced since 1900 in excess of 5 million in the United States alone. Jay Doblin mentions that the Gold Medal Company can trace their present model back to 1903. In addition, there exist British, German, Swedish, Danish, and Finnish versions of this chair. The British version, tatted up for present-day consumers in leather and walnut, is sold as the "British Campaign Officer's Chair."

In 1940 Hans Knoll purchased the design of a chair developed by Ferrari-Hardoy and Durchan Bonet. This construction of two interlinking, open tetrahedra made of steel rods, covered with a sling of leather or canvas, has since become known as the Hardoy Chair among designers, as the Butterfly Chair, Campaign Chair, Sling Chair, Egg-Head's Delight, or Safari Chair to the general public. It is an extremely comfortable indoor-outdoor easy chair, completely amphibious when using the canvas sling, lightweight, and, while not foldable in most models, at least stackable. The original Knoll-Hardoy retailed for $90 in 1940 with a leather sling. Ripoffs by competing manufacturers brought that price down, at least on the West Coast, to $3.95 in 1950. Overproduction of these ripoffs finally made the chair into a free giveaway at some supermarkets in the West and Southwest (with a purchase of $40 worth of groceries). The Hardoy Chair seems to have started as an officer's folding chair for the Italian army in 1869. It was made of naturally finished wood, brass hinges and reinforcing pieces, and a leather sling. In 1895 the Gold Medal Furniture Company produced an almost identical chair but with a canvas sling instead of leather. The first nonfolding version was produced in Germany during the early 1930s. Now during the eighties, it has been revived again with leather and pony-skin slings.

"The Sack," designed by Piero Gatti and Cesare Paolini, was introduced in Italy late in 1968. It is a leather-covered sack filled with plastic grains. The consistency of the plastic fill is such that it molds itself to the user's contours. Except

"Sacco" (the Sack) chair, designed by Piero Gatti, Cesare Paolini, and Franco Teodoro.

for the covering material, the chair carries no connotations of status. Since its introduction, copies of it, in various covering materials, have brought the price down to as little as $9.99. It seems to work well in fabric, best in the original soft, pliable Italian glove leather. A cover of vinyl or Naugahyde is probably the least pleasing because it doesn't "breathe." In 1984, the "original" Italian version still sells as an upmarket version, and do-it-yourself kits are available—and being bought briskly—from mail-order companies. Like the Director's Chair and the Hardoy Chair, it fits in superbly with today's ideas of casual living. One disadvantage of the Sack and the Hardoy Chair is that older people find it hard to get in and out of them, but what the three chairs seem to have in common (in spite of having been designed over the span of more than a century) is ease of maintenance, easy storage and portability, no concessions to status, and a low price.

Designers may not unanimously pick these three chairs as "good design." But then, the tastemakers in our society have a disastrous selection record. The Museum of Modern Art in New York is usually credited as being the prime arbiter of good taste in designed objects. To this end, the museum has published a book and two pamphlets during the last thirty-six years. In 1934 they published the book *Machine Art*. It is a heavily illustrated guide to an exhibition that was to make machine-made objects palatable to the public, and moreover the museum hand-picked these objects as "aesthetically valid." Of 397 objects thought then to be of lasting value, *396* have failed to survive. Only the chemical flasks and beakers made by Coors of Colorado still survive in today's laboratories (after enjoying a brief vogue that was museum induced, during which the intelligentsia used them as wine decanters, vases, and ashtrays).

In 1939 the museum held a second exhibition: the pamphlet *Organic Design* illustrates the various entries. Only one of seventy designs, entry A-3501, designed by Saarinen and Eames, saw further development. The box score of the 1939 exhibition was zero. However, entry A-3501 was parlayed into the Saarinen Womb Chair of 1948 and the Eames Lounge Chair of 1957, both spinoffs of that exhibition entry.

The second pamphlet deals with the 1950 international exhibition titled "Prize Designs for Modern Furniture." Only one of forty-six designs survives to this day. Since the Saarinen and Eames Chairs mentioned above sell for more than $500, their real impact on people has been negligible. But when we deal with the taste-making *apparat* of the Museum of Modern Art, a score of three successes and 510 misses is far from reassuring. What is even more startling is what the museum has missed: Mies van der Rohe's Barcelona Chair was designed in the twenties. Knoll International revived the chair in the fifties, sold it (only in pairs) at $750 *each*; it has since, at $2,000 each, become the prime status symbol of big business and graces the entrance hall of most corporate Gauleiters of industry around the world.

It is interesting to compare the many museum catalogues of "well-designed objects." Whether printed in the twenties, thirties, fifties, seventies, or eighties, the objects are usually the same: a few chairs, some automobiles, cutlery, lamps, ashtrays, and maybe a photograph of the ever-present DC-3 airplane. Innovation of new objects seems to go more and more toward the development of tawdry junk for the annual Christmas gift market, the invention of toys for adults. When plugging in the first electric toasters in the twenties, few would have foreseen that in a brief fifty years the same technology that put a man on the moon would give us an electric moustache brush, a battery-pack-powered carving knife for the roast, and electronic, programmed dildos. But there have been true originators. I can find *nothing* designed by the late Dr. Peter Schlumbohm that is not supremely well designed, thoughtfully engineered, a complete breakthrough, and unusually attractive aesthetically.

Dr. Schlumbohm, a self-employed inventor, in 1941 designed the Chemex Coffee Maker. The Chemex was to be prophetic of all Schlumbohm's later designs: a way of doing things better, more simply, and through nonelectric, usually

Left: "Chemex Coffee Maker" (1941) by Peter Schlumbohm. Pyrex glass, wood, 9″ high, manufactured by Chemex Corp., U.S.A. Collection of The Museum of Modern Art, New York. Gift of Lewis and Conger.

Right: "Water Kettle" (1949) by Peter Schlumbohm. Pyrex glass, 11″ high, manufactured by Chemex Corp., U.S.A. Collection of The Museum of Modern Art, New York. Gift of the manufacturer.

nonmechanical, means. By restudying applied physics, he was able to develop a way of making better coffee more simply. Since its introduction in 1941, many copies of the Chemex system have appeared in other countries, notably the Melitta in Germany, as well as several Swedish systems. The coffee maker was followed in 1946 by a cocktail shaker, in 1949 by a glass water kettle that boils water faster because of its configuration, in 1951 by an electric "filter-jet" fan, and by many other items, such as snow goggles and a dual-purpose tray. Everything designed by Schlumbohm (who died in 1957) was reasonably priced.

Turning to toys, there are few in 1984 that are well designed, inexpensive, and at the same time specifically related to the discovery cycles of growing children. There are reasons for this. The 1982 Christmas market saw both the introduction and the demise of video games. In 1981 a similar failure ended the three year sway of electronic games. Remote-controlled cars on indoor miniature race tracks still sell but have assumed a minor position in the market similar to that still held by model railroads. Barbie dolls (with Barbie's boyfriend Ken and a whole host of other minuscule subsidiary characters, clothes, fashion cars, Barbie swimming pools, and so forth) have dominated the doll market for thirty years now. Mattell's inventor and designer of Barbie dolls has recently publicly repudiated his own designs (*All Things Considered*, 7 October 1983), saying that they fostered a sexist view of women and that children were encouraged to buy ever-increasing numbers of accessories for the dolls.

Toys for smaller children, babies, and toddlers are frequently well conceived, as is the case with Fisher-Price or the spinoffs from *Sesame Street*. But here new moral considerations enter. Many such toys are made of cheap plastic and stain, break, or wear out quickly. Playing with them the child cannot help but to assimilate certain values: things are badly made, quality is unimportant, garish colors and cutesy decorations are the norm, and when things wear out they are to

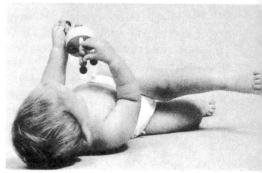

be pitched and replacements arrive miraculously. (It could be the work of a Ph.D. thesis to compare the faith in the magical reappearance of new toys by small children with the near identical beliefs of the Cargo-Cult among primitive island people in the South Pacific.)

Sesame Street is a program that cannot be legally shown in most northern and western European countries. The reasoning is as follows: the members of the Television Workshop, noticing that small children were more interested in commercials than in programs, devised commerciallike scenes to explain simple words, the letter *A*, the number *7*, or whatever. Although children learn something about letters, words, and numbers, they can at the same time be shown to quickly become acculturated to commercial messages as such. These commercials, harsh and strident, create (intentionally or not) passive miniconsumers ready for whatever commercial trash is dumped on them by the hardy hookers of the advertising profession.

"Fingermajig" (far left) and "Threading" (this page) toys designed by Jorma Vennola, Finland. "Turning" (top left) and "Pushing" (near left) toys designed by Jorma Vennola and Pekka Korpijaakko, Finland. Courtesy: Creative Playthings, Princeton, New Jersey, and Los Angeles, California.

Children, especially small ones, need to experience quality, permanence, and delightful materials in their toys. I should especially like to commend a series of simple wooden toys from Finland. These were designed to give both pleasure and training in such skills as twisting, turning, threading, pressing, and pushing and were designed by Jorma Vennola and Pekka Korpijaakko. Several summers ago, Jorma Vennola greatly helped in the invention, design, development, and building of the first portable play and training environment for children with cerebral palsy (CP-1). This environment is pictured and described elsewhere in this book. While working on the environment, Jorma Vennola also developed his "Fingermajig." Jorma brought his first prototype to one of our meetings: a purely tentative design made in wood. It had such great promise as a pure fun toy—yet an excellent training game for both retarded and normal children—that I strongly urged him to market it.

The final version consists of two plastic halves, each the exact shape and size of one of the halves of an old-fashioned bicycle bell, connected into a ball-like configuration. Through a series of holes a number of dowels protrude by about one and one-half inches each. The dowels push in and then bounce back out again, since a small rubber ball acts as backstop in the heart of the device. The toy comes in eight bright colors. Children love its wonderful feel and resiliency. It provides superb exercise for the hand muscles for all children, as well as those with cerebral palsy, some types of paraplegia, and myasthenia gravis. Being elegantly simple and nonmechanical, it does not wear out or need repairs. It floats (making it also one of the few well-designed bathtub toys). With its bright colors, it is a wonderful toy for play in the snow. Best of all, after being shipped from Finland it is comparatively inexpensive. Some stores in the United States have lately sold the Fingermajig as a toy in their children's department. An "executive pacifier" (which is the same Fingermajig sprayed in chrome finish) is available at nearly ten times as much among Christmas gifts. Creative Playthings is to be commended for marketing these toys, but much of the credit must go to Kaija Aarikka, who first began producing and selling them in Helsinki.

There are designs that are needed for things that are needed now. Often design is neglected because a better technology seems on its way. But when a blind man needs a better writing tool for taking notes in Braille, it is little use telling him that in ten years tape recorders the size of a cigarette pack will cost less than $10. First of all, he needs the writing tool *now;* second, present-day monopolistic practices make such projections of future prices highly suspect. After all, it is monopoly agreements and price-fixing that result in a hearing aid consisting of an earpiece and a pocket-sized amplifier, which cost around $10 to produce, to retail for $750. Because few people seem inclined to think up and develop the type of products really needed, I have explained many in the following passage. I must apologize for listing them in a sort of "designer's shorthand." To describe each and every product would fill many volumes. Some of these products have already been designed by students and are illustrated in this book. What we are all looking for are ways of facilitating their production.

Health care, disease prevention, and diagnostic devices provide a good starting place for products needed now. Although enormous improvements have been made by 1984 in heart-lung machines, electronic monitors for operations, and much else, simple and more modest diagnostic devices still need careful rethinking. Fairly sophisticated instruments, like the electric and pneumatic-powered drills and saws for performing osteoplastic craniotomies (designed by C. Collins Pippin), are illustrated elsewhere in this book and have inspired other similar instrumentation over the last fourteen years. But much can be done on an even simpler, almost "gadgety" level. Take fever thermometers for example. In 1984 there are several fairly cumbersome electronic probes that—while taking temperature quickly—need extra time to clean or perform battery checks, and cost around $30. Although inexpensive Band-Aid-like strips can be placed on the forehead of a child, these are

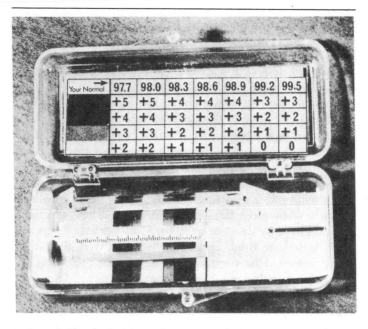

Your Normal →	97.7	98.0	98.3	98.6	98.9	99.2	99.5
	+5	+5	+4	+4	+4	+3	+3
	+4	+4	+3	+3	+3	+2	+2
	+3	+3	+2	+2	+2	+1	+1
	+2	+2	+1	+1	+1	0	0

A color-coded box with a linear magnifier holds the thermometer and permits readings by illiterates. Designed by Sally Niederauer, as a student at Purdue University.

fairly expensive over the long run and only give *approximations* of temperature. None exist that are colorcoded so that people unfamiliar with numbers can find what their temperatures are. *All* thermometers on the market are hard to read for the elderly and people with poor eyesight (an illustration shows a possible improvement). What about a thermometer that makes it possible for a blind person to take and determine his own temperature? This could be done through a simple sound code.

Anxiety-prone patients tend to unconsciously raise their own blood pressure. With dozens of new electronic devices for taking one's own blood pressure, as well as similar coin-operated product's in airports and supermarkets, nothing has yet been developed that is *soothing*.

The introduction of chip technology and microprocessors has given us dozens of small gadgets that monitor heartbeat and pulse rate, but there is still an enormous potential for other autodiagnostic instruments that enable men and women to perform simple tests of oxygen exchange, urinalysis, lung capacity, and so on. (In this connection it is interesting that the 80 cents worth of instructions, devices, and package that is sold in pharmacies for self-testing for pregnancy retails for *precisely* the same amount that most doctors charge to perform this test.) There is no diagnostic device for quickly, accurately, and inexpensively obtaining galvanic skin responses. A fountain-pen-sized probe would do the job.

Crutches are badly designed; braces could easily be designed to be less costly and offer greater adjustability to differing body proportions. Better canes for the blind were redesigned for the first time by Robert Senn; they are described and pictured in this book. Unfortunately Bob Senn's cane for the blind has been neglected in favor of enormously costly and inaccurate electronic "sensing-canes." These are heavy, work marginally at best, and have not yet reached consumers.

Over the last ten or so years there has been a great proliferation of exercising devices. These range from exercising equipment for healthy people to such welcome special equipment as racing wheelchairs that permit some of the handicapped to participate in marathons. But exercising vehicles specifically designed for children with cerebral palsy, paraplegia or quadraplegia, myasthenia gravis, and other debilitating diseases began to appear only late in 1983 on the market in the United States. They were originally pioneered by my students and myself in Sweden and the United States and are more fully discussed and illustrated in another chapter.

Although by 1984 prescription pill containers that are difficult for children to open are given away free, this was not always true. During the fifties and sixties more than 500 small

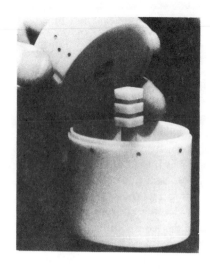

Pillbox designed to be tamperproof, so that small children are denied access to pills. Designed by David Hausman, as a student at Purdue University.

children died annually because they overdosed themselves with pills and capsules. To change this David Hausman developed a childproof medicine container under my direction in 1970 (pictured here). Tests on children proved that they could not open it since it was based on the inability of children to "read" a series of color-coded dots around the cylinder. Unfortunately Hausman's pillbox, being made of hard nylon, proved so expensive in tooling costs that it was never made. It *did* give rise however to all the "push-and-turn" or "lift-and-twist" pill containers we are all familiar with and that are now compulsory in this and other countries. These pill containers are cheap enough to be given away free but have two major drawbacks:

1. Elderly people, or those suffering from arthritis, find them impossible to open (as do the blind). This is also a problem for illiterate or non-English-speaking people (according to *Time* nearly thirty percent of people living in the United States are functionally illiterate, and eighteen percent are Spanish speaking).
2. Any determined child can open them.

There is still no childproof "safe" for medicines kept in the home. There is no tamperproof "safe" for household cleaners, bleaches, detergents, and other chemicals in the home.

Let me quote from an earlier book of mine, now out of print:

> The compulsory introduction of "childproof" containers for all prescription drugs in the United States, West Germany, Canada and a few other countries has not entirely solved the problem. One of our graduate students designed the first prototypal "Pill-safe" in 1965. Since then lid-controlled, less expensive pill jars have been made, but now children still manage to poison themselves by drinking bleach, detergents, and other household chemicals, or by chewing on fabric-softening rags. The obvious answer lies in a cabinet that stores all such materials and is lockable.
>
> However, a chest locked with a key or combination lock isn't the right answer either. Often an elderly family member may need a heart-ailment remedy quickly, without fiddling with locks and keys. Or a severely arthritic grandfather, say, may be unable to operate a key. To solve the problem, our students in Denmark designed chests that took advantage of children's inability to spread their tiny hands across a given space, yet permitted adults, even severely crippled ones, instant access. A news conference was held in Copenhagen and a half-hour TV show interviewed some of the students. As a direct consequence of the newspaper and TV coverage, passage of a new law seems probable in Denmark, making such cabinets (with ergonomically designed latches that are childsafe) compulsory in all apartments and houses rented or sold.
>
> We have been able to push this concept somewhat further, so that the government of New Zealand is also considering steps to make such a safety cupboard compulsory. The Standards Association of New Zealand, an advisory group to the government, has prepared a draft amendment to its model-building bylaw which, if tested and approved, will require a cupboard that must be installed in all new homes and flats, and cannot be opened by children. The same cupboard must be "lockable" without a key, thus giving access to adults who are severely arthritic or in other ways need fast access without fumbling for keys.

In Britain, Tim Lloyd, another postgraduate student, designed a do-it-yourself cabinet lock that is easily installed and will defeat any child's attempt to open it. This lock will convert any existing chest, cabinet or storage unit into a "safe" area in a few minutes. In an earlier book, we have shown even simpler do-it-yourself conversions. (V. Papanek and J. Hennessey, *How Things Don't Work*. New York: Pantheon Books, 1977, pp. 15–17.)

In 1980 we restudied the whole problem of dispensing pills. We decided to stand the problem on its head: A pill container was designed *specifically so that it would open easily for elderly blind people, severely crippled by arthritis deformans.* Having achieved this much, we then developed it so that small children still couldn't manage to get it open (see illustration).

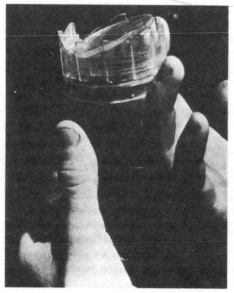

New pill safe. Completely child-proof, the pill safe was developed specifically for easy access by blind, elderly people crippled by arthritis. First prototype designed under the author's direction by Wendell Wilson, a masterclass student at the Kansas City Art Institute.

Blind adults need an instrument on which to take notes in Braille. At present they are faced either with using an expensive and bulky typewriter (since they cannot see, the typewriter needs extra controls) or using a wholly inadequate pocket stylus and slate. This instrument is small enough to be carried. However, as the impressions are made in a *downward* direction and Braille is *raised*, everything has to be written *backward*. A team of two graduate students at Cal Arts, James Hennessey and Solbrit Lanquist, designed an inexpensive, pocket-sized Braille writer. But blind people also need more meaningful work than making baskets and brooms. It could become the job of the designer to develop manufacturing processes directly related to the often impressive skills of the blind.

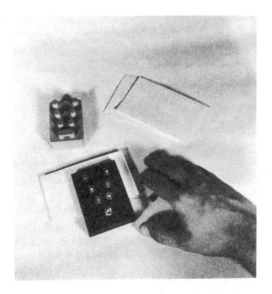

Writing instrument for the blind that is a major improvement on models now existing. Designed by Solbrit Lanquist and James Hennessey, as graduate students at California Institute of the Arts.

There are many other groups that we have singled out and called deprived, disadvantaged, or retarded. Their skills must be investigated to lead to the design and development of things for them to do. Let me stress again that members of the group actually concerned must in each case be part of the design team.

Beginning in 1970 we began a long-range development of a "Sensory Stimulation Wall." This wall, designed with two former students, Charly Schreiner of Purdue University and Yrjö Sotamaa of Helsinki, was developed for normal and re-tarded children and published by the magazine *C.P. Crusader* as a do-it-yourself project for parents of children with cerebral palsy. Since then—and always with the help of children and their teachers and nurses—many other versions of this wall have been built and are continuing to be developed. Let me briefly describe the idea. Essentially the wall is a space grid two-by-five feet and one foot deep. "Plugged" into this wall are ten one-foot cubes. Each "does" things. They squeak, show multifaceted reflections, are three-dimensional interior "feel-ies" for the hand to explore, switch on lights, and much else. This unit can live in the nursery or daycare center, lying on one of its five-foot-long sides. Children as young as one year can explore the unit and play with it. As the child grows older or new skills develop, new types of cubes, such as aquariums, rear-projection slide screens, and electronic toys, can be added or substituted by the teacher. Specific skills, such as lacing, buttoning, tying, or working a zipper, buckles, or snaps can be taught.

In a later chapter an environmental exercising and play cube that was built for handicapped children in Finland is pictured and discussed. What about other cubes? Experimen-tal cube child-care centers, cubes that can be used under water and midwater, and knock-down cubes that can be used for play, testing, and diagnostic purposes? When university stu-dents (another exploited group) move into an old apartment, they needlessly spend much money to make it habitable. The services of such an apartment are often indispensable: running water, a toilet and bathtub, heating, a kitchen complex, windows, and room for storage. Much money and time is spent on painting walls and floors, paint that eventually remains behind as an improvement for the slum landlord. And of course there are many people living in slums who cannot afford any improvements. Interior living cubes can be constructed that will make it possible to combine sleeping, working, and sitting surfaces into an aesthetically manageable entity that uses all of the resources of the apartment itself in an ancillary way only, but shuts them out visually. Friends of mine have constructed three such cubes (one to sleep, eat, and entertain in; one for work; and one as a play environment for the baby; each eight feet cubed) and installed them in their rambling, ugly, slum apartment in Chicago. They moved the cubes (knocked-down and packaged flat) to a new, equally inexpensive and ugly tenement in Buenos Aires in 1970, where it improved their environment sufficiently to motivate them to move it once more, to Brazil, in 1980.

This is probably the place to mention the excellent work done by RFSU Rehab in Sweden. They have developed cutlery for people with impaired strength and movement, especially those suffering from rheumatoid arthritis. To this RFSU Rehab has also added a "normal" set of cutlery that looks fairly similar to the clinical set, thus permitting patients to eat with their family or in restaurants without feeling conspicuous. The Rehab people in Sweden have also developed handle extenders, tap-handle or faucet turners, pens, and crutches for the handicapped. In developing countries I have helped the World Health Organization to develop do-it-yourself crutches and wheelchairs that are in use in India and Malaysia. A full discussion of such devices is offered in the chapter "Virtuous Design" in Edward Lucie-Smith's *A History of Industrial Design* (New York: Van Nostrand Reinhold, 1983).

According to the best estimates there are at present about 200 million people (worldwide) who are bedridden, would like to read, but cannot turn the pages of a book. Seven different page-turners are available in Sweden, three in the

United States; none, except very expensive projection systems, work well. After designing one, we might also link it to a small overhead opaque projector and keep prices low.

What are meaningful, constructive activities for the elderly? Surely shuffleboard is not the only option. The aged need furniture that is easy to get into or out of. This furniture should be low in cost, easy to clean, and easy to maintain. In the retirement villages of Florida and the West Coast there live hundreds of cabinet-makers, designers, and craftsmen, whose most challenging stimulus is the weekend canasta tournament. The furniture can be designed and built by the client group involved. The relationships of seat-to-back, seat-to-arms, reclining angle, and so forth, must be appropriate for the elderly.

Handicapped people, the elderly, and some children need walking aids. Most walkers available at present are dangerous, unwieldy, and expensive. *Any* compassionate and well-trained fourth-year design student could design a better walker than any that is now available, in less than one hour. This has now been done by a student in Malaysia with W.H.O. help. His walker is locally made of bamboo or wood, on a village crafts level. (See *A History of Industrial Design*.)

An ambulance can cost as much as $28,500. Where are well-designed, low-cost inserts that would convert any station wagon to an ambulance for use during a national emergency? With the number and prices of ambulances now, this particular national emergency began about twenty years ago!

During the sixties and seventies I carried out experiments at *Konstfackskolan* in Stockholm dealing with the relationship between the handicapped and their environment. Fully documented by *Form* magazine, we showed that people in wheelchairs, as well as many on crutches and with strollers, can't use pay telephones or revolving doors or buy articles of their choice in a supermarket, where many shelves are placed too high or too low to be reached with ease. Stairways needed to be replaced by ramps. In the intervening ten years, this picture has changed greatly. Pay telephones in northern Europe,

Canada, and the United States have been placed in lower positions, many ramps have been built to accommodate those in wheelchairs, and other important control areas such as light switches and elevator controls have also been lowered. But much else needs to be done. Most ramps in the United States were simply added to comply with laws governing the handicapped. Both the materials selected for these ramps, as well as their angle of incline, frequently leads to their icing up or becoming slippery during the winter or with heavy rain storms. Street crossings are still impossible in most smaller cities in the United States for people with strollers, baby carriages, and prams or in wheelchairs. Kitchen sinks are generally too high for children, short people, the elderly, and those in wheelchairs. This also holds true for kitchen shelves, desk tops, and other working surfaces. Nothing has been done about shelves in supermarkets—surely the same ingenuity that puts tantalizing displays of sweets and the *National Enquirer* at checkout points, and moves the most necessary staples such as milk, butter, and bread into the rear of the store to force customers to pass *all* the aisles, could also deal with making general merchandise barrier free.

In a vertical black slum in Chicago, built in the fifties, black women are forced to walk a round trip of nearly five miles to shop at the nearest supermarket. Public transport is unavailable. If a woman is pregnant, she has to rest her parcels on the head of her unborn baby on the way back. The architectonic and hydraulic problems of pregnancy are also permanent problems of the obese. Such simple chores as taking a bath and getting out of bed create a host of imbalances. Yet the tools to make life easier for these people have not been forthcoming.

Highly specialized work often calls for highly specialized equipment. As a case history, at Cal Arts we discovered that dancers and dance students could relax their legs more efficiently by elevating them as much as possible. No seating unit (with the partial exception of the ill-fated Barwa Lounger of 1939) exists for this function. By making dancers and dance

The conventional and a new way for carrying groceries. Developed by the author for pregnant women.

students (the client group) part of the design team, a graduating student, Douglas Shoeffler, developed a relaxing chair that does the job. In the first picture it is shown in a normal seating position. In this mode it can also be used like a rocking-chair. In the second illustration it is in a "high-speed relaxation" mode. Just by putting one's arms behind one's head, one tilts the chair to the second position. Many of these chairs have been built and sold to professional dancers or students at cost. It also helps relax the tired legs of waitresses, nurses, and so forth. (Do-it-yourself diagrams, instructions, drawings, and a materials list for building the High-Speed Relaxation Chair are given on pp. 32–33 of the author's *Nomadic Furniture.*)

One of the most dangerous vehicles in the United States is the school bus. It is unsafe, giving insufficient protection to children and driver. The excellent German buses that exist for this purpose are not bought, and American transportation firms are unwilling to build a better vehicle, since local school boards have to operate on low budgets. Hence thirty-year-old deathtraps rattle down the twisting mountain roads of North Carolina, where a local law permits them to be driven by fifteen-year-olds.

In the early to mid-seventies I worked as a design consul-

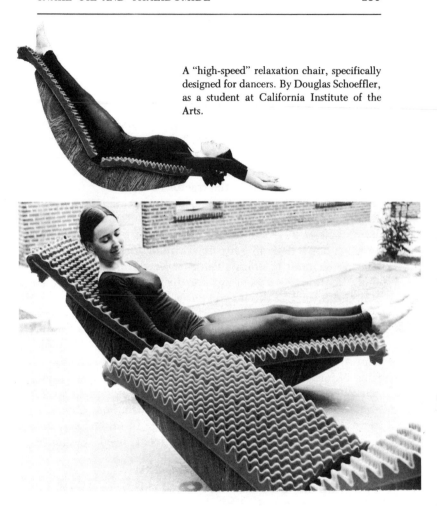

A "high-speed" relaxation chair, specifically designed for dancers. By Douglas Schoeffler, as a student at California Institute of the Arts.

tant for the Volvo automobile company of Gothenberg, Sweden. We designed some school buses to be marketed in the United States. These vehicles were enormously safe and comfortable and provided for in-transit lessons for the children. The oil crises of 1973 and 1976, as well as the reduction of educational budgets in the United States, stopped the design development cold.

Most farm accidents occur with tractors. *All* farm machinery and farm implements are unsafe. It has been my sad task to appear as an "expert witness" in cases involving farmers maimed or killed in tractor accidents. The manufacturers of farm machinery have now installed roll bars and they have been forced by multiplying law suits to provide some minimal safety devices. But the emphasis of the sales department seems to lie in such gimmickry as providing graphic equalizers for in-board stereo systems in the tractor's cabin.

With the number of boating accidents that affect small children and babies, it is amazing that no "automatic face-up" life jackets exist.

Much needs designing for the Third World. Let me repeat that we cannot sit in plush offices in New York or Stockholm and plan things for them and for their own good. Nevertheless, the purpose of this lengthy list is merely to interest people in what can and needs to be done. Power sources, light sources, cooling and refrigeration units, vermin-proof grain storage facilities, simple brick-making and pipe-making systems (for irrigation, waste disposal, and so forth), the same kind of inexpensive conversion system that will turn cars and trucks into ambulances that was mentioned earlier: these are some of the needs. But there is much else: communication systems, simple educational devices, water filtration, and immunization and inoculation equipment need design or redesign.

Some lighting designed for dental surgery and operating theaters in the "bush" have been developed by me for several clients, one of them in Australia. These are now available in Indonesia, Malaysia, the Philippines, and Papua New Guinea. A new refrigeration unit for bulk food storage on a village level is given in Chapter Ten. A communication/education device was developed by me for use in the countryside of Tanzania and Nigeria. *All* of these tools were designed with the cooperation of rural people in the country they were destined for and, in most cases, while I lived there.

With perfectly useful vehicles, such as buses, railroad cars, trains, ferry boats, and steamers, lying all over the place and not being used for anything, their redesign as movable classrooms, vocational re-education centers, emergency hospitals, and so forth, seems warranted. Old ferryboats might ply some of the tributaries of the Amazon River serving as clinics that provide birth-control information, abortion counseling, x-rays, prescriptions for glasses, dental care, and treatment for venereal diseases—just to give one possible example.

But most of the needs of the Third World will have to be solved there. Our responsibility as designers lies in seeing that emerging nations don't emulate our own mistakes of misusing design talent as an ego trip for the rich and a profit trip for industry. There is new hope that developing countries can solve their own design problems now, with little or no help from foreign "experts." Working with Mr. Paul Hogan of the Irish Export Board, we organized a month-long international meeting for industrial designers at Geneva, Switzerland, in the mid-seventies. This was done under the auspices of the United Nations. Designers and design administrators from twenty developing countries worked together on design and took lengthy field trips to Czechoslovakia, Denmark, and England. They also listened to formal presentations from industrial design offices and governmental agencies by delegates from India, Australia, the U.S.S.R., Canada, and the Irish Republic. At the end of the month an unexpected yet marvelous result emerged: a designer from Egypt offered a job to a young man from Ecuador and a graphic designer from Ghana accepted work in Southeast Asia. In other words, there was a horizontal exchange of experts who themselves came from developing countries. The myth that only the high-tech expert from the developed world could help was finally exploded.

American women seem to be willing to explore natural

childbirth and Lamaze methods. There are slide series now of fake classical sculptures showing Lamaze positions; yet good graphic information (in the form of slides or simple schematic drawings) doesn't exist. The actual films of childbirth (natural or otherwise) usually induce only a swooning spell in husbands who watch them.

Once children are born, their health is frequently neglected in some Third World countries, because there are few doctors, nurses, and clinics. Through intelligent design it has been made possible to simplify diagnosis for malnourished children. The process is so simple that it can be performed in less than a minute by parents or even school children. The diagnostic tool, which is called the Shakir Strip, is self-made by the people and can be produced for less than one-fiftieth of one cent. The Shakir Strip was designed for the International Institute of Child Health (see illustration).

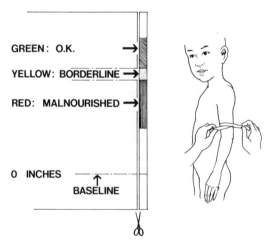

Shakir Strip. Cut from thin, colored plastic sheets to self-diagnose malnutrition. Designed for the World Health Organization. Drawing by Smit Vajaramant.

In transportation we can now take a large step backward. As a child I was lucky to be one of the few passengers in the *Graf Zeppelin*. It was both a luxurious and thoroughly delightful experience, which colored all my childhood memories of travel. These giant dirigibles consisted of a large passengers' gondola, which housed the captain's bridge, dining rooms, staterooms, and spacious corridors. The engines were housed in separate nacelles that, like the passengers' gondola, hung suspended from the gigantic aluminum structure. They were placed more than 100 feet aft of the passengers' cabins. Both vibration and engine noises were negligible, and the dirigible, being lighter than air, needed only a slight push to go in the desired direction. Unlike today's jet, it did not rip through the air. In the late thirties, the zeppelins were phased out because of several accidents. But with our new technology, we may be able to bring them back; we now have gases that are less flammable or inert, thereby eliminating disaster. It would radically reduce pollution across the North Atlantic run, provide a safe and unbelievably comfortable alternative mode of travel, and add merely a few hours to the journey. It would be a perfect supplement to today's jets and certainly a better solution than the Concorde. Supersonic jets appeal to people desperately afraid of flying, who would like to reduce their death-fear from eight hours to three. Dirigibles would give a safer and more comfortable alternative that is ecologically more responsible.

My experience with the *Graf Zeppelin* also has taken on new life. My conviction that slower is better when high-speed alternatives exist, led me in the fifties, sixties, and the beginning of the seventies to advocate the return to sailing ships, as well as bringing back dirigibles for cargo and more leisurely, comfortable air travel. Now two companies, American Skyship Industries Inc. and Unsworth Transportation International Inc., are planning to use European technology to build dirigibles once more. Across the Canadian border "Lighter Than Air Systems Inc." is building the Skyship 500 in Toronto for the U.S. Coast Guard.

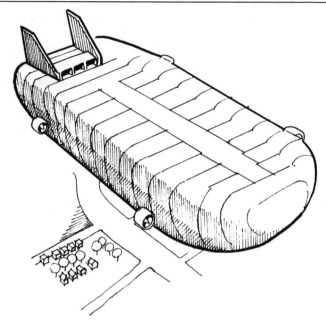

Dirigible cargo transporter, developed by Cargo Airships Ltd., London. Will carry 500 tons at 100 mph. Cruising range is global with air-to-air refueling. Drawing by Smit Vajaramant.

The dirigible American Skyship will be a "rigid airship," which means a football-shaped craft, skinned in aluminum, and filled with helium. The company's proposed R.30A will be 413 feet long, have a range of 3,500 miles, and have a carrying capacity of twenty-two tons.

Fuel efficiency is one reason for the re-emergence of dirigibles today; another is the logic of setting low-cost, slower, and more comfortable transportation against high-speed devices that are expensive to operate, like the Concorde (Associated Press, 6 March 1983).

The alternative to doing things faster is always to slow down. To bring back sailing ships for the North Atlantic run is perfectly feasible. The big difficulty with sailing ships was the manpower needed to work the rigging. Today all that can be automated. The second drawback to sailing ships was lack of speed. Today, as we can push people and goods across the ocean in a third of a day flying a jet, an alternative method seems possible here. I am delighted to find that both West Germany and the German Democratic Republic are developing such ships. Experimentation still continues on this side of the Atlantic. John L. Eyre is presently working on the first of these transAtlantic sailing ships for the United States in Bermuda. His design is partially based on the experiments of a German aeronautical engineer, Wilhelm Prolss, who christened his sail carrier the DynaShip. The DynaShip Corpora-

Cargo-carrying sailing ships with computer-steered rigging. Drawing by Smit Vajaramant.

tion of Palo Alto now owns patents in North and South America. William Warner says:

> The DynaShip is all moon buggy stuff. It's not beautiful. Electric motors set the sails, not men aloft. Everything is all push buttons. A world-wide weather routing service tells the ship where to go from satellite photographs, not the skipper's nose for wind. Computers determine how the sails are set (Associated Press, 15 October 1978).

John Eyre's vessel would be similar in some ways. Both are recent developments, stemming from rising oil prices during the seventies.

Although at the time of this writing oil prices are falling, there is no question that world oil supplies are diminishing quickly. By the end of the century the oil shortage will have become permanent and no longer related to political considerations.

Considering all the areas my list touches upon, one might assume that I feel that the problems of the world can be solved through design. Nothing could be further from the truth. All I am saying is that many problems could be eased through the talents of design intervention. This will mean a new role for designers, no longer as tools in the hands of industry but as advocates for users.

Near the end of 1983 I received a letter from Alastair Best, Editor-in-Chief of the magazine *Designer*, which, being read in more than 125 countries, is the most influential magazine on design in the world. The best way to end this chapter is to quote him directly: "I was particularly interested to hear that you are revising *Design for the Real World*, as it seems to me that *the gulf between developed north and underdeveloped south is greater than ever, and the cynicism and irrelevance of much work undertaken by the design professions is even worse than when the book was written.*" (Italics supplied.)

The disparity between north and south is indeed becoming worse. The United Nations established an ideal target amount that would have each of the technologically developed countries contribute 0.7 percent of their GNP to developing countries. Although the amount contributed increased—despite a worldwide recession—between 1981 and 1982, only four countries actually reached the UN minimal recommendation or exceeded it. These countries were Holland, Sweden, Norway, and Denmark, in that order. Although Washington politicians correctly tell us that the United States contributes the largest single dollar amount, in terms of the percentage of our Gross National Product we actually contribute to the poor countries, the United States ranks fourteenth out of fifteen high-tech countries; we are trailed only by Italy, and our own contribution is less than 0.3 percent of our GNP. In order of contribution the countries are: Holland, Sweden, Norway, Denmark, France, Belgium, Austria, West Germany, Canada, Britain, Finland, Japan, New Zealand, the United States, and Italy (O.E.C.D., *Geo* magazine, November 1983).

Part Two

HOW IT COULD BE

7

Rebel with a Cause:

Invention and Innovation

.

> When you make a thing, a thing that is new, it is so com-
>   plicated making it
> that it is bound to be ugly.
> But those that make it after you,
> they don't have to worry about making it.
> And they can make it pretty, and so everybody can like it
> when the others
> make it after you.
>
> PICASSO (as quoted by Gertrude Stein)

The most important ability that a designer can bring to his work is the ability to recognize, isolate, define, and solve problems. My own view is that designs must be sensitive to what problems exist. Frequently the designer will "discover" the existence of a problem that no one had recognized, define it, and then attempt a solution. The number of problems, as well as their complexity, have increased to such an extent that new and better solutions are needed.

At this point I should like to do three things: to attempt to explain why it is becoming critically important to encourage innovation, to define what is meant by creative problem solving, and to suggest specific methods.

151

The word creativity has become trendy over the last two decades, opening the door to a strange collection of absurdities. On my desk lies a paper entitled "Creative Aspects of Pre-Colombian Pottery." It sheds a good deal of light on pottery and might be of compelling interest to any pre-Colombian potter now working—however the dry scholarly dissection of thinking processes assumed by its author are of little help in the process of innovation. A university in southern California offers a course under the title "Remedial Creativity 201"! The mind boggles. Shelter magazines, addressing themselves to bored, middle-class housewives, consistently feature articles on "Creative Closets," "Creative Barbecue Pits," or "Twenty Creative Ways of Cooking a Country-Style Quiche." Brushing this trendy misuse of the word creative aside, we need to examine what creativity really is.

Our ways of thinking can be divided into various modes. There is *analytical* thinking (How long will it take me to drive from here to there, assuming a heavy rainstorm and stopping for lunch?). We engage in *judgmental* thinking (Which of these three steaks looks rarest?) and *routine* thinking (Given a specific temperature for the tempering of a steel alloy, what thickness is required to hold up a bridge?). In this last thinking mode we are encouraged to look up the correct answer at the back of some technical manual.

Routine thinking is a process that seems to go with the territory of being an engineer. This may be the reason why I have been retained to teach two-day seminars in "Creative Problem-Solving Techniques" to industrial engineering companies in the United States, Finland, Germany, and England for many years. Other professions seem less routinized in their problem-solving behavior.

And finally there is *creative* thinking. This seems to occur in three different ways. There is the sudden, momentary insight—the "spark of genius"—that sometimes comes to us in a blinding flash of revelation. Neither psychologists nor the innovators themselves have a clear explanation of this process.

We have a good deal of documentation for the second way

of finding a new solution: the discovery that comes to us in a dream. Scientific literature is filled with descriptions of this process: a researcher trying hard to develop a new insight, going to sleep and awakening with a lucid solution clear in his mind. This mechanism too is not understood, my own conviction is that such revelations are *intuitive*, that is: a marshalling of facts awaiting synthesis on a subconscious or preconscious level.

We are here concerned with the third mode: a systematic, solution-directed search for a new way of doing things.

Arthur Koestler has explored such acts of innovative thinking in his *Insight and Outlook* (1949) and later expanded this into possibly his most rigorous and definitive work *The Act of Creation*. Koestler finds similarities between humor and wit (through comic simile), "the art of discovery" (through analogous thinking), and the "discovery of art" (through metaphor). In each case he has established that the new insight occurs through an act of *collision*. He has named these moments of discovery as the "HaHa!, AhHa!, and Ah . . . !" reaction (as shown in the diagram below).

His working definitions of the creative act are excellent:

"The creative act consists in combining previously unrelated structures so that you get more out of the emergent whole than you put in."

Or:

"Perceiving of a situation or idea in two self-consistent but mutually incompatible frames of reference or associative contexts."

To meet problems in a new and creative way has been part of the biological and cultural endowment of our species for millions of years. But, as we live in a society that places a high

"Haha-aha-ah" curve. After Arthur Koestler.

value on conformity, our creative responses have been blunted or stifled—frequently an innovative reaction will be dismissed as mere eccentricity.

Although the ability to solve problems has been an inherent and desirable trait throughout human history, mass production, mass advertising, media manipulation, and automation are four contemporary trends that have emphasized conformity and made creativity a harder ideal to attain. In the twenties, Henry Ford, attempting to reduce the price of his cars through standardized production methods, is reputed to have said, "They [the consumers] can have any color they want as long as it's black." Through curtailing color choices, the price of individual automobiles was lowered by some $95, but consumers had to be persuaded that black is a desirable color.

This spirit of conformity has accelerated at an amazing rate. The demands on the individual to conform come from all directions: not only do the national, state, and local governments understandably enforce certain standards of behavior, but there are pressures from neighbors in suburban areas, conformist trends in school, at work, in church, and at play. What happens if we are unable to operate in so aggressively conformist an environment? We "blow our top" and are taken to the nearest psychiatrist for help. The first thing this specialist in human thought and motivation may want to say to us (if not in so many words) is "Well, now, we must *adjust* you." And what is adjustment, if not another word for conformity? This is not to argue for a totally nonconformist world. In fact, conformity is a valuable human trait in that it helps to keep the entire social fabric together. But we have made our severest mistake in confusing *conformity in action* with *conformity in thought.*

Extensive psychological testing has shown that the mysterious quality called "creative imagination" seems to exist in all people but is severely diminished by the time an individual reaches the age of *six.* The environment of school ("You mustn't do this!" "You mustn't do that!" "You call that a drawing of your mother? Why, your mother only has *two* legs." "Nice girls don't do things like that!") sets up a whole screen of blocks in the mind of the child that later inhibits his ability to ideate freely. Of course, some of these prohibitions have social value: moralists tell us that they help the child establish a conscience; psychologists prefer to call this the formation of the superego; religious leaders call it a sense of right and wrong, or soul.

However, society can go to amazing lengths to create greater conformity and protect itself from whatever the current mainstream is pleased to call "deviants." In 1970 Dr. Arnold Hutschnecker suggested in a memo to President Nixon that all children between the ages of six and eight be tested psychologically to determine if they *might* have the kind of tendencies that would turn them toward becoming criminals later in life. The underlying suggestion was that some of these children be tranquilized heavily and maintained in that condition, much as millions of elderly patients in retirement homes are kept under sedation to ease the work of the nursing staff.

Too many blocks can effectively stop problem-solving. (These blocks will be examined in detail later in this chapter.) The wrong kind of problem statement can also block effective solutions. The saying "Build a better mousetrap and the world will beat a path to your door" is a case in point. What is the real problem here, to *catch* mice or to *get rid of them*? Suppose my city is overrun by rodents, and I *do* invent a better mousetrap. As a result I may have ten million captured mice and rats to contend with. My solution may have been highly innovative; it was the original problem statement that went wrong. The real problem was to *get rid* of mice and rats. It might be far better to broadcast an ultrasonic or subsonic beam over every radio and television set for a few hours, which, while harmless to other living creatures, would sterilize all rats and mice. Some weeks later the rodents would be gone. (This raises the ethical question as to whether rats and mice should be permitted to watch television.) It would raise the environmental question to what extent some small rodents are important links in the ecosystem.

However, most problems requiring immediate and radical new solutions lie in areas that are quite new.

Chad Oliver, in his science-fiction novel *Shadows in the Sun*, says

> . . . he had to figure it out for himself. That sounds easy enough, being one of the familiar figures of speech of the English language, but Paul Ellery knew that it was not so simple. Most people live and die without ever having to solve a totally new problem. Do you wonder how to make the bicycle stay up? Daddy will show you. Do you wonder how to put the plumbing in your new house? The plumber will show you. Would it be all right to pay a call on Mrs. Layne, after that scandal about the visiting football player? Well, call up the girls and talk it over. Should you serve grasshoppers at your next barbecue? Why, nobody does that. Shall you come home from the office, change into a light toga, and make a small sacrifice in the backyard? What would the neighbors think?
>
> But—how do you deal with a Whumpf in the butter? What do you do about Grlzeads on the stairs? How much should you pay for a new Lttangnuf-fel? Is it okay to abnakave with a prwaatz?
>
> Why, how silly! I never heard of such things. I have enough problems of my own without bothering my head with such goings on.
>
> A Whumpf in the butter! I declare.
>
> *A situation completely outside human experience* . . . .

We live in a society that penalizes highly creative individuals for their nonconformist autonomy. This makes the teaching of problem-solving discouraging and difficult. A twenty-two-year-old student arrives at school with massive blocks against new ways of thinking, engendered by some sixteen years of miseducation, a heritage of childhood and pubescence of being "molded," "adjusted," "shaped." Meanwhile our society continuously evolves new social patterns that promise a slight departure from the mainstream but without ever endangering the patchwork of marginal groups that make up society as a whole.

First we must understand the psychological aspects of problem-solving. While no psychologist or psychiatrist can yet point to the exact mechanics of the creative process, more insights are becoming available. We know that the ability to generate new ideas freely is a function of the unconscious and that it is the associative faculty of the brain that is at work. The ability to come up with many new ideas is inherent in all of us, regardless of age (with the exception of senility and anility) or so-called IQ level (always excepting true morons). However in being able to associate freely, multidisciplinary abilities are indispensable. The quantity of knowledge, the quality of memory and recall can also enrich this process. All this helps to look at things in new ways. A new way of looking at things can be enhanced enormously through a thorough understanding of a second language. For the structure of each language gives us different ways of dealing with and experiencing realities.

It is perfectly reasonable to say "I am going to San Francisco" in English. The same statement can be made in German ("Ich gehe nach San Francisco"), but it makes no sense linguistically. In German a qualifier must be added, for instance: I am *flying* to San Francisco, I am *driving* to San Francisco. In Navajo and the Eskimo languages such statements must be even more specifically qualified to make sense: "I (alone, or with two friends, or whatever) am driving (sometimes I will drive, sometimes my friend will drive) (by cart, by sled) to San Francisco (then I will return and my friend will drive on)." By bringing more than one language to bear on a problem, we obtain depth.

If we are forced to wear a temporary eye patch, we have to drive more carefully: our depth perception is gone, since we see the landscape from one vantage point only. To view the road (or a problem) in full depth, we have to look at it from two different observation posts simultaneously. Optically both eyes together perform this service—this is also the principle of a range-finder on a camera. Intellectually the morphological and structural differences between two languages provides us with two similar vantage points, permitting us to use triangulation in viewing a problem. Whether the language studied is German, Finnish, Swahili, music, Fortran, or Basic matters little.

We can list the inhibitors that keep us from solving tasks in new and innovative ways. They are:

1. Perceptual Blocks
2. Emotional Blocks
3. Associational Blocks
4. Cultural Blocks
5. Professional Blocks
6. Intellectual Blocks
7. Environmental Blocks

Each can be explained simply through examples.

1. *Perceptual Blocks*: As the name implies, these inhibitors lie in the area of perception. A tone-deaf person labors under perceptual blocks when trying to hear music, with a deaf person the block has become total. There are scores of such physical blocks, from color blindness, astigmatism, and strobismus to true blindness or hysterical aphasia. These blocks lie well beyond the scope of this book. But consider the fairly familiar figure opposite.

Some people see a white goblet against a black background. Others see the profiles of two black people against a field of white. (It is interesting to note in this figure-ground-relationship problem that American blacks tend to see the second interpretation first.) No matter: *all* people can see either picture.

The second illustration is less familiar. The majority of people can identify a pretty young woman, dressed in a style of around 1890, wearing a motoring veil, and with her face provocatively turned away.

The simultaneous image of a mean old witch is less appar-

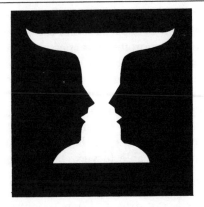

Perception problem in figure-ground relationship. After Koffka.

Old Hag—Young Girl? A classical figure in perception.

ent, and many people have to struggle before recognizing her. Now what was a black choker around the young girl's throat has become the uncompromisingly mean mouth of the witch. The young beauty's left ear and her snub nose have turned into the eyes of the old hag. (It seems that people discover what they want to see more easily.)

Again both pictures are visible to everyone but only *ad seriatim*. While anyone, once having recognized both images, can flip back and forth between them at will, it takes a good deal of training to be able to view both images *simultaneously*.

When asked how many squares are in the figure below, the majority of people say sixteen. A few, counting the encompassing "meta-square," will see seventeen.

Actually there are thirty squares of various sizes, but it's *easier* to just recognize seventeen.

2. *Emotional Blocks*: In a society that values conformity, people readily learn that "you don't stick your neck out," and "you don't rock the boat." A simple experiment will convince the reader that emotional pressures are strong in group situations. Ask a group of twenty-five or thirty people if any of

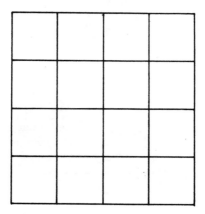

How many squares?

them does bird-watching as a hobby. Eliminate these bird-watchers, and then ask the remaining people: "How many of you can identify or differentiate among thirty different birds?"

Few if any hands will be raised in assent. The fact of the matter is that most normal six-year-olds recognize between thirty and thirty-five birds; most adults can easily differentiate or identify sixty or more, as the following list of sixty will show.

Chicken	Flamingo	Penguin
Owl	Goose	Eagle
Duck	Parrot	Parakeet (Budgerigar)
Woodpecker	Swallow	Hummingbird
Pheasant	Seagull	Peacock
Cornish Game Hen	Stork	Kingfisher
Raven	Pelican	Sandpiper
Swan	Robin	Sparrow
Cardinal	Kiwi	Quail
Blackbird	Crow	Cockatoo
Dodo	Hawk	Nightingale
Pidgeon	Tucan	Ptarmigan
Vulture	Heron	Bluebird
Lyrebird	Emu	Cormorant
Finch	Lark	Albatross
Grouse	Dove	Puffin
Guinea Fowl	Jay	Starling
Egret	Wren	Condor
Bittern	Ostrich	Falcon
Canary	Turkey	Kestrel

Individuals in a group audience are under a great emotional pressure. They don't "stick their neck out," afraid that they may be asked to identify some unusually exotic bird. It is an excellent example of emotional blocks at work.

3. *Associational Blocks*: Associational blocks operate in those areas where psychologically predetermined sets and inhibitions, often going back to our earliest childhood, keep us

from thinking freely. A well-known experiment will illustrate this point.

In one of our Eastern colleges a five-foot-long steel pipe, one-and-one-half inches in diameter, was fixed into the concrete floor of a laboratory, with twelve inches of the pipe below floor level and four feet stuck straight up. A ping-pong ball was then inserted into the pipe, so that it would rest at the bottom, five feet from the top. A miscellaneous collection of tools, utensils, and gadgets was placed in the room. One thousand students were introduced into the room one at a time—each was asked to find some method for getting the ping-pong ball out of the pipe. The attempts to solve the problem were as various as the students themselves: some tried to saw through the pipe, which proved too strong; others dripped steel filings on to the ping-pong ball and then went "fishing" for it with a magnet, finding that the magnet would adhere to the pipe wall long before it could be lowered all the way down. Others tried to raise it with a wad of chewing gum on a string, but the ball would inevitably drop off. To stick a series of soda straws together and try to "suck" it up also proved impossible. Sooner or later almost all of the students, 917 out of 1,000 (a respectable performance indeed) found a mop and a bucket of water in a corner, poured the water into the pipe, and floated the ball to the top. This, however, was only the control group.

A second series of 1,000 students were then asked to solve the problem again; conditions remained unchanged with one exception. The bucket of water was removed, and the psychologists substituted an antique rosewood table on which a finely cut crystal pitcher of water, two glasses, and a silver tray rested. Only 188 out of the second group succeeded. Why? Because nearly eighty percent of this group failed to "see" the water. The fact that a crystal pitcher standing on a rosewood table is more noticeable than a pail in a corner is obvious. Still, the second group failed to make the associational link between water and flotation. The associational connection was much more difficult to make with the handsome pitcher than with the bucket, even though we normally don't pour water out of a bucket to float ping-pong balls either.

A third version of the test removed *both* the pail of water and the pitcher. A suprisingly large number, nearly 50 percent, of these (male) undergraduates still solved the problem correctly by urinating into the pipe.

Shortly after the end of World War II, Raymond Loewy Associates designed a small home fan and succeeded in making the action truly noiseless. To their consternation, consumer response forced them to introduce a new gear into the fan that would give off a slight sound: the average American associated noise with cooling action and felt that a totally noiseless fan did not provide enough cool air.

4. *Cultural Blocks*: As the name implies, these are imposed upon an individual by his cultural surrounding. And in each society a number of taboos endanger independent thinking. The classic Eskimo nine-dot problem, which can befuddle the average Westerner for hours, is solved by Eskimos within minutes, since Eskimo space concepts are quite different from ours. Professor Edward Carpenter explains how the men of the Aklavik tribe in Alaska will draw reliable maps of small islands by waiting for night to close in and then drawing the map by listening to the waves lapping at the island in the dark. In other words, the island's shape is discerned by a sort of aural radar. We are sometimes confused by Eskimo art, for we have lost the Eskimo's ability to look at a drawing from all sides simultaneously.

While living with an Eskimo tribe some years ago, I received magazines through the post. I found that my Eskimo friends would form a circle around me, while I looked at pictures or read. Neither in igloo nor hut *was there any jostling for positions*. My friends could read (or view pictures) as easily and quickly upside-down or sideways as if "correctly" positioned by nonEskimo standards. I noticed that those Eskimos living in cabins would frequently hang pictures upside down or sideways. (Norman Rockwell covers from the *Saturday Evening Post* were a favorite, being story-telling illustrations.)

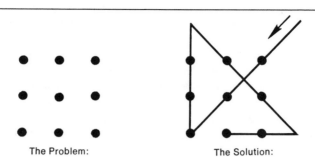

The Problem: The Solution:

The Eskimo Nine-dot Problem

Nonlinear, aural space perception imposes fewer vertical and horizontal limitations on the Eskimos' world-view. Carpenter has suggested that this may account for the immediate ease Eskimos exhibit in working with electronic devices.

It seems to me that this is a species-specific survival characteristic in the far North. I have accompanied Eskimo hunting parties, which, after the hunt, headed across fifty or more miles of featureless terrain to return to their group of igloos. There was seemingly no visual differentiation between snow-laden sky, the snow falling, or the covered ground itself. To miss the igloos by even 200 feet would have resulted in death from exposure. But both my friends and their sled dogs reacted to minute stimuli of changing moisture and wind and

Eskimo print: "Spirits (*Tornags*) Devouring Foxes." Author's collection.

invariably found the way back to the encampment. (Eskimos are equally astonished by our ability to cross Bloor Street in Toronto or Times Square in New York.)

A design problem involving cultural blocking was stated by a client of mine (a manufacturer of toilet bowls) as follows: while the average American changes his automobile every two-and-a-half years, gets a new suit about every nine months, buys a refrigerator every ten years, and even changes his residence about every five years, he never buys a new toilet bowl. If one could design the sort of bowl that would make people want to trade in their old one, industry would benefit. At first sight this seemed a phony job, calling for artificially created obsolescence. And two answers would immediately come to the mind of the "stylist." The "Detroit approach": possibly providing the bowl with tailfins and vast chrome ornamentation. Another would be the "toilet bowls are fun" approach: imprinting the surface with, say, little flowers or birds. But intelligent research soon showed that *all toilet bowls are too high* (medically speaking). Ideally, people should assume a lower, squatting position when using a toilet. After much research, a new, lower bowl was designed and built. In spite of the obvious medical and sanitary advantages, in spite of the fact that now a real reason existed for buying new toilet bowls, the design was rejected. The manufacturer felt that the cultural block in the public mind was too great and that it would be impossible for him to advertise his new and better product. It can be shown that this was a true U.S. *cultural* block: my design was eventually produced by a subsidiary company and advertised in the press in the Nordic countries, where it sold well and provided a prototypal object for other manufacturers. By 1982 I noticed that the majority of Northern European toilet bowls had followed suit. (This is fully illustrated and well described in Luigi Bearzotti's article: "W.C." in *Ottagono*, No. 73, June 1984, Milano, Italy.)

Cultural taboos about elimination processes have made other developments difficult: toilet tissue is made of paper that uses enormously large quantities of water in its manufacture.

For reasons now obscure, rolls of toilet paper are a given width. By reducing this by one inch, millions of gallons of water would be saved daily in the manufacturing process, without cutting down on the function of the tissue. Yet this is another idea that is ecologically sound but has gone begging.

Whenever the concept of recycling body wastes is brought up (for instance in a discussion of space capsules or space stations), people become disturbed. (It is useful to remember that, on Liferaft Earth, everything we breathe, drink, eat, wear, or use, has gone through billions of digestive systems since the planet was first formed.) Cultural blocks about this affect our thinking; our thinking affects our acts. We think of streams and lakes as "polluted by urban wastes"; we use words like "sludge" and "solid waste" and are appalled to find that our water sources are "poisoned" by human excrement. We are confused (as with the better mousetrap mentioned earlier) about whether we want to get rid of excrement or just separate it from our drinking supply.

The entire field of *anaerobic and aerobic digestion* has received more study, research, and application. Major scientists are involved in rigorous work with methane-generating processes. In the early seventies only occasional paragraphs appeared in *The Whole Earth Catalog* about solitary British eccentrics who manage to power their automobiles from chicken droppings, alerting the public about the gigantic energy sources that can be mined from our bodily processes of putrefaction, digestion, and waste-making. Now research technology has developed a prime-energy convertor that, by using anaerobic digestion systems, can make a house independent of external connections. In 1973, looking through the newspapers of communes and alternative societies, I thought it pathetic that much of their gear (transformers, pumps, high-fidelity components, light generators, projectors) still had to plug in somewhere. The use of biological recycling for energy has now made true independence possible.

By 1969 much of this had already been proven experimentally. Dr. George W. Groth Jr. maintained 1,000 pigs in confinement on his farm near San Diego, California. The pig manure operates a ten-kilowatt war-surplus generator, which provides all the electricity needed for both light and power. The liquid manure pit has been capped, and the sewer gas is tied to a gas engine. Hot water from the engine's cooling system runs through 300 feet of copper tubing coiled inside the pit. A temperature of between 90 and 100 degrees Farenheit is maintained, which provides the best temperature for maximum "digestion." A tiny pump, running off the fan-belt pulley, circulates the water. A complete digestion cycle takes about twenty days, but, once the process is an ongoing one, it is also continuous. Besides providing electric power, the system has virtually no odor and attracts no flies. Finally, the manure at first breaks down into simple organic compounds like acids and alcohols. Ultimately, as there is no air, it breaks down into water, carbon dioxide, and methane gas. Experiments of this sort have also been tried in Europe, Asia, Africa, and Latin America.

By 1983 methane digesters are working in communities and farms all over the world. It seems clear that this design strategy is giving us a way of using human and animal waste by converting it into power sources and recycling what is left. (But even now it is curious that what little has been written about it has appeared mostly in technical journals, the underground press, and alternative life-style papers where cultural blocks are less inhibiting.)

5. *Professional Blocks*: Sometimes, specific professional training may establish truly crippling blocks. When shown the front elevation and the right side elevation of an object (as shown) and asked to draw a correct plan view or perspective, architects, engineers, and draftsmen usually fail at a higher rate than people untutored in these fields. Finding the correct solution to this problem can also teach us *how* we solve problems. Both answers shown are correct. It is possible to diagnose how a solution was reached: either through a species of creative analysis or through sudden insight (depending on

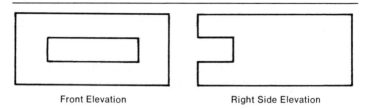

Front Elevation   Right Side Elevation

Object Visualization Problem

which answer is given). The reasoning behind answer number one runs somewhat as follows: "The right side elevation is wrong; it should be a center section. I must therefore find a figure where the theoretical center section and the right side elevation are identical. After selecting an equilateral triangle as the answer, I see that the front edge will show up as a line in the front elevation. By rounding this off, the line disappears and the problem is answered correctly." The second answer is equally correct but, mathematically speaking, much more elegant. It is discovered through sudden insight and intuition.

Needless to say, the particular professional block that keeps people from answering this problem correctly (using either solution), lies in their assuming a false, ninety-degree relationship, and visualizing the figure as being rectangular or square. "Rectangularity" or "squareness," then, is the basic block that the solver himself has built into the problem.

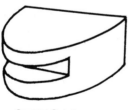

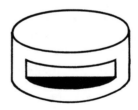

Correct Solution: "Elegant" Correct Solution:
Deductive Reasoning   Sudden Insight

Object Visualization Solutions

Professional blocks can also be illustrated by the following anecdote: Two engineering students are finishing their graduate work at MIT. One evening John visits Michael in his rooms and is amazed to see an entire wall covered by a huge "attribute-listing" chart. This chart lists the names of various young ladies, Joan, Cheryl, Mary, Jennifer, and so forth, along the left margin. The top line lists attributes: "has money," "cooks well," "good-looking," "intelligent," "trained in engineering," "good in bed." To John's questions, Mike replies: "I've been asked to start teaching at Stanford, and I felt this would be a good time to get married. So I've listed all the young women I know with their attributes and—true to engineering tradition—have put check marks across significant correlations." John is impressed and, noticing that one young woman in particular has accrued most of these distinctions, says, "I guess you'll marry Mary?" "No," replies his friend fastidiously, "you see, *I don't like her!*" Michael overcame his professional block.

6. *Intellectual Blocks*: Over-intellectualization frequently keeps us from recognizing the nub of a problem and makes it difficult to choose the best method for reaching a solution.

Arthur Koestler cites the following puzzle:

> At sunrise one morning a Buddhist priest begins to climb a holy mountain. There is only one narrow path that spirals its way to a meditation chamber at the top. The priest interrupts his upward path frequently to rest, to meditate and pray. Being elderly it takes him the entire day to reach the summit. There he spends several days in meditation and fasting. He starts his way down, again at sunrise, walking more briskly this time and with fewer and shorter rests.
>
> Is there *a spot* along the path that the priest will occupy at precisely the same time of day in both trips? Answer yes or no.

Answers to this simple puzzle are usually equally divided between yes and no. The correct answer of course is yes. It is interesting to note that those who have opted for the negative fight furiously and irrationally on behalf of their solution. In this case, the intellectual interest lies in *how* the problem was solved. By far the simplest way is to mentally add a second priest and collapse time into one day. Visualize *two* priests— one at the bottom and one at the top—both starting their journey at the same moment (sunrise). It is obvious that at some time and at some point they will meet along this single path, regardless of each other's speed. This point is the spot along the path, the time of meeting is the time. The answer is yes.

You may have chosen a visual image as your method of thinking. In that case you probably also solved it. One can equally well imagine a plot on a graph of each priest's position as a function of time. The two graph lines will have to intersect at a common time and position.

If you chose verbalization, you probably failed. Even after knowing the "visual solution," if you again think about it in a verbal manner, the problem will become confusing and obscure.

Here is another example of an intellectual block:

> Envisage a large piece of paper the thickness of a sheet of typewriter paper. Fold it in half in your imagination, resulting in two layers. Now fold it once again (having four layers) and continue folding it over upon itself fifty times. How thick would the 50-times-folded paper be?

In reality it is impossible to fold any piece of paper (regardless of size or thickness) fifty times. But for the sake of this problem, imagine you can do it.

Most people guess "two to three inches."

The correct answer is approximately 50,000,000 miles, or more than half the distance from the earth to the sun. The *first fold* gives a stack two times the original thickness. The *second* results in two by two the original thickness; the *third*, two by two by two times the original thickness. If you are somewhat mathematically inclined, you will see that the answer to the problem is 2^{50} times the thickness of typing paper, and 2^{50} is about 1,100,000,000,000,000.

Solving this problem *visually*, as with the priest on the sacred mountain, you would fail. It is impossible to correctly envisage fifty folds. *Verbalization* also leads to difficulties. If you are familiar with *"doubling problems,"* you saw that the answer would be enormously large but could still not place a correct value on it. In this case the best strategy is mathematics.

7. *Environmental Blocks*: From Proust's cork-lined room to the noise of the editorial office at the *Washington Post* is a major step. Environmental blocks, that is, the extent to which the environment influences your problem-solving behavior positively or negatively, differ from person to person. My twelve-year-old daughter can do rigorous exercises in mathematics while listening to symphonic music. My older daughter, Nicolette, writes and edits training manuals in an environment that must be completely quiet and peaceful. Personally I find that I operate best with phones ringing, frequent interruptions, and a great deal of visual distraction. (This may be based on my having started my writing career as a reporter for a busy morning paper.)

You are best able to determine yourself the ideal environment for problem solving in your case.

These points will recapitulate what has been established so far:

1. With constant pressure toward less individualism and greater conformity forced upon our society by mass advertising, mass media, mass production, and automation, the ability to solve problems in new and unexpected ways is becoming increasingly rare.
2. In a fast-accelerating, increasingly complex society, the designer is faced with more and more problems that can be solved only through new basic insights.
3. Design graduates leave our schools with some know-how, a great many skills, and a certain amount of aesthetic sensitivity but with almost no method for obtaining any basic insights.

4. They find themselves unfit to solve new problems because of perceptual, emotional, associational, cultural, professional, intellectual, and environmental blocks. These blocks are the direct result of the constantly accelerating rat race toward conformity and so-called adjustment.
5. This race is not only inimical to all true design creativity but, in a wider sense, violates the very survival characteristics of the human species.
6. The various blocks are not inherited parts of the personality structure but rather learned, limiting, and inhibiting factors.

Our job then becomes one of establishing methods of doing away with these blocks. Although it is difficult to make a definitive list, since there is enormous overlap between different methods, I shall list eight:

1. Brainstorming
2. Synectics
3. Morphological Analysis
4. Sliding Scales
5. Bisociation
6. Trisociation
7. Bionics and Biomechanics
8. Forcing New Thinking Patterns

1. *Brainstorming*: This is probably the most widely known problem-solving method. The emphasis in a brainstorming team is on *quantity* of ideas rather than quality. The team members are asked to *suspend their judgment sense* during the actual working session. A team of six to eight people can be randomly assembled within an organization; the problem is then explained, and they then sit around a table trying to generate as many ideas as possible and list them regardless of merit. The theory behind the concept is simple. It is assumed that if only *one* solution to a problem exists, the originator will always feel protective towards it. Should it later prove

unworkable, he or she will be blocked from contributing new insights by unconsciously attempting to merely ring variations on the original thought.

Since no idea can be prejudged, an enormous quantity of ideas is generated. To a problem statement like "How can we increase sales of personal computers?" a team will frequently contribute 300 to 400 unevaluated concepts. These ideas are then slowly processed through a series of criteria (also brainstormed by the team) until final implementation. It is significant that brainstorming was invented by Alexander Osborne, of BBD & O, an advertising agency. Because of its advertising background, the system lends itself primarily to solving "soft" problems, that is, problems in behavior, marketing, or motivation. Technical problems tend to be encumbered by so many important limitations that these very considerations form a type of prejudgment. The reader will find a complete explanation of brainstorming in Sidney Parnes' *Creative Behavior Guide Book* (New York: Charles Scribner's Sons, 1967).

2. *Synectics*: William J.J. Gordon developed this second team problem-solving method while leading the Invention Research Group for Arthur D. Little. A synectics team, unlike brainstorming, requires a strong team leader; furthermore, team membership is permanent, and the members of the team are carefully chosen to represent at least two disciplines each. Synectics works best with technical and scientific problems and is much more rigidly structured than brainstorming. I have worked with synectics modes in Cambridge, Massachusetts; since this system is closely tied to biology, I have given some examples in the following chapter. Those interested are referred to Bill Gordon's *Synectics* (New York: Harper & Bros., 1961), or, for a less self-serving analysis, George Princes's *The Practice of Creativity* (New York: Macmillan/Collier Paperback, 1978).

3. *Morphological Analysis*: This system, unlike brainstorming and synectics, is a method of *individual* problem-solving. Morphological analysis is a good deal simpler than its pretentious name. Developed by a West Coast advertising guru, it

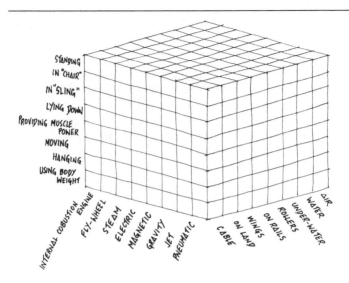

Morphological-analysis Matrix

consists of a three-dimensional graph in the form of a cube (as shown).

Since each of the three parameters consists of eight small squares, forming a larger square of 64, the entire construct results in a sort of super-cube containing 512 boxes. The late Professor John Arnold gave an example of using it to provide a new concept for personal transportation. In our illustration I have chosen power source, medium in which the vehicle operates, and gross means of locomotion.

If we now look at each of the 512 boxes resulting from the conjunction of the three parameters, we find a series of "solutions." Some of these will unavoidably be duplications of already existing systems: a steam-driven device, running on rails with seated passengers—in other words, a railroad. In another box we will find a jet-propelled device operating under water with people reclining on couches. This yields us an idea for high-speed underwater transportation. Another cube generates the suggestion for a fly-wheel-powered vehicle with people standing up in it and operating on a hard surface. Seemingly this gives us still another new approach. Later research will show that this system is in use for buses in Switzerland—nonetheless it may force an American transportation designer to think in new and unfamiliar ways.

From the above it will be clear that this is no more than the externalization of a sort of memory aid, a sort of "paper computer." But there is one advantage: we still are completely unable to design a computer *with a random hunting circuit.* Until we do, and that prospect seems unattainable now, we need to use the associational powers of the brain in selecting useful answers from among the 512 possibilities contained in the super-cube.

4. *Sliding Scales*: I developed this *individual* problem-solving system out of my impatience with the small number of possibilities that morphological analysis offers. It is another "paper computer," although it happens to be made of wood. As shown in the illustration, it consists of twelve tally-sticks that move in grooves against one another, somewhat in the manner of an old-fashioned slide-rule. Using peel-off labels it is possible to insert twenty or so different limitations of a problem in architecture or design on each stick, with all of the limitations still confined to just *one* general area. This might be material, process, or whatever. Sliding the individual sticks up or down, it is then possible to read a line across. This will yield twelve combinations out of a possible 240 juxtapositions (as shown in the photograph on page 176).

But wait. The unit shown is but *one* out of eighteen identical ones (each of which consists of twelve tally sticks—each stick has twenty or so further parameters written in). These other seventeen devices each stand for major design considerations, such as economics, social consequences, aesthetic criteria, and safety factors. These eighteen boards, each with 240 juxtapositions, hang next to each other in a vertical file. By working all eighteen boards and reading not only the linear

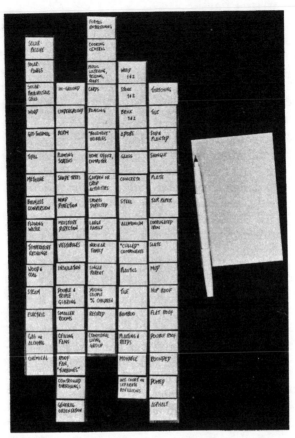

Sliding scales, arranged to solve an architectural problem. Photo by John Charlton.

solution on each board but also *reading through all eighteen three dimensionally*, we are looking at nearly 4,400 possible combinations.

Sliding scales give a much larger choice than morphological analysis. Although useful in searching for problem solutions, they are still fairly unwieldy. Both systems are basically "paper computer" checklists, and rely on a guiding, goal-directed, and selective brain to make choices. Unfortunately the sheer mechanics—simple as they are—get in the way.

Finding all such systems cumbersome, I have spent a good deal of time trying to develop a simple and elegant way of turning the brain to solution finding (and problem finding) with no mechanical intrusions. I also felt that the number of ideas obtained should be unlimited—as it is in normal intensive thinking—rather than arbitrarily tied to 512 or 4,400 possibilities.

Arthur Koestler's theory of bi-association (the engineered collision between two incompatible sets of ideas) was explored by him and myself in the years since his original publication of *Insight and Outlook*. Through meetings and letters we refined the phrase to *bisociation*. Over the last ten years I have both practiced and taught my bisociation technique, which seems to fill my original prescription for an elegant system without mechanical distraction.

5. *Bisociation*: The individual problem-solving method is best explained through an actual example. A simple chart is shown, with the object to be designed listed to the left of the vertical line. To the right six or seven "response words," that is, nouns arbitrarily picked from a dictionary or provided by a coworker, are written down. *It is important that these nouns not be connected in the designer's mind with the object under design consideration.* To organize the solutions discovered, these are arranged under headings on the extreme right of the page. Classifications I normally use are:

NOW (a product or system that can be made immediately)

2-5 YEARS (a concept not quite ready for immediate production)

5-10 YEARS (an answer leading to long-range product or system planning)

R & D (a solution that sounds reasonable, the feasibility of which may have to be determined by the Research & Development department)

GIMMICKS (Sometimes an idea results that has nothing to do with the product itself but rather develops a new merchandising gimmick.)

OTHERS (Frequently ideas may emerge that don't solve the specific design problem at all. Nonetheless they may be innovative answers to problems beyond the scope of the inquiry and may be developed for other clients.)

Let's see how it works in practice. Below are typical bisociation forms. The one on the right at the start of the problem, the same form on the left upon completion:

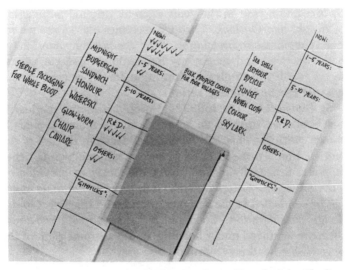

Two bisociation charts. Photo by John Charlton

The object chosen to be designed is a chair. The response words offered are ventriloquist, sex, eagle, orchid, bicycle, sunset, and ice cream.

It will now be my task to bring the concept of chair-to-be-designed into an artificial and forceful collision with each of the response words in turn. The technique used is a sort of free stream-of-consciousness flow.

> Chair/Ventriloquist: ventriloquists use dummies . . . window-display dummies . . . figures in a wax museum . . . back to window dummies . . . they used to be made of papier-mâché

. . . kids use papier-mâché in nursery school . . . in chair design
compound curves can be achieved only with difficulty in mass
produced plastic shells . . . here's the idea: we can construct
an enormously comfortable easy chair for normal use, or even
for a specific subgroup such as severely handicapped people
. . . by using a chicken wire armature we can create any compound curve configuration we want to, wet newspapers and
glue (papier-mâché) can be worked in over the armature . . .
We can now make one-of-a-kind individual chairs easily for
the first time in history (the wire and papier-mâché shell can
be covered with foam and fabric in a conventional manner).
Enter under NOW.

Chair/Sex: a delightful activity . . . Freud's "prime deter-
minate" . . . pleasure . . . pregnancy . . . pregnant women
. . . pregnant women's stomachs expand . . . they go back to
"normal" after delivery . . . here's the idea: since seating comfort depends on positional changes, we can design a continuously yet randomly expanding and contracting back portion of
a chair. This can be done hydraulically or mechanically. Enter
under NOW for chairs; enter under R & D for dentists' chairs
and under OTHERS for seats in automobiles, buses, trains,
and aircraft.

Chair/Eagle: the eagle is a national symbol . . . it is also a
bird of prey . . . prey . . . pray . . . . No redesign has been
done on church seating, including prayer stalls. Enter under
NOW . . . but I want to continue . . . back to bird . . . when
birds sit on a telephone wire, they don't fall off when they go
to sleep, why? . . . as their leg muscles relax with the onset of
sleep, their bones and claws lock . . . as they wake up, mus-
culature takes over before bones unlock . . . . This can become
a locking and unlocking swivel base for chairs. Enter under
NOW.

Chair/Orchid: orchids are flowers . . . flowers are beautiful
. . . this morning I saw a magnificent Bonsai . . . cut flowers
. . . flowers are plucked . . . an enormous amount of money
and research has been expended to make auditorium and
classroom chairs that stack . . . the problem is with the leg
structures . . . . Here comes the solution: why not have the
seat-back terminate in a single leg? Classroom or auditorium
flooring could be built with one-and one-half-inch holes; chairs

could be plucked . . . plugged . . . into the floor as needed, into any configuration, and unplugged again. Floor receptacles for chair legs, one and one-half inches in diameter, would be 36 inches apart and could be closed with a stopper when not in use. Since this demands architectural predesign, enter under 2-5 YEARS.

Chair/Bicycle: bicycle seats still needlessly uncomfortable . . . simple redesign is possible using new ergonomic data. . . enter under OTHERS . . . . Here comes a second idea: a bicycle seatlike "perch" could provide excellent temporary seating for assembly line workers. Enter under NOW.

Chair/Sunset: great beauty . . . changing colors . . . some of the beauty of sunsets caused by pollution . . . particulate matter in the air . . . spots . . . the leopard does not change his spots . . . but the chameleon does . . . How? . . . melanic deposits in the epidermic layer rise to the surface, depending on background coloration . . . this can be done in plastics through the insertion of encapsulated pigments . . . If phototropic, a variably colored or changing color chair would result. Enter under R & D.

Chair/Ice Cream: ice cream is chilly . . . cold . . . hot . . . warm . . . the technology of electric blankets can form the surface of a chair easily . . . Less than pennies a day can give us warm easy chairs and sofas, reducing heat needs in a living room. Since warmth rises the chair will keep occupants comfortable. A timely idea: enter under NOW and R & D.

A balance sheet will show that I have developed nearly a dozen new and original ideas—most of them patentable—in less than six minutes. This is an idea flow of better than one new idea every thirty seconds!

The best thing about bisociation is the fact that it can be learned in the length of time it has taken you to read about it. The reason is fairly simple: *all* of our minds work this way nearly *all* the time when hunting for ideas. All that this bisociation technique accomplishes is to *externalize* the process by making a list. Without the list, the mind tends to wander, seeking more beguiling images than a new chair.

If you try this out, and it doesn't work for you the first time, just substitute seven different response words.

One final note: it is possible to feed your design concept through this list a second time. Our first solution was chair/ventriloquist leading to a compound curved papier-mâché chair design. We can now take this entire concept and start again at the top:

> Compound Curved Chair/Ventriloquist: ventriloquist . . . dummy . . . sits on ventriloquist's lap . . . small . . . child-sized . . . handicapped children . . . . Here comes the idea: a clinical and adjustable chair for retarded children. It can be made of a number of sections (each in comfortable curved configurations). These can then be plugged together in a limitless number of combinations, each of which caters to the specific handicap and body size of one particular child. Enormously individualized clinical seating through a type of mass production. Enter under NOW.

And so forth.

This is an elegant system, which I have used, without exception, on everything I have designed for more than a decade.

6. *Trisociation*: This variation of sliding scales and bisociation uses my icosahedral dice. (An icosahedron is a regular solid with twenty faces, each an equilateral triangle.) A series of parameters can again be established; as under morphological analysis or sliding scales various concepts can be assigned to colors of dice and to numbers from zero to nine (twice on each die). One roll of *three* dice yields 8,000 forced associations, one roll of *four* dice gives 160,000 possibilities.

7. *Bionics and Biomechanics*: It has been explained that many of the ideas and methods in synectics come from the field of biology. The reader will also have noticed that many of my bisociational "triggers" in the example given above came from the field of nature. In my opinion the use of biological prototypes in design is profoundly justified. The entire following chapter is given over to this concept.

8. *Forcing New Thinking Patterns*: By repeatedly facing
students and young designers with problems far enough removed from everyday reality so as to *force* them into entirely
new thinking patterns (new cortical associations), by constantly pointing out to them the nature of the various blocks,
it is possible to help them realize their creative design potential. By forcing them into solving problems that have never
been solved before, problems that lie outside normal human
experience, a habit pattern is slowly established, a habit pattern of solving problems without the interference of blocks
(since, with problems removed from everyday experience,
blocks cannot operate), and these habit patterns are then carried over into the solving of *all* problems, familiar or not.

What constitutes a totally new problem, outside all previous human experience? If we are asked to design some fab-
ulous animal unlike any we are familiar with, we will
probably end up with something possessing the body of a
horse, the legs of an elephant, the tail of a lion, the neck of
a giraffe, the head of a stag, the wings of a bat, and the sting
of a honeybee. In other words, we have really put a lot of
familiar things together in a totally unworkable, unfunc-
tional, unfamiliar way. This is *not* solving a problem. If, on
the other hand, we are asked to design a bicycle for a man
with three legs and no arms we can now solve a specific functional problem, far enough removed from any previous experience, to become valuable in this context.

It was my good fortune to study and assist the late Professor
John Arnold at M.I.T. Arnold pioneered in this field with students in engineering and product design. Most famous of his
problems is probably the Arcturus IV project: here the class
is given voluminous reports regarding the inhabitants of the
imaginary fourth planet in the Arcturus system, as well as the
planet itself. An extraordinarily tall, slow-moving species de-
scended from birds, these mythical inhabitants possess many
interesting physiological characteristics. They are hatched
from eggs, possessed of a beak, have birdlike, hollow bones,
with three fingers on each hand and three eyes, the center one

of which is an x-ray eye. Their reaction speed is almost ten times as slow as that of human beings; the atmosphere they breathe is pure methane. If a class is now asked to design, say, an automobilelike vehicle for these people, totally strange, new limits for design are immediately established.

Obviously a gasoline gauge is unnecessary, since the Arcturians can always see through the gas tank with their x-ray eye. What about a speedometer? Top speed will have to be around eight miles per hour because of their slow reaction speed. Perceptually, however, such a people would experience the gradations of speed (up to eight miles per hour) much as we experience the speed range in our own automobiles. The answer here then seems easy: subdivide a speedometer dial. But what kind of a numerical system would people use who have three fingers on each hand and three eyes: decimal, duodecimal, binary, sexagesimal? As these vehicles will be built on earth and exported to Arcturus IV, should they use a standard gasoline engine shielded against a methane atmosphere, or must a new type of engine, specifically designed to operate optimally in methane, be designed? What of the overall shape of the vehicle? Should it be egg-shaped (a simple and sturdy form when aerodynamics are of no importance), or would the egg be the worst possible shape in terms of vehicular safety because the Arcturians would perceive it, psychologically speaking, as a return to the womb, lulling them into a false feeling of security? Maybe our design consideration then becomes one of a shape as unlike an egg as possible—a difficult order to fill indeed!

Arcturus IV is just one of many problems evolved by Professor Arnold, and, from this all-too-brief analysis of some of the possible approaches to it, it will be seen that, while fantastic and science fictional in content (especially three years before *Sputnik*), it is a serious approach to creative problem solving.

It can be seen from the foregoing that the "how" in teaching design creativity must consist largely of establishing a milieu in which new approaches can flourish. But schools tend to preserve the cultural *status quo*, by disseminating whatever mass of data is currently acceptable as "truth." Education rarely concerns itself with the *individual* human brain; rather, the tremendous variation in human minds is taken into account only as something to be flattened out so that the particular curriculum or theory in vogue at the moment can be "sold" with minimal effort. We have failed to recognize that discovery, invention, original thought are culture-smashing activities (remember $E = mc^2$?) whereas so-called education is a culture-preserving mechanism. By its very nature, education, as it is now constituted, cannot sponsor any vital new departures in any facet of our culture. It can only *appear to do so* to preserve the sustaining illusion of progress.

One of the major problems is that "newness" often implies experiment, and experiment implies failure. In our success-oriented culture, the possibility of failure, although an unavoidable concomitant of experiment, works against the matrix. The history of progress is littered with experimental failures. This "right to fail," however, does not absolve the designer from responsibility. Here, possibly, is the crux of the matter: to instill in the designer a willingness to experiment, coupled with a sense of responsibility for his failures. Unfortunately, both a sense of responsibility and an atmosphere permissive of failure are rare indeed.

A more ideal creative design environment will consist of habituating designers and students to work in areas where their many blocks and inhibitions cannot operate, and this will imply a high tolerance level for experimental failure. Furthermore, it must mean the teaching and exploring of basic principles that, by their nature, have no immediate application. This calls for a suspension of belief in ready answers, and in the glib, slicked-up kitsch that characterizes most of the design work coming out of schools and offices.

We need not journey to Arcturus IV to face designers and students with something completely outside their familiar experiences. All we have to do is to design for the poor, the sick, the elderly, the disabled. For while designers have addressed themselves to the fads of the middle and upper bourgeoisie, we have lost sight of the fact that a very substantial part of our population is discriminated against in design.

I am questioning, then, the entire currently popular direction of design. To "sex-up" objects (designers' jargon for making things more attractive to mythical consumers) makes no sense in a world in which basic need for design is very real. In an age that seems to be mastering aspects of form, a return to content is long overdue.

Much of what is suggested throughout this volume in the way of alternative areas for attack by designers also has the useful quality that it will be new to designers and students alike. If (within the meaning of this book) we do that which seems right, we will also develop our ability to see things in a new way and to do things that are new.

8

The Tree of Knowledge:

Biological Prototypes in Design

> *A bird is an instrument working according to mathematical law, which instrument it is within the capacity of man to reproduce with all its movements.*
>
> LEONARDO DA VINCI

One source that never seems to go out of style is the handbook of nature. Here, through biological and biochemical systems, many of the same problems mankind faces have been met and solved. Through analogues to nature, man's problems can be solved optimally.

The ideal solution to any design problem is to achieve "the most with the least" or, to use George K. Zipf's happy phrase, to employ "the principle of least effort."

Bionics means the use of biological prototypes for the design of man-made systems. To put it more simply: to study basic principles in nature and then apply these principles and processes to the needs of mankind.

Dr. Edward T. Hall states in *The Hidden Dimension* that "man and his environment participate in molding each other. Man is now in the position of actually creating the total world in which he lives, or what the ethologists refer to as his biotype. In creating this world he is actually determining *what kind of an organism he will be.*"

A simple problem will show that more than a designer with a modicum of good taste is needed: several years ago a new low-cost plough was designed, built, and distributed in areas of Southeast Asia that commonly use a forked stick weighted down by a rock to till the soil. After a few years it was discovered that the ploughs were not in use—they were rusting away. In the religious beliefs of the inhabitants, metal makes the soil "sick" and offends the Earth-mother. I recommended that the ploughs be dipped in a plastic compound similar to Nylon 60. Since neither the people nor the Earth-mother were offended by plastics technology, the ploughs were finally accepted and used.

The point of this anecdote? A cross-disciplinary design team, including anthropologists, engineers, biologists, and psychologists, would have prevented the original misdesign. Shifting to a technically more sophisticated level, one can see that the dry, acrid sound and the need to reduce the number of seats available at Lincoln Center after architectural spaces were reduced might have been avoided had musicologists and habitual concertgoers been part of the design team (see William Snaith's *The Concert Hall Syndrome*). Acoustics engineers and architects were too involved with decibel levels and square foot costage to be able to *listen* and to think about the audience.

At present industrial and environmental designers form the focus of any design team. Their status as key synthesist in a design situation is not based on their being better informed or more creative; rather, they assume the role of comprehensive synthesist by the *default* of all other disciplines. For education in all the other areas is a matter of increasing *vertical specialization.* Only in industrial and environmental design is education still *horizontally cross-disciplinary.*

While the designer in a given team may know far less about psychology than the psychologist, far less about economics than the economist, and very little about, say, electrical en-

gineering, he will invariably bring greater understanding of
psychology to the design process than the electrical engineer.
He will also predictably be better informed about electrical
engineering than the economist. He will become the bridge
between the disciplines.

The basic tenets on which this chapter is based are:

1. That the design of any product unrelated to its sociolog-
   ical, psychological, or ecological surroundings is no longer
   possible or acceptable.
2. That the design of products and environments must be
   accomplished through interdisciplinary teams.
3. That such an interdisciplinary team must also include
   end-users (consumers), as well as the workers that make
   the things designers design.
4. That biology, bionics, and related fields offer rewarding
   new insights to designers. Designers must find analogues,
   using biological prototypes and systems for design approaches culled from such fields as ethology, anthropology, and morphology.

Man has always derived ideas from the workings of nature,
but in the past this has been achieved on a rather elemental
level. As design problems have become increasingly complex
with the global proliferation of technology, mankind has become more and more alienated from direct contact with biological surroundings.

Designers and artists especially have looked to nature, but
their viewpoints have often been clouded by a romantic long-
ing for the reestablishment of some sort of primeval Eden, a
desire to get back to "basics" and escape the depersonalizing
power of the machine, or by a sentimental mystique about
"closeness to the soil."

Yet very little has been written in the area of bionics. Heinrich Hertel's *Structure, Form and Movement*, Lucien Gerardin's *Bionics*, and E. E. Bernard's *Biological Prototypes and
Man-Made Systems* were written in the sixties. Various re-

ports on bionics prepared by the armed services concern themselves with man-computer-control relationships only—dealing with the interface between cybernetics and neurophysiology. There have been a few articles in the *Saturday Evening Post*, *Mechanix Illustrated*, and *Industrial Design*, during the sixties and early seventies, but these have been largely over-simplified popularizations. Strangely enough little else in this field has been published since the first edition of this book. Karl von Frisch's *Animal Architecture*, Carl Gans' *Biomechanics*, and Felix Parturi's *Nature, Mother of Invention* are the only new books addressed to the lay reader in this area. They document in fascinating detail how innovation in design and architecture is related to biology.

Throughout history there have been exceptional designers. "A bird is an instrument working according to mathematical law, which instrument it is within the capacity of man to reproduce with all its movements," said Leonardo da Vinci in 1511. Fire, the lever and fulcrum, early tools and weapons—all these were invented by man observing natural processes, the wheel being possibly the only exception to this rule. And even here Dr. Thomasias presents a closely reasoned argument for the wheel having been derived from observation of a log rolling down an inclined plane.

During the last 100 years, and especially since the end of World War II, scientists have begun looking into the biological sciences in a search for answers and have made breakthroughs that are of enormous importance. A profound difference between design by early man and today's designs must be noted: while we may consider the first hammer an extension of the fist, the first rake a type of claw, and smile at the attempt made by Icarus to fix bird wings to himself and fly into the sun, today bionics is concerned not so much with the *form of parts* or the *shape of things* but rather with the possibilities of examining *how* nature makes things happen, *the interrelation of parts, the existence of systems.*

Thus a psychologist, shown the diagram of a control mechanism for an apparatus enabling a blind man to read by scanning letter forms and transforming them into tones, immediately recognized it as the so-called fourth layer of the visual cortex, the part of the brain responsible for Gestalt vision.

As far back as the early calculating machines, scientists recognized a similarity between the machine's function and the function of the human nervous system. With the advent of electronics, this similarity became even more startling. It is for this reason that the many applications of bionics are in the field of computer design. Here, insights from computers to human brains and from human brains to computers continue to be gained. Professor Norbert Wiener at M.I.T. worked with psychologists, physiologists, and neurophysiologists to attempt to learn more about the brain through the construction of computers, whereas Dr. Heinz von Foerster, in work with Professor W. Ross Ashby and Dr. W. Grey Walter at the University of Illinois, gained insight into the way computers ought to be constructed through his research on the design of the human brain. In the eighties neurophysiology and microelectronics are used in parallel to explore both fields.

W. Grey Walter, the British physiologist, developed simple electronic machines that responded positively to light as a stimulus. These machines will head for the nearest light source: an invention much indebted to the study of the photophiliac behavior of the common moth.

Rattlesnakes are known to biologists as pit vipers because of the two pits located in their snout, midway between nostrils and eyes. These pits contain temperature-sensing organs so delicate that they can detect temperature changes of 1/1,000 of a degree. This might be the difference, for instance, between a sun-baked stone and a motionless rabbit. A similar principle was used by Philco and General Electric in the design of the side-winder missile, an early heat-seeking air-to-air missile that homes in on the exhaust of jet aircraft.

The sensing devices of the pit viper are more sophisticated than our crude analogs. After years of research, air-to-air missiles are still inaccurate: because of a $2 million price tag real testing is not possible (ABC Evening News, 9 March 1983). Thank god we still can't approach the accuracy of a pit viper.

In 1983 the Department of Aerospace Engineering Sciences of the University of Colorado began studying the lift and thrust of dragonflies. It is their hope to use the data acquired to develop more maneuverable and fuel-efficient aircraft. Marvin Luttges heads a team of bioengineers and designers who tether dragonflies to a harness in a wind tunnel that is filled with nontoxic smoke. Photographs and films of the insects' motions are used to study dragonfly aerodynamics. When the tests are completed, the dragonflies are released unharmed. Quite aside from the application of these findings to aircraft design, this bionic area of research, known as "unsteady aerodynamic design," should also make it possible to achieve more accuracy in predicting weather, ocean-current movements, and even the direction in which air currents will carry destructive insects (*Geo*, November 1983).

Bats find their way in the dark through an echo location method: they emit a high-pitched sound that bounces off objects in their path, is picked up by their sensitive ears, and thus establishes an unencumbered flight path for them. Much the same principles are used in radar and sonar. Sonar uses audible sound waves; radar uses ultra-high-frequency waves.

An excellent result of a bionic design investigation is a remarkably accurate speed indicator for aircraft. Certain beetles compute their air speed prior to landing by watching moving objects on the ground. A study of the sense organs of these beetles has yielded an aircraft speed indicator that measures the time elapsed between a craft's passage over two known points on the ground and translates it into speed.

In the early seventies Dr. Ralph Redemske, a specialist in bionics who worked for Servomechanism Inc. in Santa Barbara, California, plated an ordinary honeybee with a thin coating of aluminum. Using a standard black background, this enabled him to make photographs (which were less fuzzy than a bee) of every detail of its complex structure. From this work, engineers created mechanical eyes modeled from those of bees, which are now used for scanning devices in computers to "read" shapes.

One of the most interesting animals that holds many different design solutions is the bottle-nosed dolphin (*Tursiops truncatus*). The dolphin uses a radar- and sonar-like navigational system that does not depend on hearing. In common with whales, it ripples its external skin surface, utilizing this effect for navigation and increasing swimming speed.

The ground effects caused by a helicopter flying in a stationary position at a distance of less than fifty feet above ground level have puzzled aircraft engineers for over a decade. Through a study of the dragonfly, these causes are beginning to be understood and have found application in spraying and ice removal by helicopters.

Energy input versus output poses interesting questions: two examples are the South American fruit bat, or flying fox, and the male of a South American beetle called *Acroncinus longimanus*. The fruit bat has a gigantic wingspread and great power, yet it uses a comparatively small energy input. The incredibly long front legs of the South American beetle utilize even less energy input and still derive great power.

I found the input-output disparity of these beetles to be a challenging problem. Eventually able to dissect several, I found a fluidic energy amplification system. It is a measure of my own biological naiveté that I gleefully assumed I had made a major theoretical breakthrough. Certainly had I dis-

Acroninus longimanus, male specimen showing elongated front legs. Author's collection.

sected these beetles some fifty years ago (at the tender age of five) I might be known today as the Father of Fluidics. But there is a serious point hidden in this anecdote: unknown to me, fluidics existed. From this it seems safe to assume that there is an infinite number of biological principles—like fluidics—lying around, waiting to be discovered.

The major emphasis in industrial and environmental design will certainly lie in an ethological and ecological approach to systems, processes, and environments. When industrial designers talk about "total design," they refer to two different concepts. First, that the design of, say, a steam iron ought to logically lead to the design of the logo, the manufacturer's letterhead, the point-of-sale display for the iron, the package, and even some control over the merchandising of the product. At other times "total design" means in-plant work: the design of the handling machinery for manufacturing the steam iron, safety devices, and traffic patterns within the plant.

But "total design" in the future will mean seeing the steam iron (as well as its factory or promotional gimmicks) merely as links in a lengthy biomorphic phylogenetic chain reaching back to heated rocks and stove irons and forward to the final extinction of the phylum "steam iron" by mass introduction of "perma-press" and "stay-press" fabrics or a radical reevaluation of clothing itself.

If the industrial revolution gave us a *mechanical* era (a comparatively static technology of movable parts), if the last hundred years have given us a *technological* era (a more dynamic technology of functioning parts), then we are now emerging into a *biomorphic* era (an evolving technology permissive of evolutionary changes).

We have been taught that the machine is an extension of a man's hand. But because of enlarging scale even this no longer holds. For 5,000 years, a brickmaker was capable of making 500 bricks a day. Technology has made it possible for one man, with the right kind of backup machinery, to make 500,000 bricks a day. But biomorphic change obsolesces both the man and the bricks: we now extrude building skin surface, i.e., sandwich panels that include heating, lighting, cooling, and other service circuits.

The total chain of design can probably be best explained anecdotally. Consider the fact that the absorption of 10,000 pounds of Radiolaria establishes 1,000 pounds of plankton, that 1,000 pounds of plankton establish 100 pounds of small marine animals, that these in turn create ten pounds of fish, and that it takes ten pounds of fish to put one pound of muscle tissue on a human being. The frictional losses in the system are simply staggering. With 168,000 species of insects in North America there is six to eight times as much insect protein living in a forty-acre field as beef protein represented by grazing cattle thereon. Actually, we do eat flies; it's just that we process them through grass, cows, and milk first.

It may be argued that the average industrial designer or design engineer concerned with research and development lacks a sufficient background in the biological sciences to utilize biology as a meaningful source of design. If we attempt to define the word bionics in its narrowest sense, on a cybernetic or neurophysiological level, this may be true. But all around us are manifestations in nature and primitive structures that have never been properly investigated, exploited, or used by designers, biological schemes that bear investigation and are accessible to anyone free for a walk on a Sunday afternoon.

Take seeds, for instance. A simple maple seed (*Aceraceae saccharum*), when released from just a few feet off the ground, will fall in a spiral pattern. This method of air-to-ground delivery has so far never been applied in any significant way. An interesting application of the maple seed's flight characteristics, discovered by George Filipowski, led to a new method of extinguishing forest fires or getting fire-extinguishing modules into inaccessible parts. An artificial maple seed some eight and two-thirds inches long was constructed out of inexpensive, ultralightweight plastic. The seed portion contained a fire-extinguishing powder. Experimentation and investigation showed that when maple seeds (artificial or real) were released above a fire, they would naturally be caught up in the thermal updrafts above the flames. If, on the other hand, the seeds were *forced* below the updraft area and into the semivacuum below, their flight pattern would re-establish itself, and they would fly toward the hottest part of the fire. To return to the plastic maple seeds. Thousands of these encased in time-sacks can be dropped from aircraft. The sacks rip open once they have plunged to below the updraft area. Thousands of plastic maple seeds circle toward the hottest part of the fire, and here, their casing consumed by the flames, the fire extinguisher is released. This is by no means a way to put out forest fires. It is, however, a way of getting at canyons and other areas that are normally not accessible from the ground or to smoke-jumpers. It has been tested successfully in British Columbia.

Reforestation of the extreme northern tundra areas of Alaska, Canada, Lapland, and the Soviet Union, as well as the restocking of these areas with fish, can be achieved through water-soluble maple seeds that contain seed spores or fish eggs. Naturally these artificial maple seeds can also include nutrient solutions, serve as thermoprotectors, or carry fertilizer. This system too has been tested successfully by the Department of Wildlife and Natural Resources in Canada.

The random spreading of almost any material can be achieved through artificial maple seeds; tolerances are reassuringly broad: I have constructed artificial maple seeds that performed optimally with a wingspread up to forty-six inches. At the other end of the scale, maple seeds only one-eighth of an inch long can be operational.

The seed of the white ash (*Fraxinus americana*) has characteristics very similar to those of the maple seed. In still air the seed falls almost straight down, spinning in a tight area. In a strong wind the seed will travel horizontally or, because of its lightness, climb for a period of time while spinning rapidly. If the seed's mass were concentrated into a small solid sphere, it would fall much faster, due to the decreased surface area, which would decrease the frictional drag acting on the body. However, if the seed were a hollow sphere of the same mass and with the same surface drag but did not spin, it would fall still faster. Thus we see that the spinning actually helps to slow the seed's descent. This is due to the fact that in spinning, the seed uses energy that would otherwise contribute to its rate of descent.

Basswood seeds (*Tilia americana*) are distinguishable by their unusual flight pattern. The "wings" force a spinning motion as the seeds slowly descend, drifting with the wind in spite of the (comparatively) great weight of the double-seed, which sticks out from the wing part on bifurcated extenders.

The flight characteristics of all of these spiraling seeds have not yet been studied sufficiently. The spiraling behavior of such seeds, artificially created in media other than air (water, oil, gasoline) or in near-vacuum or different gravity situations, may also prove a rich source of design concepts.

The falling Ailanthus seed (*Ailanthus altissima*) spins rapidly about its longitudinal axis, making one complete revolution while descending about one-quarter of its length. The geometry of this seed can be approximated with twisted paper (as shown). In the first simulation, the twists produced at each end are equal, which occurs only rarely in nature. In this case the seed descends, in still air, along a straight line, at approximately a forty-five-degree angle to the horizontal. If, however, the twists are unequal, as shown in the second simulation, the seed follows a path that combines a spiral action with a screwing, axial spin. The twisted end pulls air from the vicinity of the tip of the seed in toward the center of the seed. This produces a high-pressure area around and under the seed, which slows its descent. When the twists are equal, they both push the same amount of air toward the center, producing a lower pressure in the vicinity of that end. Therefore, the seed is being acted upon by unequal forces. The seed tends to slip axially toward the lower pressure area. Thus, instead of following a straight line, the seed descends in a spiral path. The combination of axial spin, slip, and spiral descent gives a very slow and almost random flight pattern to each seed. In artificial "seeds" all these characteristics, drag, spin, descent rate, yaw, slip, can be controlled.

Seeds of the wild onion (*Allium cernuum*) and the salsify plant follow radically different flight patterns. The wild onion seed is a delicate structure of radiating, lacy, umbrella-type formations. Dozens of these form a spider-web-like ball around the plant's central hub. The ball thus formed is a continuous-tension-discontinuous-compression sphere. The umbrellas are closely interconnected and inverted slightly. When released, the delicate filaments flatten out and lose their convexity. Each individual "parachute," released from the C-T-D-C sphere, performs a neat somersault, to keep its own "shroud-lines" from becoming entangled with other seeds. They fall like tiny parachutes, only at a much slower rate. Because, unlike parachutes, they possess a flat, disk-shaped top consisting of scores of finely interlaced hairs, their rate of fall, directionality, and so forth may be applicable to uses far different from those of conventional parachutes. Their lacy mantle also would foil radar detection.

Anchorage, grappling, and hook-closures are other seed characteristics. In Chapter Six we looked at the use of artificial burrs for erosion control or as "sand anchors" in the Sudan. The common cocklebur (*Xanthium canadense*) will cling to an animal's fur or, for that matter, to a man's trousers when he walks across a field in autumn. The specific hooking action has been adapted to Velcro nylon closure strips for clothing. Here a female surface of tiny loops and a male surface of tiny hooks are biaxially oriented. When pressed together, they can be pulled apart only in one direction and resist parting along all other axes. This principle has also been adopted for the upper-arm bands used in determining blood pressure; also, American astronauts wear the male part on the soles of their feet to walk on drop-cloths, consisting of the female part, that are lashed to the exterior of a space capsule, permitting them to walk in a null gravity situation.

Explosive-force seeds—seeds that, because of the interior construction of the seed pod, are hurled twenty feet or more—

provide another new and useful area of research. Specifically the seed of a small berry, *Hubus arcticus*, growing only in the Lapland section of Finland, would repay investigation. Closer to home: seeds of the squirting cucumber (*Ecbellium elaterium*) attain a muzzle velocity of ten yards per second and attain a flying speed of nearly twenty miles per hour. *Cyclanthera explodens*, a member of the pumpkin family, stores its seeds under a pressure-tension of sixteen atmospheres, exploding its seeds at speeds of sixty-five miles per hour.

The growth characteristics of almost any plant can provide the solution to innovative design problems. Thus we can learn from the growth of an ordinary green pea. If peas are permitted to "go to seed," a string at the back of the peapod ceases to grow. Since the rest of the pod continues to enlarge, soon it very slowly opens, and the pea seeds are slowly raised above the level of the pod. A manufacturer of children's suppositories was persuaded to adopt this as a packaging method. Hitherto, each suppository was separately wrapped in silver foil, eight to a box. The parent, unwrapping them, might find three-quarters of the glycerine under his fingernails, with the suppository now desterilized. A package of polyethylene was purposely miscast to solve this problem. The package was cast so that the "memory" of the plastic was its open state. The sterile suppositories, but with all need for wrapping gone, would now be inserted, and a high-impact styrene closure would slide over the top. The small polyethylene package would now be under tension. Its purposeful miscasting acts like the string on the back of the peapod. When the styrene top is gently slid off, the package opens very slowly and the suppositories are gently forced up and out. Closing the package merely means squeezing it gently together (thus forcing the remaining suppositories back down) and sliding the styrene retainer-top back on.

Nothing has been said about insulating, heat-storing, protection from cold, and many other properties possessed by seeds.

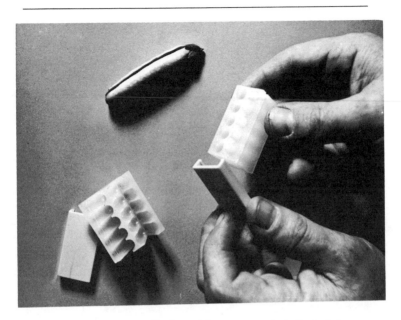

This package was bionically derived from a pea pod. Author's design.

During the late seventies and early eighties I have continued research into the protective capacity of seeds. The seed pods of a number of trees and shrubs burst open in the late summer, and the seeds emerge attached to a fluffy cotton-wool-like substance that permits the wind to carry the seeds over great distances. What is interesting here is that the tightly packed fluff, when fully extended, occupies a volume more than forty times as great as while in the pod. Such studies have led to the development of an improved mailing bag for precision devices, as well as research centered around the possibility of actually *growing insulation around camera lenses, instruments, and electronic devices.*

Before ending the discussion of seeds, I should also mention the sheer fun and adventure of bionics. We originally began by writing to botany departments of major universities in Eu-

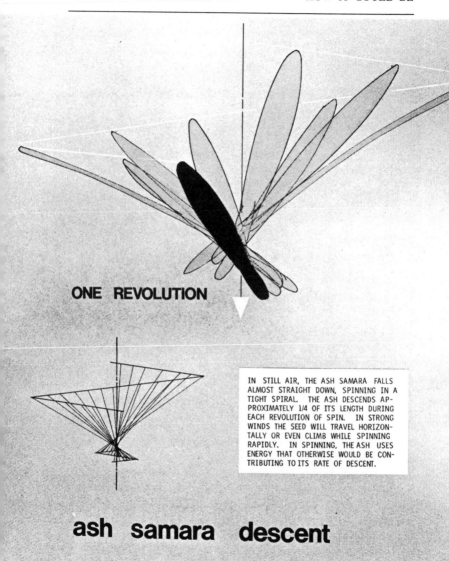

ONE REVOLUTION

IN STILL AIR, THE ASH SAMARA FALLS ALMOST STRAIGHT DOWN, SPINNING IN A TIGHT SPIRAL. THE ASH DESCENDS APPROXIMATELY 1/4 OF ITS LENGTH DURING EACH REVOLUTION OF SPIN. IN STRONG WINDS THE SEED WILL TRAVEL HORIZONTALLY OR EVEN CLIMB WHILE SPINNING RAPIDLY. IN SPINNING, THE ASH USES ENERGY THAT OTHERWISE WOULD BE CONTRIBUTING TO ITS RATE OF DESCENT.

ash samara descent

Three examples of research into aerodynamic behavior of seeds. Graduate-team research under the author's supervision by Robert Toering, John K. Miller, and Jolan Truan, as students at Purdue University.

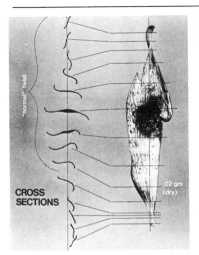

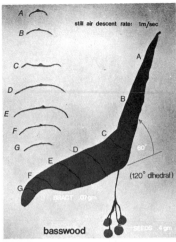

rope and North America, carefully explaining our interest in seeds as storage devices, explosive mechanisms, air-to-ground delivery systems, gliders, parachutes and fliers. Seventy replies received were discouraging: each university botany department explained that such gross structural characteristics were unimportant when compared to the study of plant genetics. Several colleagues suggested that what we tried to find out might have been of interest to "some morphologists at some German university a hundred years ago"—but not presently. Nonetheless we continued classifying seeds according to flight and dispersion characteristics. Now, more than fifteen years later, it seems that *we have become the experts!* My two former graduate assistants and I routinely receive scientific inquiries from the same universities that originally dismissed our work as frivolous.

An equally large area for bionic design investigation lies in botanic architecture, such as growth patterns, cells, the growth rate of bamboo shoots, the architecture of a rose, various stem configurations of plants, and properties of mushrooms, algae, fungi, and lichen. Regarding this last item let

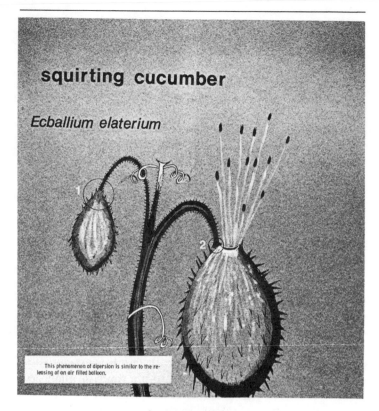

Squirting cucumber

me discuss an example (with indebtedness to William J. J. Gordon and synectics).

When repainting the interior of buildings, the cost of paint, labor, and eventual depreciation has to be considered. Paint is a substance that looks good when first applied to the wall, but as time goes on it deteriorates. Let's try (still with Bill Gordon) to isolate the problem: is it possible to find a substitute that, when applied to the wall, may look unpleasant at first but will be self-improving and self-maintaining? The answer is not far away. Lichen (a symbiotic growth relationship between algae and fungi) exist naturally in a selection of "de-

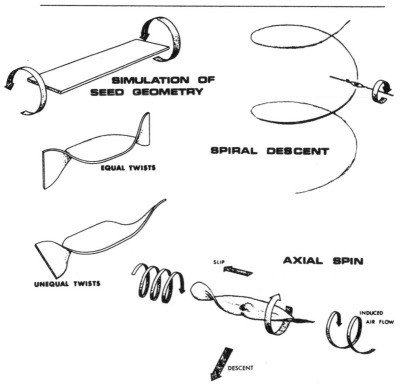

SIMULATION OF SEED GEOMETRY

SPIRAL DESCENT

EQUAL TWISTS

UNEQUAL TWISTS

SLIP

AXIAL SPIN

INDUCED AIR FLOW

DESCENT

An example of research into the aerodynamic properties of seeds in flight.
This example is the ailanthus seed. Graduate-team research by John K. Miller
and Jolan Truan, Purdue University.

licious decorator colors." (Bright oranges, purples, flaming
reds, subtle grays, verdant greens—the list consists of 118
colors.) We could theoretically select the lichen of our color
choice, spray it on a wall (together with a nutrient solution),
and just sit back and relax. Obviously the wall may be a
splotchy looking mess at first, but, as the lichen begin to grow,
an even color will result. Unfortunately, the designer may be
obliged to speculate as to whether people can be motivated to
enjoy shaggy walls. But a serious application is possible.
Nearly all lichen grow to a height of approximately one and
a half inches, and are not affected by temperature extremes

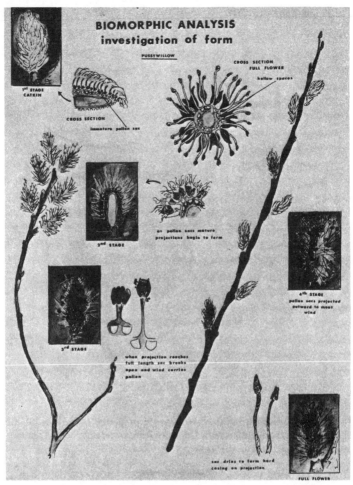

such as −30 degrees or a blistering 146 degrees Farenheit. (Cryptoendolithic lichens even grow at −158 degrees!) One direct use would be to plant them, instead of grass, in the center median of the New York Thruway. Because mowing costs of the New York Thruway Authority amount to some $2.5 million annually, this would be a great saving indeed. Furthermore, color-coding might be brought into play: the Berkshire cutoff could be planted in, say, blue, and the Ohio cutoff in red.

The shaggy wall paint has finally found an application: lichen pigment is an excellent wall covering for art galleries. Walls that would normally need to be constantly repainted to hide nailholes now become "self-healing." It is being used by galleries in West Berlin, Amsterdam, Yugoslavia, and elsewhere.

The growth patterns of the pussy willow have led a student to evolve a seed-planting tool that could be used in those areas

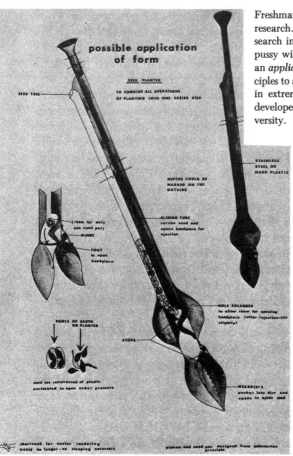

Freshman student project in bionic research. The first plate shows research into the configuration of a pussy willow. The second plate is an *application* of these basic principles to a device for planting seeds in extremely hard soil in underdeveloped countries. Purdue University.

of the world where the soil is poor and hard. This simple hand tool, utilizing a basic bionic principle, could be of great use specifically in Central India, Shansi, and Sinkiang, Niger, N. E. Nigeria, and Chad, as well as the Mongolian Republic. Furthermore, the tool is simple and maintenance free, so that it can be used even by relatively unsophisticated people.

In an entirely different area, let us see what can be developed from crystallography. If asked to fill two-dimensional space completely with polygons of the same type and size, there are only three ways in which the job can be done: grids of equilateral triangles, squares, or hexagons. Even though the number of polygons is infinite, we cannot derive a complete "space-fill" from others. Octagons, for instance, require small squares for fill-ins; with pentagons the job is impossible.

If we attempt the same thing in three-dimensional space, there are again only a very limited number of possible solutions. We can use bricks, which are, after all, a type of square-ended prism. For the same reason we can also utilize equilaterally triangular-ended prisms or hexagonal prisms. Proceeding with any of these three systems, we have merely built a two-dimensional construct in space: any of these three grid patterns will result in a wall as high or long as we wish; its depth, however, will be that of *one* brick. True integration in three dimensions has not taken place.

If we derive our shape from the field of crystallography and semiregular polyhedra, we will find that there is one shape, and one shape only, that makes a stable, fully three dimensionally integrated space grid possible: the tetrakaidecahedron.

Tetra (four) kai (and) deca (ten) hedron: a fourteen-sided polyhedron consisting of eight hexagonal and six square faces. A number of these will cluster easily in space because of their angles of incidence and adherence. If we examine one of the shapes, we will find that it is rounder than a cube but squarer than a sphere. It can resist pressure (either from without or from within) better than a cube but not as well as a sphere. Rather, not as well as a single sphere: If we were to cluster a series of spheres of the same size (balloons for instance) like a cluster of grapes and subject them to equal and steady pressure by submerging them in water, we would find that little pressure areas (in the form of convex, spherical, triangular pyramids) build up between our balloons. If pressure is permitted to build up more the balloons will collapse into their most stable shape: a cluster of tetrakaidecahedra. The tetrakaidecahedron, in fact, is the idealized shape of the human fat cell, as well as many other basic cellular structures.

A series of tetrakaidecahedra were handed to students for design exploitation. Many new design solutions resulted. By building huge tetrakaidecahedral cells thirty-eight feet in diameter, it is possible to construct a suboceanic shelter area for men and materials that might be used for subocean mining or oil drilling. Each cell had three floor levels; a cluster of between thirty and ninety of these cells would constitute a suboceanic station housing 200–300 scientists and workers.

By reducing the diameter of the cells to one-eighth of an inch, a new type of radiator for an automobile was evolved, exhibiting more surface areas and containing more water.

A folding, semipermanent vacation house, sleeping twenty, could, in its knockdown stage, be transported in a standard VW camper or Dormobile.

Using thirty-eight-foot-diameter tetrakaidecahedra, a central tower could be erected, eleven units or 418 feet tall. Twenty-eight more units of the same size could then be attached in spiral form, surrounding the central core. With each unit being trilevel, the result is a luxury apartment building. The central core tower would carry stairways, air-conditioning conduits, elevators, water, heat, and electricity. In addition, any given central core unit (also being trilevel) would house bathrooms, kitchens, and other service rooms, each level housing rooms for the closest cantilevered spiral unit. The three floors of the exterior spiral unit could be given over to living, entertainment, and sleeping areas, with the hexagonal roof of each acting as a combination heliport and garden. Because of the ease with which further omnidirectional units can

Tetrakaidecahedra: archimedian solids that close-pack in three-dimensional space.

be "plugged in" or, for that matter, "unplugged," each te-trakaidecahedron that is part of the exterior spiral could easily be air-lifted and plugged in other core units in different areas of the world. The same construction might also serve as a con-tractable or expandable grain silo.

When the first visual model of this structure was removed from its base, I attached a line to it and dragged it through water. It has excellent motion characteristics in water. This suggests the possibility of constructing huge hollow tetrakai-decahedra out of ice (reinforced with algae), pumping them full of crude oil, and towing a string of these spiral clusters across the Atlantic by submarines, thus eliminating the need for tankers.

The most elegant technological use, however, lies in the field of space stations. Assume that a basic cluster of tetrakaidecahedra (each trilevel and thirty-eight feet in diameter*), numbering forty-eight single units, were to be put in a locked orbit 200 miles above earth. This unit could house a labor force of 300 men. If we now place further single cells in orbit, we will find that (because of the many angles of incidence and adherence, mentioned above) 300 workers can attach another fifty units in a twenty-four-hour work period. At this point the station (which incidentally would provide enough centrifugal spin to give a semblance of earth's gravity) will house 600 people. After two days of work it will house 1,200 workers, 9,600 at the end of five days, 307,200 at the end of ten days, and 9,830,400 at the end of fifteen days. In other words, it would be possible to absorb entire large populations in two weeks, *with all of these people housed in trilevel structures*. Now give the whole construct a push, and when it arrives at, say, Mars, Alpha Centauri II, or Wolf 359, it will be possible to decant people *and their homes*, establishing a city at the same speed as people can be landed.

I am presently working on a research project that explores tetrakaidecahedra. It attempts to use the shape for the construction of grain silos that will be less subject to spontaneous grain dust explosions. Such explosions cause the loss of many lives each year and destroy millions of dollars worth of grains and cereals in farming regions. By compartmentalizing grain into smaller tetrakaidecahedra units, grain can be transported in these new containers by truck, rail, or barge. On arrival these cells plug together to form the silo tower—they can again be removed without the dangers attendant upon the decanting of grain.

*The thirty-eight-foot-diameter module has been established as a "principle-of-least-effort" structure. In other words, it exploits sandwich-skin panels to their utmost. Larger constructs are feasible, of course, but only with a sharp rise in cost.

Much of the early research on the tetrakaidecahedron was done during 1954–1959. Other exploitations of crystalline forms are possible. William Katavolos of New York suggested that cities could be "grown." With breakthroughs in Russian crystallography since 1970 and our increased abilities to grow large hollow crystals, it may be possible, before long, to "seed" an entire city and move in when it is fully grown.

The snub rhomboicosadodecahedron, consisting of eighty equilateral triangles and twelve pentagons, lends itself quite naturally to the erection of dome structures. While such domes bear a generic resemblance to Buckminster Fuller's geodesics, they are in fact simpler to erect, for all sides are straight and of equal length, all angles identical.

Even if we mention some random thoughts on shell structures and sea shells, regeneration, exoskeletal structures, various propulsion systems in fish, the swimming behavior of snakes, "free" soaring in flying fish, we will barely touch the surface of a few of the areas that will yield to bionic design development.

The articulation of a snake's skeleton found an application in a variable curve ruler designed for Keuffel and Esser Company. Again it may be worthwhile to point out that bionic design application *never means copying by establishing a visual analog*. Rather, it means searching out the basic, underlying organic principle and then finding an application.

A whole group of beetles: *Propomacrus bimucronatus, Euchirus longimanus, Chalcosoma atlas* and *Forma colossus, Dynastes hyyllus* and *centaurus, Dynastes hercules* and *Granti horn* and *Neptunus quensel*, the *Megasomae* (*elephans, anubis, mars, gyas*), and the *Goliathi* (especially *Goliathus Goliathus drury, atlas, regius klug, cacius, albosignatus, meleagris,* and the *Fornasinius fornasinii* and *russus*, as well as the *Meoynorrhinse* and *Melagorrhinae*, the *Macrodontiae*, and especially the *Acrocinus longimanus L.* (males only), have "front-end handling mechanisms" that are startling in their variety and challenging in their complexity. None of these has ever been intelligently exploited.

Direct bionic design is made possible through ethology. John Teal, professor of human ecology at the University of Alaska in the seventies, investigated the mating behavior and domestication of the musk ox. With forty-eight chromosomes, the musk ox is badly named: it is not an ox but related to the goat and antelope, and there is no musk. The fur of the musk ox works better than wool in terms of moisture shedding and heat retention. John Teal has set himself the rather unusual job of domesticating musk oxen and eventually giving the results of his studies to Eskimo tribes and Laplanders all across the northern tundra belt of the world. A completely new human ecology and new social patterns have emerged among these northern people, based on a spinning and weaving trade. The normal ratio of the musk ox birthrate was three females to one male, a problem that has now been eliminated through multiple-birth-hormone injections. One of the reasons why Dr. Teal's work is so unusual is that musk oxen have not been domesticated in almost 6,000 years.

Speculations about the possible future domestication of microbes may open entire new vistas in design-planning, bionically, for medical applications, environmental controls, waste elimination, pollution management, and so forth.

In some areas of design, almost direct translations of natural phenomena can be used. In Dusseldorf in 1940, a gigantic vertical turning machine was constructed by having the interior "sperm" machine build the rest of the machine around itself.

The cross-channel flight of *Gossamer Albatross* (a muscle-powered solar airplane) in 1981 shows that the intermixing of two or three separate biological principles—Arthur Koestler's "collision"—can lead to the fulfilment of one of mankind's oldest dreams: human-powered flight.

Greater London, with a population close to that of New York City and with an unbelievably primitive and leaky water supply system, nonetheless uses only one-fourth as much water as is consumed in New York. The reason is a biomorphic one. D'Arcy Wentworth Thompson quotes Roux in formulating the following empirical rules for the branching of arteries and leaf venation:

1. If an artery bifurcates into two equal branches, these branches come off at equal angles to the main stem.
2. If one of the branches be smaller than the other, then the main branch or continuation of the original artery makes with the latter a smaller angle than does the smaller or lateral branch.
3. All branches which are so small that they scarcely seem to weaken or diminish the main stem come off from it at a large angle, from seventy to ninety degrees.

The water supply of London was laid out according to the above rules and, in spite of marginal losses, represents a biologically stable system. New York City's water supply, by contrast, is a right-angled grid. This looks beguiling on paper (especially to engineers) but works less efficiently, creating turbulence and "frictional losses."

In some fields "bypassing" characteristics are beginning to make their appearance. Sonic thesia, a system used recently in dental work, equips the patient with a pair of stereo earphones through which he listens to prerecorded music. A third stream broadcasts a continuous screaming or wailing sound which the patient has to tune out continuously with a pain control. The patient becomes so task-oriented that little or no pain is felt because nerve endings and pain receptors are being bypassed.

When a telephone operator broke in on you in the phone booth making your nickel telephone call in the thirties, it was still good business to do so. With fully automated equipment, communication satellites, and a lack of operators, this is no longer cost-effective even on a long-distance basis. In 1970 Bell Telephone Systems proposed to use standard billing per month, which would permit unlimited station-to-station direct-dialing calls anywhere on the continent.

This idea is now being reconsidered. With the dismemberment of the Bell telephone system into decentralized, separate entities, AT&T has put forward several proposals. All of these cluster around the concept that billing the customer costs *more* than his or her phone call: it is suggested once more that direct-dial long-distance calls be billed at a token figure, whereas the cost of any operator assisted call might increase by as much as 200 percent.

Telephones and other communication devices constitute an invisible environment, suggesting Marshall McLuhan's "Global Village" concept. But it is in the design of actual environments that design teams, including architects, city planners, landscape designers, regional planners, and the occasional sociologist, have operated traditionally.

It is precisely in the area of environmental design that bionic approaches and biological insights gleaned from the most recent research in ecology and ethology will be most valuable. As we attempt to survive in the regional smear reaching from Kansas City to St. Louis to Chicago to Cleveland to Erie to Buffalo, we also participate in mass-producing inhabitants of prisons, slums, redeveloped slums, mental institutions, and $150,000 condominiums. The subtle interaction of all these types, as well as their interaction with the dominant culture, has yet to be studied, interpreted, and understood.

Insights will come from frightening studies performed over the last twelve years, with animals under conditions of stress and extreme crowding. *Fatty degeneration of the heart and liver; brain hemorrhage; hypertension; atherosclerosis with its attendant effects of stroke and heart attack; adrenal deterioration; cancers and other malignant growths; eye strain; glaucoma and trachoma; extreme apathy, lethargy, and social nonparticipation; high abortion rates; failure of mothers to tend their young; extreme promiscuity among the barely pubescent; a rise in sexually deviant behavior, and the emergence of a new sexual subtype given to impressive and colorful, but superficial, displays of virility, though in reality asexual;* this may sound like a list of what some think of as moral decay or the ailments of modern urbanized people, but it is not. The symptoms listed above have been observed in such widely divergent animals as Minnesota jackrabbits, Sika deer, Norway rats, and several species of birds. The common denominator is stress syndromes caused by overcrowding. Similar behavior patterns have also been observed among concentration camp inmates and prisoners, causing Dr. John Calhoun of the National Institute of Mental Health to coin the accurate and lethal phrase "pathological togetherness." With greater crowding, all these problems have increased enormously. Up to now environmental planning has sublimely disregarded all this.

Industrial and environmental design are fields in which schools should be ideologically in the forefront of the profession. Professional society meetings that endlessly and fruitlessly attempt to *define* industrial design might take another look at the sciences. Electricity, after all, is never defined but is described as a function; its value being expressed in terms of relations—the relation between voltage and amperage, for instance. Still, people identify themselves as electrical engineers, or electricians, seemingly without any loss of identity. Industrial and environmental design, too, can be expressed only as a function; its value, for instance, being expressed in terms of relations: the relation between human ability and human need.

9

Design Responsibility:

Five Myths and Six Directions

One cannot build life from refrigerators, politics, credit statements and crossword puzzles. That is impossible. Nor can one exist for any length of time without poetry, without color, without love.

ANTOINE DE SAINT-EXUPÉRY

Industrial design differs from its sister arts of architecture and engineering. Whereas architects and engineers routinely solve real problems, industrial designers are often hired to create new ones. Once they have succeeded in building new dissatisfactions into people's lives, they are then prepared to find a temporary solution. Having constructed a Frankenstein, they are eager to design its bride.

One basic performance requirement in engineering hasn't really changed too much since the days of Archimedes: be it an automobile jack or a space station, it has to work, and work optimally at that. While the architect may use new methods, materials, and processes, the basic problems of human physique, circulation, planning, and scale are as true today as in the days of the Parthenon.

With accelerating mass production, design has become responsible for all of our means of communication, transportation, consumer goods, military hardware, furniture, packages, medical equipment, tools, utensils, and much else. With a present worldwide need of 650 million individual family living units, it can be safely predicted that even "housing," still built individually by hand, will become a fully industrially designed, mass-produced consumer product by the end of the century.

Buckminster Fuller made an early start toward mass-produced housing with his Dymaxion House (experimentally produced by the Beech Aircraft Company in Wichita, Kansas) in 1946. Later came his Domes, which started a whole generation of "Dome freaks" busily building geodesic carbuncles with a dismaying capacity for leaking covers. Other attempts came through an intelligent reappraisal of trailers stacked vertically three units high. These experiments were carried out under grants from Housing and Urban Development in Lafayette, Indiana, in the mid-sixties. The most promising mass-produced house now is manufactured in Japan by Misawa Homes. These buildings can be put together in hundreds of different configurations, are inexpensive and quickly built, and are made with a new kind of concrete.

Even now the contemporary architect is frequently no more than a master assembler of elements. *Sweet's Catalogue* (twenty-six bound volumes that list building components, panels, mechanical equipment, and so forth), occupies an honored place on the shelves of an architect's working library. With its help, he fits together a puzzle called "house" or "school" or whatever by plugging in the components—designed, for the most part by industrial designers, and listed conveniently among the 10,000 entries in *Sweet's*. Quite naturally architectural offices use computers and merely feed all of *Sweet's* pages, as well as the economic and environmental requirements of the job, into the computer. The computer assembles all the bits, relates all the information to square-foot costage, and comes up with the solution. With endearing candor, some architects have taken pains to explain that "the computer does an excellent job."

By contrast, as in the case of the TWA Terminal at Kennedy International Airport, the architect may create a three-dimensional trademark, an advertisement through which people are fed, but whose function it is to create a corporate image for the client, rather than provide comfort and facilities for passengers. Having myself been trapped at the TWA Terminal during a fifteen-hour power blackout, I can vouch for the inappropriateness of this sculptural environment to process people, airplanes, cars, food, water, waste, or luggage.

The lacy mantles and Gothic minarets of Edward Durell Stone and Yamasaki are little more than latter-day extensions of the Chicago Fair of 1893. Frothy trifles, concocted to reinject romanticism into our prefabricated, prechewed, and predigested cityscape, can nonetheless be revealing. For who could see Yamasaki's soaring Gothic arches at the Seattle Science Pavilion without realizing that here science was at last elevated through glib design clichés to the stature of religion? One almost expected Dr. Edward Teller to appear one Sunday morn, arrayed in laboratory vestments, and solemnly intone "$E = mc^2$."

One of the difficulties with design by copying, design through eclecticism, is that the handbooks, the style manuals, and floppy disks continuously go out of style and become old-fashioned and irrelevant to the problem at hand. Furthermore, it is not just aesthetics that is eliminated in designing via *Sweet's* and/or the computer. "The Concert Hall and the Moonshot Syndrome," by William Snaith in his *Irresponsible Arts*, gives an excellent example of how design fails when it relies exclusively on copying and computer-generated models.

If the need for some 650-million housing units around the world is to be met, surely the answer lies in rational rethinking of what housing means—or can mean—and the developing of totally new processes and concepts.

The architect as heroic master builder and the architect who defiles this fair and pleasant land with gigantic sterile file cabinets ready to be occupied by interchangeable people are both anachronisms.

When Moshe Safdie designed and built Habitat, an example of a radically new type of shelter, for the Montreal Exposition of 1967, he was among the first architect-planners who attempted to use a modular building system intelligently. Habitat has often been faulted for being both too expensive and too complex. In reality Habitat is probably the least ex-

Modular housing, shown first in the terraced houses and gardens of Habitat Montreal, then on the first site of Habitat Puerto Rico on San Patricio hill in Hato Rey, San Juan. Courtesy: M.I.T. Press and Tundra Books of Montreal. Photos by Jerry Spearman.

pensive and at the same time most varied *system* that can be devised, and it is instructive to note that the Canadian Exposition Board made it impossible to build more than one-third of the units. The strength of Habitat lies in the fact that once a large amount of money has been invested in basic building and handling equipment, the system then begins to pay for itself as more units are built. For a fuller understanding of the Habitat system, see Safdie's two newer projects in Puerto Rico and Israel (see also R. Buckminster Fuller's *Nine Chains to the Moon*, p. 37).

In clothing design, as in architecture, the industrial designer has entered the field through the back door, creating disposable work gloves (2,000 to a roll), ski boots, space suits, protective throwaway clothing for persons handling radioactive isotopes, and scuba gear. Lately, with the introduction of "breathing" and therefore usable leather substitutes, much of the boot, belt, handbag, shoe, and luggage industry, too, is turning to the product designer for help. New techniques in vacuum forming, slush molding, gang turning, and so forth, make mass-production design possible for products traditionally associated with handcrafted operations.

The lesson of this book, to design for people's *needs* rather than their *wants*, can be applied to clothing design as well. Fashion design is much like automotive styling in Detroit: applying Band-Aids to cancerous sores. Women have been permanently disabled by wedgies, elevator shoes, stiletto heels, and pin heels. The influence of girdles on women's diaphragms, digestive systems, and pulmonary abilities could lead to a book by itself. But there are genuine needs here as well: the design of clothes for handicapped children and adults making it possible for them to dress or undress themselves—resulting in greater pride and self-confidence. Most fashion is designed for people who are seventeen years old or, more disastrously, their middle-aged brothers or sisters fancying themselves as teenagers. Little or no clothing is designed for the elderly, the obese, people who are unusually short or very tall.

Satisfying the need for tools, shelter, clothing, breathable air, and usable water is not only the job and responsibility of the industrial designer but can also provide enormous new challenges.

Mankind is unique among animals in its relationship to the environment. All other animals adapt *autoplastically* to a changing environment (by growing thicker fur in the winter or evolving into a totally new species over a half-million-year cycle); only mankind transforms earth itself to suit its needs and wants *alloplastically*. This job of form-giving and re-shaping has become the designer's responsibility. A hundred years ago, if a new chair, carriage, kettle, or a pair of shoes was needed, the consumer went to the craftsman, stated his wants, and the article was made for him. Today the myriad objects of daily use are mass-produced to a utilitarian and aes-thetic standard often completely unrelated to the consumer's need. At this point Madison Avenue must be brought in to make these objects seem desirable.

How the smallest change in design can have far reaching consequences can be explained through example. Automotive designers in Detroit might set themselves the goal to make car dashboards more pleasing through a symmetrical arrange-ment of all control knobs, and by relocating ashtrays, air con-ditioning controls, and wiper and heater switches. The results? *As many as 20,000 people killed outright and another 80,000 maimed on our highways during any given five-year span.* These 100,000 deaths and accidents would be caused by the driver having to reach only eleven inches further, diverting attention from the road for an extra second or two. These fig-ures are an extrapolation of the Vehicular Safety Study Pro-gram at Cornell University. In 1971 a General Motors executive said: "GM bumpers offer 100 percent protection from all damage if *the speed of the car does not exceed 2.8 miles per hour.*" (Italics supplied.) Meanwhile the president of Toyota Motors has built a $445,000 shrine to "honor the souls of those killed in his cars" (quoted in *Esquire*, January 1971). By 1982 I saw many small shrines and memorial tablets built by the president of Honda in Japan to victims of accidents in their cars.

In late April 1983 the National Highway Traffic Safety Administration stated that General Motors might have to recall 5 million midsize cars and trucks made in 1978–1980. Should this recall be ordered, General Motors would have the distinction of having been involved in the three biggest recalls in history: in 1971 6.7 million GM cars and light trucks had to be recalled, followed by a recall of 6.4 million midsize cars in 1981. This would mean that GM had to recall a total of nearly 19 million vehicles—*or nearly half of its entire production*—due to design and engineering mistakes.

Consider the home appliance field. Refrigerators are not designed, aesthetically or even physically, to fit in with the rest of the kitchen equipment. Rather, they are designed to stand out well against competing brands at the appliance store and scream for the consumer's notice. Once bought, they still shrilly clamor for attention in the user's home—destroying the visual calm and unity of the kitchen.

Through wasting design talent on such trivia as mink-covered toilet seats, chrome-plated marmalade guards for toast, electronic fingernail-polish dryers, and baroque fly-swatters, a whole category of fetish objects for an abundant society has been created. I saw an advertisement extolling the virtues of diapers for parakeets. These delicate unmentionables (small, medium, large, and extra large) sold at one dollar apiece. A long-distance call to the distributor provided me with the hair-raising information that 20,000 of these zany gadgets were sold each month in 1970.

In all things, it is appearance that seems to count, form rather than content. Let's unwrap a fountain pen we have just been given. At first there is the bag provided by the store. Nestled in it is the package, cunningly wrapped in foil or heavily embossed paper. This has been tied with a fake velvet ribbon to which a pretied bow is attached. The corners of the wrapping paper are secured with adhesive tape. Once we have

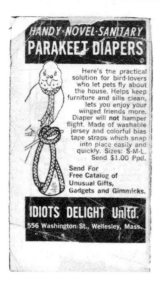

Advertisement for diapers to be used for parakeets. Author's collection.

removed this exterior wrapping, we come upon a simple gray cardboard sleeve. Its only function is to protect the actual "presentation box." The exterior of this little item is covered with a cheap leatherette that looks (somewhat) like Italian marble. Its shape conjures up the worst excesses of the Biedermeier style of Viennese cabinetry during the last and decadent stages of that lamentably long period. When opened, the vistas thus revealed would gladden the heart of Evelyn Waugh's *The Loved One*, for they match the interior appointments of a Hollywood-created luxury coffin to a nicety. Under the overhanging (fake) silk lining and resting on a cushion of (phony) velveteen, the fountain pen is at last revealed in all its phalliform beauty. But wait, we are not yet done. For the fountain pen itself is only a further packaging job. A recent confection of this type (selling for $150.00) had its outer casing made not of *mere* silver, but of "silver obtained by melting down ancient 'pieces of eight' " recovered, one must assume, at great expense from some Spanish galleon fortuitously sunk near the Parker Pen factory three centuries ago. A (facsimile) map, giving the location of the sunken ship and tastefully printed on (fake) parchment, was enclosed with each pen. However, whatever the material of the pen-casing, within it we find a polyethylene ink-cartridge (manufacturing cost, including ink, 3¢) connected to a nib.

In the case of the silver pen cited above, the retail price of the silver pen in its package is approximately 145,000 percent higher than the cost of the basic writing tool. We may say that inexpensive pens are, after all, available and that the example mentioned merely illustrates "freedom of choice." But this freedom of choice is illusory, for the choice is open only to those to whom the difference between spending $150 or 39¢ is immaterial. In fact, a dangerous shift from primary use and need functions to associational areas has taken place here, since in most ways the 39¢ ball-point pen outperforms the $150 one. Additionally the tooling, advertising, marketing, and even the materials used in packaging represent such an exercise in futile waste-making that it is not acceptable except to a pampered elite.

This is *not* an argument against comparatively high prices that are a result of outstanding quality. My own fountain pen (a German *Mont Blanc*) was given to me by my father on my tenth birthday; it has given me excellent service—with two minor repairs—for nearly forty-four years and is still working well and is unusually handsome.

The example of pens could be easily duplicated in almost any other area of consumer goods: the packaging of perfumes, whisky decanters, games, toys, sporting goods, and the like. Designers develop such trivia professionally and are proud of the equally professional awards they receive for the fruits of such dedicated labor. Industry uses such "creative packaging"—this, it is useful to note, is also the name of a magazine addressed to designers—in order to sell goods that may be shabby, worthless, or just low in cost, at grossly inflated prices.

In 1981 Americans for the first time paid more for the packaging that contained their food than was paid to farmers as net income, according to the Department of Agriculture's

Economic Research Service. Twenty-three billion dollars was paid for food packaging by consumers in 1981 compared with a net farm income of nineteen point six billion. This is expected to rise year by year. Here are some examples:

> A beer can (or bottle) costs five times as much as the beer it holds.
>
> A potato chip bag, table syrup bottle, chewing gum wrapper or soft drink bottle cost twice as much as the foods they contain.
>
> A breakfast cereal package, soup can, frozen food box, baby food jar, or dessert box costs one-and-one-half times as much as the foods inside. (Associated Press, 20 September 1982; Department of Agriculture *National Food Review*, 7 July 1981).

In communication and transport, other new challenges emerge globally. Nearly twenty-two years ago I was approached by representatives of the United States Army and told of their practical problems concerning parts of the world (like India) where entire village populations were illiterate and unaware that they lived in, and were part of, a nation-state. Unable to read, and without enough power for radios or money for batteries, they were effectively cut off from all news and communication. In 1962 I began to design and develop a new type of communications device.

An unusually gifted graduating student, George Seegers, did the electronic work and helped to build the first prototype. The resulting one-transistor radio, using no batteries or current and designed specifically for the needs of developing countries, consisted of a used tin can. (As illustrated in this book, a used juice can is shown, but this was no master plan to dump American junk abroad: there is and was an abundance of used cans all over the world.) This can contained wax and a wick that burned (just like a wind-protected candle) for about twenty-four hours. The rising heat was converted into enough energy (via thermocouples) to operate an

Radio receiver designed for the Third World. It is made of a used juice can and uses parafin wax and a wick as power source. The rising heat is converted into enough energy to power this nonselective receiver. Once the wax is gone, it can be replaced by more wax, paper, dried cow dung, or anything else that will burn. Manufacturing costs on a cottage-industry basis: 9 cents. Designed by Victor Papanek and George Seeger at North Carolina State College.

earplug speaker. The radio was, of course, nondirectional, receiving any and all stations simultaneously. But in emerging countries, this was then of no importance: there was only *one* broadcast (carried by relay towers placed about fifty miles apart). Assuming that one person in each village listened to a "national news broadcast" for five minutes daily, the unit could be used for a year until the original paraffin wax was gone. Then more wax, wood, paper, dried cow dung (which has been successfully used as a heat source for centuries in Asia), or for that matter anything else that burns could continue to keep the unit in service. All the components: earplug

The same radio as on previous page but decorated with colored felt cutouts and seashells by a user in Indonesia. The user can embellish the tin-can radio to his own taste. Courtesy UNESCO.

speaker, hand-woven copper radial antenna, an "earth" wire terminating in a (used) nail, tunnel-diode, and thermocouple, were packed in the empty upper third of the can. The entire unit was made for just below 9¢ (1966 dollars).

It was much more than a clever little gadget, constituting a fundamental communication device for preliterate areas of the world. After being tested successfully in the mountains of North Carolina (an area where only *one* broadcast is easily received), the device was demonstrated to the Army. They were shocked. "What if a Communist," they asked, "gets to the microphone?" The question is meaningless. The most important intervention is to make information of all kinds freely accessible to people. After further developmental work, the radio was given to the U.N. for use in villages in Indonesia. No one, neither the designer, nor UNESCO, nor any manufacturer, made any profit or percentages out of this device since it was manufactured as a "cottage industry" product.

In 1967 I showed color slides of the radio at the *Hochschule für Gestaltung*, at Ulm in Germany. It was viewed with dismay because of its "ugliness" and its lack of "formal" design. Of course, the radio *was* ugly. But there are good reasons for this. It would have been simple to paint it (gray, the people at Ulm suggested). But painting it would have been wrong: I felt that ethically I had no right to make aesthetic or "good taste" decisions that would affect millions of people in Indonesia, members of a different culture.

The people in Indonesia decorated their tin-can radios by pasting pieces of colored felt or paper, pieces of glass, and shells on the outside and making patterns of small holes toward the upper edge of the can. In this way it has been possible to bypass "good taste" and to design directly for the needs of the people by "building in" a chance for them to make the radio truly their own through design participation.

It is more than twenty years now since the tin-can radio was first used. Two decades later, the people of Indonesia use normal broadcasting channels; in Bali and Java ordinary stereo AM-FM radios are used by nearly everyone—much as anywhere else. One of the original tin-can radios is still on view as a sort of historical artifact in the museum at Jakarta. However I am told the radio is still used in West Irian (the Indonesia-ruled western half of Papua New Guinea). West Irian is at a stage of development comparable to that of the rest of Indonesia two decades ago.

The story of the tin-can radio shows that it is possible—or at least was possible—to practice decent and ethical design intervention in a developing country. But it must be emphasized that the intervention was small and on a village level. Large-scale design in the Third World by outsiders has never worked. During the fifties large design offices, such as Joe Carreiro of Philadelphia, Chapman and Yamasaki of Chicago, and others, performed design development in Third World countries at the request of the State Department. But most of their work was a sort of "win the minds and hearts of the countryside" operation: they helped to design and manufacture craft-based objects that would appeal to American consumers. In other words, they did not design for the needs of people in India, Ecuador, Turkey, or Mexico; instead they worked for the fancied wants of American consumers. The fallacy of this approach has been shown in an earlier chapter. During the seventies and early eighties similar large-scale designs have been carried out in developing countries, this time predominantly by architects. When a developing nation is cluttered up with large buildings and consumer objects all designed and developed somewhere else, the effects tend to be disastrous. The verdict is already in for Iran; it is about to be pronounced in the Philippines; for most of Latin America the jury is still out.

If we turn from the real and fancied needs of developing countries to our own cities, we see a similarity between expectations that constantly rise and a decaying reality.

Our townscape bears the stamp of irresponsible design. Look through the train window as you approach New York, Chicago, Detroit, Los Angeles. Observe the miles of anonymous tenements, the dingy, twisted streets full of cooped-up, unhappy children. Pick your way carefully through the filth and litter that mark our downtowns or walk past the monotonous ranch houses of suburbia where myriad picture windows grin their empty invitation, their tele-vicious promise. Breathe the cancer-inducing exhaust of factory and car, watch the strontium-90 enriched snow, listen to the idiot roar of the subway, the squealing brakes. And in the ghastly glare of the neon signs, under the spiky television aerials, remember: this is our custom-designed environment.

How has the profession responded to this? Designers help to wield power to change, modify, eliminate, or evolve totally new patterns. Have we educated our clients, our sales force, the public? Have designers attempted to stand for integrity and a better way? Have we tried to push forward, not only in the marketplace, but by considering the needs of people?

Listen in on a few imaginary conversations in our design offices:

> "Boy, wrap another two inches of chrome around that rear fender!"
>
> "Somehow, Charlie, the No. 6ps red seems to communicate freshness of tobacco more directly."
>
> "Let's call it the 'Conquistador' and give people a chance for personal identification with the sabre-matic shift control!"
>
> "Jesus, Harry, if we can just get them to PRINT the instant coffee right on to the paper cup, all they'll need is hot water!"
>
> "Say, how about roll-on-cheese?"
>
> "Squeeze-bottle martinis?"
>
> "Do-it-yourself shish-kebab kits with disposable phenolic swords?"
>
> "Charge-a-plate divorces?"
>
> "An aluminum coffin communicating 'nearness-to-God' (nondenominational) through a two-toned anodized finish?"
>
> "A line of life-sized polyethylene Lolitas in a range of four skin shades and six hair colors?"
>
> "Remember, Bill, the corporate image should reflect that our H-bombs are always PROTECTIVE!"

These imaginary conversations are quite authentic: this is the way designers talk in many offices and schools, and this is also the way in which new products often originate. One proof of authenticity is that of the eleven idiocies listed above, all but two—charge-a-plate divorces and protective H-bombs—have by now become available.

Is this just a hysterical outburst, directed toward some of the phonier aspects of the profession? Aren't there designers working away at jobs that are socially constructive? Not enough. Few articles in the professional magazines or papers presented at design conferences deal with professional ethics or responsibilities going beyond immediate market needs. The latter-day witch doctors of market analysis, motivation research, and subliminal advertising have made dedication to meaningful problem-solving rare and difficult.

The philosophy of most industrial designers today is based on five myths. By examining these, we may come to understand the real underlying problems:

1. *The Myth of Mass Production*: In 1980, 22 million easy chairs were produced in the United States. Dividing this number by the 2,000 chair manufacturers, we find that, on the average, only 11,100 chairs could have been produced by each manufacturer. But each manufacturer has, on the average, ten different models in the line; this reduces our number to only 1,000 or so chairs of one kind. Since furniture manufacturer's lines change twice a year (in time for the spring and autumn market showings), we see that, on the average, only 500 units of any given chair were produced. This means that the designer, far from working for 235 million people (the market he is trained to think about), has, on the average, worked for 1/5,000 of 1 percent of the population. Let's contrast this with the fact that in underdeveloped areas of the world there exists a present need for close to two *billion* inexpensive, basic seating units in schools, hospitals, and houses.

2. *The Myth of Obsolescence*: Since the end of World War II, an increasing number of responsible people at the top levels of management and government have voiced the myth that, by designing things to wear out and be thrown away, the wheels of our economy can be kept turning *ad infinitum*. This nonsense is no longer acceptable. Polaroid cameras, even though new models routinely replace earlier ones, don't become obsolete since the company continues manufacturing film and accessories for them. The German Volkswagen has moved into a leading position in supplying the transportation needs of the world by carefully refraining from major style changes or cosmetic jobs. The Zippo lighter sells far better than all other domestic lighters combined, even though (or could it be because?) the manufacturer guarantees to repair or replace its case and/or guts for life. There is ironic justice in that. For it was in 1931 that George Grant Blaisdell, a nonsmoking American, noticed that some of his friends carried windproof, dependable, Austrian cigarette lighters that

sold in chain stores for twelve cents. He tried importing them directly and selling them at one dollar apiece, but, with a public unwilling to pay that much during the Depression, he stopped. He waited for the expiration of the Austrian patent and began producing it in 1935 with a lifetime guarantee. The Zippo lighter has moved from an item made on $260 worth of secondhand tools, in a $10 room in Brooklyn, to a production level of 3 million units per year. Since so many of our products are made obsolete by technology, the question of *forced* obsolescence becomes redundant and, in terms of scarce raw materials, a dangerous doctrine.

3. *The Myth of the People's "Wants"*: Never in recent times have the so-called wants of people been investigated as thoroughly by psychiatrists, psychologists, motivation researchers, social scientists, and other miscellaneous tame experts, as in the case of the ill-fated Edsel. That mistake cost $350 million and led one comedian to quip that the mistake "was being handled by the Ford Foundation."

"The people want chrome, they like change," except that Volkswagen, Honda, Renault, Volvo, Saab, Mercedes Benz, Datsun, Toyota, and Fiat have exploded that idea thoroughly. So thoroughly, in fact, that over the last twenty years, Detroit has had to start producing compact cars whenever foreign imports began to seriously affect American sales figures. As soon as foreign imports began to drop off, compact cars were again advertised as "the biggest, longest, lowest, most luxurious of them all." This stylistic extravaganza has now again increased the number of small Japanese and European imports coming into this country.

The myth of the people's wants continues to be used by industry and some designers. With the oil crises of 1973 and 1978 behind us, we are early in 1984 facing the possibility of still another shutoff due to the Iraqi-Iranian war. The people have demonstrated their wants by buying subcompacts and— insisting on quality—buying many of these cars from Japan. But in the real world of multinationals, mass unemployment in Detroit, and economic downtrends, other facts assume

Where are they now?

A comparison of automobiles of 1949. Advertisement by Volkswagen of America, Inc.

greater importance. Three of the four big car makers in America have now associated themselves with European or Japanese companies to produce high-quality subcompacts cooperatively. Meanwhile Japan has limited itself to exporting a smaller number of cars to the United States, and this has directly led to a fine irony: the Japanese now export larger and more luxurious cars to the United States, so that their profits can increase with a smaller number of units exported.

4. *The Myth of the Designer's Lack of Control*: Designers often excuse themselves by explaining that it's "all the fault of the front office, the sales department, market research," and so forth. But of more than 200 mail-order, impulse-buying items foisted on the public in 1983, a significantly large number were conceived, invented, planned, patented, and produced by members of the design profession.

In the magazine *Products That Think* (no. 12, JS&A Corporation), an electronically heated ice-cream scooper designed in France is offered for $24. The "Electronic Burger" (in the same issue) is, according to the description, "an AM radio shaped like a hamburger with its speaker at the bottom of the bun." One assumes the speaker has been placed there so that the sound is barely discernible. As mentioned earlier, a $30,000 solid gold telephone was available from Diners Club for the 1983 Christmas market. For $149 an overnight electric trouser-warmer is available under the title "Hot Pants."

These 1983 items recall one of my all-time favorites: "Mink-Fer," a tube of deodorized mink droppings sold at $1.95 in 1970 as a Christmas fertilizer for "the plant that has everything."

5. *The Myth That Quality No Longer Counts*: While Americans have for years bought German and, later, Japanese cameras, Europeans now line up to buy Polaroid cameras and equipment. American Head skis are outselling Scandinavian, Swiss, Austrian, and German skis around the world. Sales of Schlumbohm's Chemex Coffee Maker are diminished only somewhat by a recent German copy of it. The United States Universal Jeep designed by Willys in 1943 (since modified, and sold by American Motors) is still a desirable multipurpose vehicle; the only competition to its descendants comes from the British Land Rover and the Japanese Toyota Land Cruiser, both updated and improved versions of the Jeep.

The one thing these and some other American products that

still command world leadership hold in common is a radical new approach to a problem, excellent design, and the highest possible quality.

Something can be learned from these five myths. It is a fact that the designer often has greater control over his work than he believes he does, that quality, new concepts, and an understanding of the limits of mass production could mean designing for the majority of the world's people, rather than for a comparatively small domestic market. Design for the people's *needs* rather than for their *wants*, or artificially created wants, is the only meaningful direction now.

Having isolated some of the problems, what can be done? At present there are entire areas in which little or no design work is done. They are areas that promote the social good but call initially for high risk and, to begin with, low return. All that is needed is a selling job, and that is certainly nothing new to the industrial design profession.

Here are some of the fields that design has neglected:

1. *Design for the Third World*: With the global increase in population over the last twenty years, nearly three billion people stand in need of some of the most basic tools and implements.

In 1970 I said that more oil lamps were needed globally than ever before. By 1984 this lack has become even more acute. *There are more people without electric power today than the total population of earth before electricity was generally used.* In spite of new techniques, materials, and processes, almost no radically new oil or paraffin lamps have been developed since Thomas Edison's day. In northeastern Brazil the local population began adapting used electric light bulbs to burn oil for illumination in the late seventies. The *Nordestinos* have difficulty understanding why light bulbs have to go through an electric cycle before being cut down into a container for oil. And it is a fact that Brazil now has to import used bulbs into the northeastern states where oil lamps exceed electric bulbs.*

*See "Papanek 1983" pp. 148–149.

Eighty-four percent of the world's land surface is completely roadless terrain. Often epidemics sweep through an area: nurses, doctors, and medicine may be only seventy-five miles away, but there is no way of getting through. Regional disasters, famines, or water shortages develop frequently; again aid can't get there. Helicopters work but are far beyond the money and expertise available in many regions. Beginning in 1962, a graduate class and I developed an off-road vehicle that might be useful in such emergencies. We established the following performance characteristics:

a. The vehicle would operate on ice, snow, mud, mountain forests, broken terrain, sand, certain kinds of quicksand, and swamps.
b. The vehicle would cross lakes, streams, and small rivers.
c. The vehicle would climb forty-five-degree inclines and traverse forty-degree inclines.
d. The vehicle would carry a driver and six people, or a driver and a 1,000-pound load, or a driver and four stretcher cases; finally it would be possible for the driver to walk next to the vehicle, steering it with an external tiller, and thus carry more load.
e. The vehicle could also remain stationary and, with a rear-power takeoff, drill for water, drill for oil, irrigate the land, fell trees, or work simple lathes, saws, and other power tools.

We invented and tested a completely new material, "Fibergrass." This consists of conventional chemical fiberglass catalysts but with dried native grasses, hand-aligned, substituting for expensive fiberglass mats. This reduced costs. Over 150 species of native grasses from many parts of the world were tested. By also inventing new manufacturing logistics, it was possible to reduce costs still more. Various technocratic centers were to build components: heavy metal work was to be done in Egypt and Libya, Central Africa, Bangalore (India), and Brazil. Electronic ignitions were to be made in Tai-

Mock-ups and working models of two vehicles designed and built under the author's direction at Konstfackskolan in Stockholm,
Sweden. These vehicles were explorations in
transporting materials over rough terrain by
muscle power alone. One of them (designed
by James Hennessey and Tillman Fuchs) is a
proposal for an inner-city run-about and
shopping vehicle. It will carry two people
and 200 pounds. Courtesy: *Form* magazine.

wan, Japan, Puerto Rico, and Liberia. Precision metal work
and the power train were to be done in the Chinese Democratic Republic, Indonesia, Ecuador, and Ghana. The Fibergrass body would be made by users on a village or cottage
level, all over the world. Several prototypes were built (and
are illustrated), and it was possible to offer the vehicle to
UNESCO at a unit price of less than $150 (1962 dollars). But
this is the point where ethical considerations became important: Although the prototypal vehicle worked well, and computer analysis by the U.N. told us that close to ten million
vehicles could be used initially, we realized that we were con-

Off-road vehicle, discontinued for ecological reasons, designed by student team under the author's direction, School of Design, North Carolina State College, 1964.

niving at ecological disaster. The net result of going ahead would have meant introducing ten million internal combustion engines (and consequently pollution) into hitherto undefiled areas of the world. We decided to shelve the off-road project until a low-cost alternative power source was available, which still has not happened.

(Historical note: Since I do not believe that patents work toward the social good, photographs of our vehicle were published in a 1964 issue of *Industrial Design* magazine. Since then, more than twenty-five brands of vehicles of this type, priced between $5,500 and $8,000, have been offered to wealthy sportsmen, fishermen, and (as "fun vehicles") to the youth culture. These vehicles pollute, destroy, and create incredible noise problems in wilderness areas. The destructive ecological impact of the snowmobile is detailed in Chapter Ten.)

General Motors, Mercedes Benz, Volvo, and others are now manufacturing off-road vehicles for many developing countries. While these vehicles bring about some benefits to the countries involved, they also violate some of the ecological standards that made us withdraw our own vehicle. Furthermore they tie the economy of Third World countries to corporations from the rich countries through direct import or franchise deals. There are notable exceptions to this: Volkswagen production in Mexico, Brazil, and other developing countries operates with reassuring autonomy.

As a result of our concern for pollution, we began exploring muscle-powered vehicles together with a group of Swedish students at *Konstfackskolan* in Stockholm. The Republic of North Vietnam moved 1,100 pound loads into the southern part of that country by pushing such loads along the Ho Chi Minh trail on bicycles. The system worked and was effective. However, bicycles were never designed to be used in just this manner. One of our student teams was able to design a better vehicle made of bicycle parts. The new vehicle is specifically designed for pushing heavy loads; it is also designed to be pushed easily uphill through the use of a "gear-pod" (which can be reversed for different ratios, or removed entirely). The vehicle will also carry stretchers and, because it has a bicycle seat, can be ridden. Several of these vehicles plug into each other to form a short train (see photographs and sketches).

When students suggested the use of old bicycles or bicycle parts, they regretfully were told that old bicycles also make good transportation devices and that parts are always needed for replacement or repair. (The students may have been influenced somewhat negatively by the fact that a design student won first prize in the Alcoa Design Award Program by designing a power source, intended for Third World use, made of brand-new aluminum bicycle parts.)

Consequently we designed a new luggage carrier for the millions of old bicycles all over the world. It is simple and can

be constructed in any village. It will carry more payload. But it will also fold down in thirty seconds (see illustration) and then can be used in its other capacity for generating electricity, irrigation, felling trees, running a lathe, digging wells,

These drawings show that the muscle-powered vehicle can be plugged together into a short train. It also comes apart, and the geared power pod is reversible so that the vehicle can be pushed uphill under heavy loads. It can also carry stretchers or, with the power pod removed, be used like a wheelbarrow. Designed under the author's direction by a student team in Sweden, it could be used in underdeveloped areas to propel heavy loads, similar to the loads pushed on bicyles along the Ho Chi Minh Trail in North Vietnam. Photos by Reijo Rüster. Courtesy: *Form* magazine.

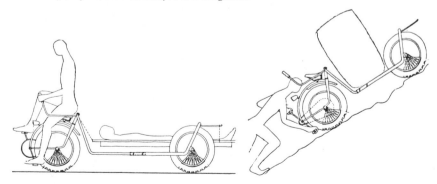

As bicycles are needed as transportation devices in the Third World, this luggage carrier was designed to flip down and be used as a temporary power source when needed. Its construction is within the scope of the most modest village technology. Designed by Michael Crotty and Jim Rothrock, as students at Purdue University.

and pumping for oil. Afterward the bicycle can be folded up again and returned to its primary function as a transportation device. Except that it now has a better luggage carrier.

A Swedish student built a full-size sketch model of a vehicle that is powered by the arm muscles and can go uphill. This in turn led us at Purdue University to design an entire generation of muscle-powered vehicles that are specifically designed to provide remedial exercise for handicapped children and adults (see photographs).

2. *Design of Teaching and Training Devices for the Retarded, the Handicapped, and the Disabled*: Cerebral palsy, poliomyelitis, myasthenia gravis, mongoloid cretinism, and many other crippling diseases and accidents affect one-tenth of the American public and their families (20 million people) and approximately 400 million people around the world. Yet the design of prosthetic devices, wheelchairs, and other invalid gear is by and large still on a Stone Age level. One of the traditional contributions of industrial design, cost reduction, could be made here. At nearly every drugstore one can buy a transistor radio for as little as $8.98 (including import duties and transportation costs). Yet as mentioned previously, pocket-amplifier-type hearing aids sell at prices between $300 and $1,100 and involve circuitry, amplification elements, and shroud design not radically more sophisticated than the $8.98 radio.

Another version of a muscle-powered experimental vehicle designed by a student in Stockholm.

Tricycle for adults with battery-power assistance. $650 each. Courtesy: Abercrombie & Fitch Co.

Hydraulically powered and pressure-operated power-assists are badly in need of innovation and design.

Robert Senn's hydrotherapeutic exercising water float is designed in such a manner that it cannot tip over. There are no straps or other restraint devices that would make a child feel trapped or limited in his motions. At present hydrotherapy usually consists of having the child strapped to a rope attached to a horizontal ceiling track. In Robert Senn's vehicle all such restraints are absent. Nonetheless, his surfboardlike device is safer (it will absorb edge-loading of up to 200 pounds), and the therapist can move in much more closely to the child. Later, I explain further ideas we have developed in this field.

3. *Design for Medicine, Surgery, Dentistry, and Hospital Equipment*: Only recently has there been responsible design development of operating tables. Most medical instruments, especially in neurosurgery, are unbelievably crude, badly designed, very expensive, and operate with all the precision of a steam shovel. Thus a drill for osteoplastic craniotomies (basically a brace and bit in stainless steel) costs nearly $800 and does not work as sensitively as a carpenter's brace and bit available for $7.98 at any hardware store. Skull saws have not changed in design since predynastic times in Egypt. The radically new power-driven drill and saw for osteoplastic crani-

A water vehicle designed for hydrotherapy of handicapped children. Designed by Robert Senn, as a graduate student at Purdue University.

otomies was tested in vet labs devoted to experiments with animals. It promises to revolutionize methods in neurophysiology.

The cost of health care is rising astronomically. Regardless of who absorbs these costs in the long run, the fact remains that a great deal of the high expense can be attributed directly to bad design.

From time to time, illustrations of new biomedical equipment appear. Almost invariably these are "hi-style modern" cabinets, in nine delicious decorator colors, surrounding the same old machine. Hospital beds, maternity delivery tables, and an entire host of ancillary equipment are almost without exception needlessly expensive, badly designed, and cumbersome.

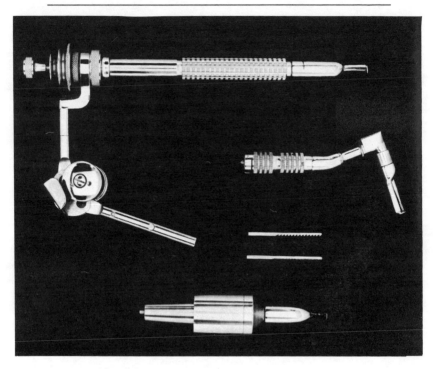

System of drills and saws for osteoplastic craniotomies. Designed and copyrighted by C. Collins Pippin, North Carolina State College.

4. *Design for Experimental Research*: In thousands of research laboratories, much of the equipment is antiquated, crude, jury-rigged, and high in cost. Animal immobilization devices, stereo-encephalotomes, and the whole range of stereotactic instruments need intelligent design reappraisal.

Companies routinely overcharge governmental purchasing agencies by percentages that are incredibly high. Before a Senate Subcommittee investigating overcharges by manufacturers to Air Force purchasing agents, a simple hexagon Allen wrench was shown (a three-inch-long piece of six-sided wire bent to a right angle at one end). This sells to the public for

12¢. With one-eighth of an inch cut off and a 1¢ rubber grip slipped on, the same vendor sells the tool to the United States Air Force at $9,602 each! A piece of thin steel wire, about three inches long, was also shown. This wire sells for 1¢ per yard, hence the retail price of a four-inch chunk is about one-twelfth of a penny each. However industry sells this plain wire to the Air Force for $7,417 each under the formidable title Antennae Motor Safety Alignment Pin! Senate hearings have established that similar overcharging sometimes amounts to price increases as large as 230,000 percent—a practice that costs American consumers an estimated total of eighteen billion dollars annually. (All figures from U.S. Senate Subcommittee hearings on defense spending and the *MacNeil-Lehrer News Hour*, 2 November 1983.)

A simple electric laboratory timer made in upstate New York sells to amateur photographers for $89.50. Research laboratories pay $750 for the same device. An electric kitchen mixer is offered to consumers for $49.95 in white enamel or in stainless steel for $79.95. For lab use the *same* unit by the *same* manufacturer lists for $485. Value engineering is a sub-branch of design that has to do with cost reduction and assessing the value of specific parts in a machine. These value engineering techniques could play an important part to change the pricing of machines and devices for laboratories. After enough Senate investigations, manufacturers might even decide to sell laboratory apparatus at an *honest* profit, instead of defrauding the public and research establishments alike.

5. *Systems Design for Sustaining Human Life Under Marginal Conditions*: The design of total environments to maintain men and machines is becoming increasingly important. As mankind moves into jungles, the Arctic, and the Antarctic, new kinds of environmental design are needed. But even more marginal survival conditions will be brought into play as sub-oceanic mining and experimental stations on asteroids and other planets become feasible. Design for survival in space capsules has already become routine.

The pollution of water and air and the problems of toxic

and atomic waste disposal also make a re-examination of environmental systems design necessary and are explored in Chapter Ten.

6. *Design for Breakthrough Concepts*: Many products have reached a dead end by now in terms of further development. This has led to "additive" design: more and more features or extra gadgets are added instead of reanalysing the basic problems and evolving new and innovative answers. Automatic dishwashers, for example, waste billions of gallons of water each year (in the face of a worldwide water shortage), even though other systems like ultrasonics for "separating-dirt-from-objects" are well within the state of the art. The rethinking of "dishwashing" as a system might make it easier to clean dishes, as well as solving one of the basic survival problems: water conservation. To this add: industrial water waste, toilets, showers.

Humidity control in homes and hospital rooms is important and can sometimes become critical. In many regions of the United States humidity levels are such that both humidifiers and dehumidifiers are needed. Such gadgets are costly, ugly, and ecologically extraordinarily wasteful of water and electricity. Researching this problem for a manufacturer, Robert Senn and I were able to develop a theoretical humidifier/dehumidifier without moving parts, using no liquids, pumps, or electricity. By combining a mix of deliquescent and antibacteriological crystals, we were able to develop a theoretical surface that would store twelve to twenty-four atoms of water to each crystal atom and release it again when humidity was unusually low. This material could then be sprayed onto a wall or woven into a wallhanging, eliminating the drain on electric power as well as noise pollution and expense of present-day systems. Experiments have continued for several years, and the device now works well. In 1982 test marketing was begun.

Problems are endless, and not enough breakthrough thinking is done. Consider the heating of rooms and houses. With heating costs rising many people have been forced to close off some rooms in their homes—especially in the Northeast of the United States—and install paraffin heaters, electric fires, or other space heaters that are only marginally safe. Add to this group of people those living in southern California, parts of Florida, Australia, and other areas where room heating is only temporarily needed. Basing my thinking on Frank Lloyd Wrights's "gravity heat," that is the fact that a warmed floor will reduce temporary and permanent heat requirements in a room, I began research in 1981 for another breakthrough answer to this. Using techniques borrowed from electric blankets, which take very little current to operate, I developed a system for modular electric rugs. Each electric rug is shockproof and measures 39 by 39 inches, and they're easily plugged together. With very low energy usage they heat a room to comfortable temperatures. They are now being experimentally worked with by one of my clients in Australia.

Breakthrough concepts are also related to people's expectations and wants, as discussed earlier in this chapter. Catheryn Hiesinger describes such a change in people's consciousness and its impact on manufacturers: "While in 1964 visitors to the New York World's Fair were presented with an exhibit of model homes called The House of Good Taste, the 1982 World's Fair at Knoxville, Tennessee, displayed TVA conservation techniques, a Victorian house remodeled with energy-saving devices and appliances, and a factory-built home with a solar-heating system, approaching if not attaining the utopia of Victor Papanek's *Design For The Real World*" (*Design Since 1945*. Philadelphia: Museum of Art, 1983).

These are six possible directions in which the design profession can and must go if it is to do a worthwhile job. Few designers have realized the challenge so far or responded to it. The action of the profession has been comparable to what would happen if all medical doctors were to forsake general practice and surgery and concentrate exclusively on dermatology, plastic surgery, and cosmetics.

10

Environmental Design:

Pollution, Crowding, Ecology

Nature has let us down, God seems to have left the receiver off the hook, and time is running out . . .

ARTHUR KOESTLER

The community of nature—that biotic community that provides mankind's environment—has been disturbed in major ways. Many examples exist of individuals deformed, mentally retarded, or crippled by pollution. We know that genetic damage has occurred following the use of Agent Orange in Vietnam. Bone cancer and leukemia have plagued people living downwind from atomic test sites in Nevada and Utah. Improper dumping of toxic wastes at Love Canal in upstate New York, Times Beach in Missouri, Stringfellow in California, and approximately 50,000 other sites has also had grave health consequences. But human generations last too long to be able to demonstrate *evolutionary* changes—*so far*.

Sometimes it is possible to use diagnostic tools from nature. Changes caused as environmental pollution spreads (or, more rarely, recedes) can clearly be shown by a certain type of moth. Nearly 150 years ago scientists in England noticed a significant change. The peppered moth (*Biston betularia*) has silvery wings with a few dark markings—since these moths sit on lichen-covered birch trees, such mimicry protects them from the birds who prey on them. In Manchester and other industrial areas heavy sulphur dioxide pollution gave rise to a new melanic form: *Biston carbonaria*. This mutant has brownish-black wings, the color of soot-stained buildings (no silver). Within fifty years the mutant form had bred true in smog-polluted areas, and the original silvery type had completely disappeared. J.B.S. Haldane founded experimental colonies in which he was able to breed both types of peppered moths (together with the intermediate form *Biston insularia*— which has an equal balance between silver and black on its wing markings—depending on the amount of pollution being introduced to his specimens). In England it was possible forty years ago to actually chart areas of heavy pollution by the type of peppered moth collected. The same has been done in the United States with *Biston cognataria*. Relatively pollution-free areas still yield the original form; the drab melanics breed true in polluted areas. But there is hope: *as cities are slowly being cleaned up, the real peppered moth, nearly pure silver, has reappeared and the mutant is dying out.*

This is not a reductionist argument, saying people are like moths. But such studies can provide biological tools for the diagnosis of sulphur dioxide pollution.

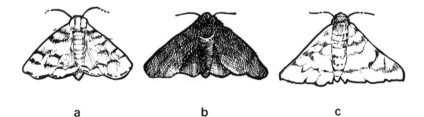

a   b   c

The Peppered Moth (*Biston Betularia*)
a. Original markings before pollution (up to 1850).
b. The mutant stage (ca. 1850–1970).
c. After pollution was eased (the last twenty years or so).
Drawings by Smit Vajaramant.

Industrial designers, industry, and governments must determine together what social and ecological harm we are doing to our communities. To say that there is something inherently wrong with technology itself is overly simplistic. We can no longer just rid ourselves of technology, since the whole world depends on it. A neo-Luddite destruction of technology would produce worldwide catastrophes that would have equally strong impacts in such high-tech centers as New York or Tokyo and in many areas of the Third World. All of us are tied into worldwide health-care, data transmission, food, and personal transport, and other systems.

Industrial "growth," if directly exported from fully industrialized countries to those that are still industrializing, has far-reaching social, ecological, ethological, and environmental consequences. Some of these consequences are malignant. Their main negative effects are pollution and alienation.

In the developed world we pay for our riches by also living with rising statistics of suicide, vandalism, absenteeism, work sabotage, "wildcat" strikes, alcoholism, meaningless violence centered around mass sporting events, crimes against the person, neglect and battering of children, unusually high divorce rates and deviant sexual behavior, drug use, loss of identity, and, finally, anomie.

When we speak about "pollution through products," the cycle is more complex than we usually think. It consists minimally of seven parts:

1. Natural resources are destroyed; moreover, these resources are usually irreplaceable.
2. The very destruction of these resources by strip-mining, open pit mining, and so forth, creates a pollution phase (1 and 2 form phase I).
3. The manufacturing process itself creates more pollution (phase II).
4. This same manufacturing process also brings about worker alienation and anomie.

5. Packaging (this is essentially a repetition of phases I and II).
6. The use of the product creates more pollution and user alienation and user anomie (phase III).
7. Finally, discarding the product creates even more lasting sources of pollution (phase IV).

The intervention of designers must be modest, minimal, and sensitive. Thus if we find that the indigo-dyeing of textiles in West Africa creates major breeding areas for tsetse flies and *Anopheles* mosquitoes and consequently an increase in malaria and sleeping sickness, the answer is *not* to get rid of the dyeing pits but to introduce biological controls.

If in Lesotho the social life of women is centered around the beating of maize, the answer is not to introduce electric maize-grinding machinery but to simplify the work and still retain the social grouping.

If it is found that the *Mukwa* (headband) with which Kikuyu women carry loads in Kenya forms permanent depressions in their skulls, we must examine the entire social context of load carrying in West Africa before introducing some insane "improvement," such as motor scooters.

In more fully industrialized countries we can often make the workers' work life more rewarding and more meaningful to them. I have been involved with companies in some of the Scandinavian countries where just paying people more money is not enough. Working with Scandinavian, as well as foreign guest workers, we found that we could improve job performance and lessen alienation by abandoning assembly lines and introducing team assembly, complete job rotation, learning various skills and languages on company time, and so on. If such work techniques are operated in the most technologically advanced countries, then they can also be built into countries that are not yet fully industrialized. To do otherwise smacks of neocolonialism and exploitation.

One way in which I can illustrate how the behavioral sciences can be used in design is through the "washing machine in the playground" syndrome. It is useless to build better playgrounds in slum areas where women have no time to supervise their children at play. Instead, we have built a playground in which there is a central, glass-enclosed observation area fitted out with washing machines and clothes dryers. Consequently, women can supervise their children at play while doing the wash and also talk with one another.

It may be questioned where the profit lies in putting washing machines in playgrounds. May I suggest that "profit" suffers from bad social accounting methods?

If design is ecologically responsive, then it is also revolutionary. All systems—private capitalist, state socialist, and mixed economies—are built on the assumption that we must buy more, consume more, waste more, throw away more. Design, to be ecologically responsible, must be independent of concern for the gross national product (no matter how gross that may be). Over and over I want to stress that, in pollution, the designer is as heavily implicated as anyone. The garbage explosion, and with it the enormous increase in toxicity, acid rain, and poisoned ground water, have outdistanced the population explosion. Professor E. Roy Tinney, director of the State of Washington's Water Research Center, has remarked, "We have not run out of water. We have simply run out of new streams to pollute."

Since this book was first written, examples of pollution have multiplied at an alarming rate; at the same time a few ways of fighting back have emerged.

In mid-July of 1969, one single 200-pound sack of the German pesticide Thiodan that accidentally fell off a barge on the Rhine was able to kill more than 75,000 tons of fish in Germany, Holland, Switzerland, Austria, Liechtenstein, Belgium, and France *and to stop a new fish population from forming for a time period that was estimated at four years but has actually lasted nearly twelve years.*

The most frightening pollution story of all, unfortunately, is somewhat complex to tell: historians have made a good case that lead poisoning was prevalent—especially among the upper classes—in ancient Rome. In 1983 Dr. Jerome Nriagu of the Canadian National Water Research Institute wrote about lead-caused madness and gout in classical Rome in the *New England Journal of Medicine*. The classic symptoms of lead poisoning: gastric diseases, kidney failure, numbness, insomnia, and constipation, seem to have been caused by contaminated spices used in the foods for the rich. Red lead was routinely added to pepper (to increase its weight and make more money); all wines had their bouquet and color enhanced with a grape concentrate that was boiled down in lead containers. "Just one teaspoon of this syrup," says Nriagu, "would have been more than sufficient to cause chronic lead poisoning." All food was prepared in lead, pewter, and lead-soldered utensils—copper vessels coated with lead were supposed to improve flavor.

The Roman aristocrat absorbed (according to Nriagu) an average of 250 micrograms of lead every day in this manner. The average American city-dweller in 1983 absorbs about fifty micrograms a day. In other words, *just living in New York, Chicago, or Los Angeles, we absorb one-fifth the daily dosage of lead that poisoned the ruling classes of ancient Rome and is thought to have led to the decadence and eventual downfall of the Roman Empire, which quantity is more than sufficient to poison us* (*Newsweek*, 28 March 1983).

Pollution problems and ecological threats that were first recognized during the sixties and seventies were often solved with quick "technological fixes." Now, a decade or two later, we have realized that many of the solutions only masked and intensified the problems. Acid rain is a case in point. When industrial pollution was first recognized by the environmental movements of the seventies, a number of seeming solutions were offered to the public.

A classic case was a steel company near Gary, Indiana. Their No. 2 smokestack created enormous environmental damages, specifically through emission of sulphur dioxide (SO_2) and nitrogen oxide (NO_x). The company fought the community tenaciously with legal maneuvers, finally carrying litigation all the way to the Supreme Court. Ultimately required to stop production, install scrubbing equipment and afterburners on their smokestacks or pay a $1,000 a day fine, their sleek corporate attorney appeared at the city manager's office with a check for $365,000, saying "Here is our fine for next year!"

Other companies merely increased the height of smokestacks, thus limiting pollution at the sources of elimination. These primary sources are located around the Chicago-Detroit-Buffalo area, with secondary sources around St. Louis and the Houston-Dallas-Ft. Worth area. The precipitation from these factories now affects an area from the extreme northeast of Canada to Galveston Bay in Texas and is heaviest in Quebec, Ontario, and the New England states. Results are easy to spot. More than half of all spruce trees in the Green Mountains of Vermont have withered or are completely denuded. The salmon in nine Nova Scotia rivers can no longer reproduce. Bronze statues in Boston and Montreal seem to be melting. A new congressional study suggests that more than 9,000 lakes and 60,000 miles of streams in thirty-four states are endangered.

But there are even longer range pollution problems caused by acid rain: the Scandinavian Union (Sweden, Finland, Norway, and Denmark) are preparing a lawsuit against the Ruhr Valley in Germany, as well as against Michigan, Ohio, Illinois, and Indiana, for extreme long-range pollution and acid rain deposited there by the jet stream. Scandinavian lakes, streams, and forests are destroyed by factory emissions from the American Midwest. Their lawsuit—the first of its kind—will be heard by the World Court at The Hague sometime in 1984.

It has been estimated that acid rain causes as much as $5 billion in environmental damage *annually* to crops, farmland, fishing, and the timber industry. In addition, acid rain damage to buildings in cities has been estimated at $2 billion in the Northeast of the United States per year and $360 million annually to the eastern towns and cities in Canada. Solutions to this horrendous damage seem to point in three directions:

1. A cleanup of the sources of emission. This would lead to enormous expenses for manufacturer and consumer alike—it would also predictably result in the loss of thousands of jobs.
2. A number of scientists and (understandably) industrialists argue that acid rain ought to be fought in the lakes and forests where it causes problems—not at the source.
3. A combination between the first two points will yield the best results. While the cost of cleanup of pollution sources is enormously high, one fact usually escapes the apologists for industry: the cost in unemployment can be even higher in the problem areas, since it affects agriculture, fishing, farming and fruit farming, timber, the construction industry, and the tourist trade.

In the Adirondacks some acidified lakes are already being neutralized with infusions of limestone. But this is at best a temporary gesture, sticking a Band-Aid on a festering wound. When Lake Holmsjö in central Sweden became heavily acidified, local residents applied for a county subsidy to treat it with calcium. New budgetary constraints prevented the county from helping. It was at this point that some unsung local hero remembered that eggshells contain high calcium levels and that a major regional bakery threw away tons of eggshells every month. The lake—a victim of acid rain—is now being treated with eggshells to neutralize the sulphuric acid threatening its aquatic life. The Uppsala University Agricultural Science Department has stated that the treatment will work if the lake isn't too far gone (*Urban Innovation Abroad*, August 1982).

From these two small-scale examples emerges a picture of a tiny band of dedicated farmers, fishermen, or ecologists trying to fight the mess made by giant corporations with home remedies. But there is no need for consumer groups to remain small and nearly impotent. We can learn from the Third World in the areas of consumer protection and citizens' initiatives.

While working in Nigeria, I was amazed at the amount of coverage the daily press gave to environmental and ecological issues. Many local newspapers—tabloid format in size—use six to eight of their sixteen pages to alert their readers to environmental problems.

The Consumers' Association of Penang (Malaysia) is possibly the strongest consumer group in the world and manages to exert greater political weight and pressure in that country than even Petra Kelley's Green Party in Germany. The association publishes both a daily and a weekly newspaper and acts as a clearinghouse on product safety, environmental protection, consumer issues, and pollution problems. They publish scores of single-issue pamphlets, have issued a number of excellent books, and have organized more than a dozen international conferences during the last ten years.

Most of the examples of environmental damage cited in the earlier edition of this book were only the first indications of present worldwide dangers. The toxic waste crisis in the United States alone has assumed terrifying proportions. There are more than 50,000 dumps and in excess of 185,000 open pits, ponds, and lagoons at so-called industrial parks around this country, receiving an estimated eighty-eight billion pounds of toxic wastes annually. Near Flint, Michigan, experts aren't even certain of what local sites contain. What little they do know gives abundant cause for alarm: traces of C-56, C-58, zinc, copper, cadmium, lead, chromium, and cyanide have leached into surrounding waters and are slowly moving toward the Great Lakes. Ground-search radar has shown that illegally dumped barrels lie at the bottom of this noxious brew and may contain hydrochloric acid. When mixed with cyanide already present in the water, a cloud of deadly hydrogen-cyanide gas would give local residents less than ten minutes to evacuate.

Newsweek magazine (7 March 1983) describes the difficulties of Bonnie Exner, a Denver housewife who formed a citizens' group out of her concern with the nearby Lowry landfill. "Strange things began to happen. Her telephone was tapped and no matter how quickly she called group meetings, a representative of the dump's owner, Chemical Waste Management Inc., was always there. Her car was tailed and chased at high speeds and a bomb was found planted in her car." It all sounds like a reprise of the Karen Silkwood story, but Bonnie Exner successfully contacted the newspapers. On examination the Lowry landfill was found to contain such known cancer-inducing substances as benzene, acitone, and trichloroethylene. It was closed by the Colorado Supreme Court; however, a state representative introduced legislation to let it be reopened.

Among the well-trimmed lawns and perpetual sunshine of California's high-tech Silicon Valley, people have always felt themselves to be living in the cleanest industrial environment in the world. Nonetheless people living in Los Paseos, California, found in 1982 that chemical cleaning solvents had seeped into local wells from an electronic firm's tank. An unusually high number of birth defects, thirteen area deaths, and medical problems ranging from skin disorders to congenital heart disease and other birth defects were noticed among 117 children. This resulted in a multimillion dollar suit against the Fairchild Camera and Instruments Corporation and the waste company.

It must be remembered that many ailments caused by toxic chemicals, such as dioxin, lead to cancers and genetic defects that may not show up for decades or several generations. In a belated attempt to make good, the Environmental Protection Agency spent $36.7 million to buy the entire town of Times Beach, Missouri, a town that has disappeared. It is beyond the scope of this book to investigate the corruption in the EPA. But *even according to the highly suspect figures of the EPA, ninety percent of the eighty-eight-billion-pound toxic wastes annually are "disposed of improperly"* (Newsweek, 22 August 1982).

The problem is not uniquely American, but the lack of will to come to grips with it is. As Rita Lavelle, a former high official in the Environmental Protection Agency said in May 1982: "It is not the responsibility of regulatory agencies to create or change economic incentives: we have to leave the marketplace alone." In West Germany, by contrast, eighty-five percent of all hazardous wastes are detoxified by treating them with mutant bacteria, physical pressure, and chemical or biological neutralizers.

The area around Seveso in Italy suffered serious toxic waste poisoning in 1976 and had to be abandoned. Now eight years later, biological neutralizers have done their work, and people are slowly being permitted to move back.

Destruction of natural resources may result from apparently benign environmental interference. In the early sixties I was involved in the Aswan Dam Building Project. One of the largest structures of its kind, the Aswan Dam project was specifically designed to provide a multitude of socioeconomic benefits. There would be, minimally, a twenty-five percent increase in cultivated land, and electrical output would double. Unfortunately, things did not work out like that. Lake Nasser (part of the Aswan development) retains most of the silt on which the rich Nile Delta farmland depends. The dam also impounds essential natural minerals needed by the ecological chain of marine life in the delta. Since Aswan first started to regulate the flow of the river in 1964, Egypt has suffered a loss of $35 million to its native sardine industry; as of the spring of 1969, there were reports that the delta shrimp fishery was also declining.

Professor Thayer Scudder of Cal Tech has reported similar results in the wake of damming up the Zambezi River in southern Africa. The designers of the dam had predicted that the loss of flood farmland would be offset by increasing fishery resources. In reality, the fish catch diminished immediately after the dam was completed, and, soon after, the lakeshore bred hordes of tsetse flies, which infected native livestock and nearly aborted cattle production.

Slowly some lessons are being learned. One plan that was mercifully never put into practice concerned the Amazon basin. Herman Kahn's Hudson Institute proposed early in 1971 that an inland sea, nearly the size of all of western Europe, be created in the center of South America. A study by the World-Watch Institute clearly demonstrated that the building of the Amazon inland sea would have destroyed one of the last large primal forests left and changed the climate of the entire southern hemisphere. I am delighted that the maniac pipe-dream of the Hudson Institute for Brazil and Colombia has finally been abandoned.

But in spite of this lesson learned, U.S. Army engineers built a series of small dams nearly across the entire northern boundary of the Everglades National Wildlife Refuge in Florida. This work was done throughout the seventies in order to irrigate the area and to provide land suitable for cattle grazing (notoriously the least efficient use of land), to appease the cattle-raisers' lobby. The result: the Everglades are drying up, wildlife is being destroyed, soil is becoming salinated, and parts of southern Florida are taking on the characteristics of a desert. And now, in the early eighties, there is still a chance that a new jetport (with its high decibel levels and pollutants) will be constructed at the southern edge of the Everglades.

We tend to overlook the fact that nearly all major disfigurements of the earth have been created by mankind. The impoverished lands of Greece, Spain, and India, the man-made deserts of Australia and New Zealand, the treeless plains of China and Mongolia, and the deserts of North Africa, the Mediterranean basin, and Chile all attest to the fact that *where there is a desert, man has been at work.* This is richly documented in Ritchie Calder's *After the Seventh Day.* Compare maps of the United States that cover the period from 1596 to the present. The earliest maps, prepared by Spanish Catholic missionaries, are of the Southwest. The desert— which now covers parts of nine states—hardly existed at all. But as trees were cut down indiscriminately, as water runoff increased, as an estimated 200 million buffalo were eradicated, as topsoil was washed away each spring, the Dust Bowls of 1830 and 1930 were created, and the deserts kept growing. The only thing that has changed is the pace of change itself. It took Alexander the Great and other conquerors nearly 1,500 years to turn Arabia and Palestine (land of milk and honey) into a desert. A mere 300 years sufficed for the American desert. And more "know-how" has succeeded, through the use of defoliation, napalm, and the diversions of rivers and streams, in altering the ecological cycle of the southern part of Vietnam in five years in such a manner that the country may become a permanent semidesert.

The tropical rain forest—that ecologically important green belt that lies between the Tropic of Cancer and the Tropic of Capricorn—is disappearing in chunks that are the size of France. Many botanists feel that mankind's future may be falling at the same rate as the trees. As the forests are destroyed, mankind may find it more and more difficult to feed itself. The tides may be altered, and the atmosphere polluted with poisonous fumes. A major energy source could die without being used, and weather cycles could change for the worse.

One scientist writes: "As technology develops ways to utilize the vast amounts of solar energy stored in tropical forest plants each day, these forests could generate as much energy in the form of methanol and other fuels, as almost half the world's energy consumption from all sources in 1970" (Norman Myers, *The Sinking Ark*).

One percent of the world's remaining tropical forests is destroyed every year—more than twenty-five percent of the lush Amazon basin has been disturbed—tropical Asia and Africa have suffered even more.

Not saving the forests in time is resulting in an ecological time-bomb. For not only are these forests the "green lungs" of the planet, they can also be replanted with fruit and nut trees that could add immeasurably to the world's food supplies.

Two men have developed a plan that might mark the beginning of the road back from ecological disaster. John Maurice (a veteran of the Royal Air Force), who has spent more than half his life with applied plant genetics, and James Aronson (another experienced plant geneticist) are planning to develop a network of nurseries that would develop fast-flowering trees that can easily be transported to remote areas and be planted there. After years of grafting, transplanting, more grafting, and using every genetic trick, these two botanists have grown several "ideal" trees: macadamia nut trees, mango, avocado, and other species. These weigh no more than two ounces in the nursery but are still hearty enough to reach maturity in *half* the normal time.

Aronson says that their breakthrough means that trees can be shipped by the thousands, each wrapped in a cigar-sized tube that contains a life-support system providing enough food and moisture for weeks. In other words: an entire infant forest could be put on the back of a burro!

Maurice's nursery is already exporting trees to Ethiopia, Tanzania, and other African states, where they arrive in excellent shape and ready for planting. Their work is now sponsored by Peru and the Missouri Botanical Garden. Their research is taking them to Mexico, Central America, South America, Hawaii, the Philippines, Indonesia, and Malaysia.

The design elegance of their reforestation work lies in its transportability. "It used to be you had to put a tree in a tin can," Aronson and Maurice say, "with a lot of soil around the roots. It might weigh twenty pounds, which is all right if you are taking it home in the back of a station wagon but is a different story if you have to put millions in an airplane."

In 1983 radio and television news programs, as well as newspapers and magazines, began to explore the "greenhouse effect." This dangerous change in the earth's climate is now modulating all our futures. The increase of pollutants in the air, created by automobile emissions and the increasingly widespread use of fossil fuels, is simultaneously warming the earth's surface and keeping most of this heat from being vented off into space. Foreseeable results include the increase of temperatures by an average of 9 degrees Fahrenheit in the northern hemisphere by the year 2040, the partial melting of polar ice caps leading to a rise in sea levels by up to forty feet, and macro and microclimatic changes affecting agriculture globally.

Although some of these changes seem profoundly fixed by now, there are parts of the problem that can be addressed through designed solutions.

One source of worldwide pollution that demands immediate design attention is the automobile. As early as thirteen years ago, Los Angeles was the first place in which the total acreage used for roads and parking places *exceeded* the amount of space given over to homes and parks. This may be the beginning of a frightening trend. Obviously, the automobile is highly inefficient in many ways; what is needed is a *designed* solution.

It would be naive and dangerous to argue for the total elimination of the automobile. A carless world may be nice to contemplate from an ivory tower, but, in large farming areas that are sparsely settled, it is an impossibility. Whether in Saskatchewan, Canada; or the Dakotas, Texas, or Wyoming in the United States; the outback farms of Queensland and New South Wales in Australia; Brazil; or the farming plains of eastern Poland, the automobile is an important tool, often the only link to services and other people.

But what *kind* of a car? With three oil crises behind us we have become accustomed to driving smaller, more fuel-efficient cars. But—as in so many other areas of living—we still wear a protective set of blinders in North America and care little and know even less about what goes on in the rest of the world right now.

We have accustomed ourselves to drive small cars made by Honda and eagerly swap miles per gallon figures with our less adventurous neighbors. In Japan, however, Honda is selling a car that gets seventy mpg in city driving conditions. This is the Honda 1983 *City*—a car unavailable in North America. Because of looming import quotas the Japanese are now exporting larger, more expensive, and less fuel-efficient cars to the United States (*All Things Considered*, 22 April 1983).

The "Shopper" do-it-yourself car. Made in West Germany. Advertising photograph by "Shopper."

Renault's *Vista* (*Vehicule econome de systemes et technologie avances*) gets ninety-four mpg and seats four passengers plus their luggage. This car is also unavailable in North America (*Design*, London, No. 409, January 1983).

A German firm is manufacturing a do-it-yourself car that gets sixty mpg and can be built by two people in one weekend, (*The Shopper*, made by Automobilwerk Shopper, G.M.B.H., in West Berlin).

But there are even more unusual experimental vehicles that have been tried and tested. Japan's Nichilava Co. Ltd. has developed a pedal-powered vehicle for short-distance travel. A four-wheel cycle enclosed in a carlike cabin, it provides greater stability than a bicycle and protects riders from the elements. It is designed to carry an adult plus packages or a child, will reach eighteen mph, and roll up a ten-degree incline with less effort than it would take to walk. Like a car it comes equipped with headlights, horn, rearview mirror, and flashers—it sells for $450.

Pedal car. Drawing by Smit Vajaramant.

In December 1982, Solar Trek, a solar-powered automobile, was driven from Perth to Sydney, roughly the distance of Philadelphia–San Diego (3500 miles). This experimental vehicle uses a one-horsepower DC electric motor powered by two normal car batteries. The batteries are constantly charged by 720 photovoltaic cells. The entire trip was trouble free, with the exception of flat tires. (*Design World*, Australia, No. 1, March 1983.)

Most imported cars are not only smaller, safer, more economical, and more innovative in design and engineering than

Electrivan: By 1968 there were more than 45,000 electrically propelled vehicles on the roads in Britain, more than anywhere else in the world. Without them and their extremely low running costs, Britons would no longer enjoy home milk delivery, garbage collection, ambulances, or street maintenance. The post office began using them some years back. Crompton Leyland Electricars have introduced this small and spunky van. It is 9 feet long and has all the usual advantages of an electric: no clutch, gearbox, radiator or oiliness, which give low maintenance cost, plus a 20-foot turning circle and built-in charger. It can do 33 mph and will carry 500 pounds. It is guaranteed for 10,000 miles or one year. Courtesy: The Council of Industrial Design, England. There seems little need for the controversy as to whether electric cars are feasible—thousands have been on the road for years!

U.S. cars, they are more carefully made. Quality control tends to be tighter at the factory. Nearly half of the states in the United States plan to sue the General Motors Corporation for installing Chevrolet engines in more expensive cars without advising customers (*Kansas City Star*, 16 October 1978).

If we envision the "car of the future," we can make fairly accurate guesses. We can assume that the typical automobile of the future (1985–2000) will be about the size of a Honda Civic. It will carry four adults in some comfort with an easy cruising speed of fifty-five mph and a top speed of about ninety mph. It will be a three-door hatchback but will be available in a slightly longer ("station wagon") version. In both models, rear seats will fold down and will be entirely removable.

The power-plant will be a laterally placed four-cylinder air-cooled aluminum block engine (as in Britain's Mini-Cooper of the sixties), making even more cargo and passenger space available. The engine will be a "clean" type, using *no* catalyst (as in the Honda CVCC and some Volvos). It will be front-wheel driven but also available in a four-wheel drive option (like the Subaru). In normal driving it will get 75–100 mpg (like Honda's *City* and Renault's *Vista*). All engine parts will be clearly labeled (as in the Subaru) for easier understanding. All major body parts will be made of fiberglass to reduce weight. Such fiberglass bodies are now standard on many custom cars and are being experimented with in Detroit, Japan, Sweden, and Germany for production models. The roof will be a sliding solar panel that will provide up to thirty percent of all energy. (This panel and conversion job is *now* available for the Honda, Subaru, and Rabbit in California.) Instrument readouts will also give pollution factors, mpg ratios, and a "gasoline consumer" gauge. (All this instrumentation is *presently* available from Germany and Sweden.) The fuel-injection and electronic ignition system will make immediate winter starts possible; this will be further helped by a permanently installed block-heater (now available and compulsory in most Canadian provinces). An electronic sensor will shut off idling engines after three minutes to prevent air pollution, especially in the winter (this feature is now available from Sweden). The car body will have a total wraparound bumper designed for high-impact absorption (similar to Scandia-Saab's cellular rubberized plastic honeycomb bumper). Seats will be ergonomically and orthopedically designed (as in Porsche and Mercedes-Benz). The car will have a six-speed manual transmission with electric overdrive. The driver's door will open in the opposite direction of most standard car doors: *backward* (like the Citroen 2CV), which will provide greater safety in entering or leaving the vehicle, as well as helping the elderly or handicapped. The passenger's door will *slide* (like the VW Microbus). A distress signaling device, operating on a police band, will become part of the radio system. Paint will be permanently protected against salt damage for ten years (as in the 1983 Porsche).

It's easy to go on and on, projecting the ideal car. But the important point is clear: a sensitive reading of the description will show that *such a car can be brought into existence right now, using existing off-the-shelf hardware!* This points to an important fact about design: often, vital and useful design concepts exist for several years (sometimes decades) before they are synthesized into a whole that makes optimal use of each concept.

The answer to worldwide transportation needs must inevitably lie in a complete rethinking of *transportation as a system*, as well as rethinking each component of that system. Some possible guidelines for the future already exist!

It has been a century since a monorail rapid-transport system was first put into daily operation at Wuppertal in Germany. The system has proved itself to be fast and clean and intrudes only minimally on the physical and visual environment. Surely, monorail systems could help ease traffic congestion in many of our large city-smears.

We are told that the average individual in the Western world values his personal and individual transportation device, and that, especially in the United States, the family automobile has become surrounded by the whole cluster of ideas—self-reliance, independence, and mobility—that once surrounded Old Paint in the days of the wild and woolly West. We have seen the automobile as a sort of super horse and blind ourselves to its drawbacks. But once we begin to consider the car as merely *one* link in a total transport system, alternative solutions can easily be found.

The average American will drive the car a distance of sixty feet around the corner just to mail a letter or drive one or two miles, once a week, to do the marketing. He or she may drive (quite alone in this huge steel coffin) a round trip of some forty miles daily to get to work. The entire family may pile into the car (two or three times a year) to visit Grandma 300 miles away. We know that at any time we can jump into a car and, by driving long hours, reach California from New York in a mere five days: this is rarely done; instead we fly and rent a car in California.

Now let us analyse this as a system. Distances of more than 500 miles can be best traversed by airplanes. Distances of between fifty and 500 miles are more efficiently served by railroads, buses, monorail systems and will be better served by other methods yet to be developed by design teams.

Many devices now exist for traveling distances of less than fifty miles, some of which have not been sufficiently exploited. New ones will be evolved by design teams. A partial listing in rising order of complexity would begin with walking. People in the United States walk a great deal more than they used to twenty or even ten years ago, so there is something ludicrous about millions of Americans solemnly jogging on a $2,995 "magic carpet" electric treadmill for ten minutes every night (*Products That Think*, no. 12, 1983). Roller skates may sound ridiculous and can be dangerous; nonetheless they are already in use in large storage facilities and factories where they don't intermix with cars. Nonpowered push scooters give excellent mobility to travelers traversing long arrival halls at Kasturp International Airport outside Copenhagen and cost 1/200 as much as the so-called people-movers that are used in other airports.

An electrically powered aluminum scooter, weighing eighteen pounds and, when folded, no larger than a bathroom scale, with a cruising range of fifteen miles, was designed and tested by an industrial design student in Chicago several years ago. This device, which would give excellent mobility without pollution or congestion in downtown areas and on large college campuses, has never been built commercially. It would allow people to get from place to place on a platform measuring nine by fifteen inches. Our industrial design student in Chicago worked alone for a period of seven months and spent a total of only $425 developing his electric, handbag-sized miniscooter. Given the $6 billion General Motors alone spends for corporate research and development each year, as well as the facilities and design talent available, we can readily see that this excellent scooter is by no means the last word in personal transportation.

As of December 1983, such a scooter, redesigned in Germany, is now also available in the United States for $995. We can expect prices to drop as mass production and mass sales reduce costs (*Products That Think*, No. 12, Dec. 1983).

Bicycles are used for movement within the fifty-mile radius we have established, both in Denmark and the Low Countries. Many of these fold; some can be carried easily. Powered bicycles with miniature gasoline engines exist; small electric drive-assist systems could be devised easily. Some of the vehicles designed by my students, for exercise and sport by both normal and paraplegic children, may point the way to new ways of transport. Mopeds, powered scooters, and motorcycles can be left out of this discussion in their present form as they are prime polluters.

Some utopian concepts, such as moving sidewalks, must be rejected at this time because power is expended in a disastrously high ratio to value gained.

By joining three systems, all of them in existence right now, we can find at least one viable alternative to the downtown clutter and traffic problem. If we combine (1) a fleet of battery-driven miniature taxis similar to the 1950 Simca with (2) a transportation credit card and computer billing of users at the end of each month and (3) a one-way wristwatch-sized radio, we have the beginning of a rational downtown transportation system. The user could summon a minitaxi to his particular location with his radio (thus eliminating the biggest argument against public transport: a long walk in the rain and then a wait at the bus stop). The minitaxi could then take him to his specific location, again eliminating approximate destinations. Payment would be via credit card and billed monthly. Even with thousands of these minitaxis in downtown areas, more land (now given over to garages, parking lots, and service stations) would be liberated. Exhaust fumes would be eliminated. Larger parts of the streets could be given over to planting, parks, and walking space. At the end of the workday, users would be brought back to downtown monorail terminals and returned to their home destinations.

Those romantic souls who would still prefer to "shift their own gears" and feel the soft purr of a high-powered sports car at their command would find themselves in a position analogous to that of horseback riders today. At garages, located in a peripheral circle around larger cities, station wagons, trucks, or open sports cars could be rented for a few hours, or days, of country driving. However, such vehicles could not be brought into built-up areas or cities.

The foregoing scenario is highly speculative and in no way pretends to present *the* answer to urban transportation problems. It merely attempts to show one of many possible solutions and, at the same time, show how the designer and the design team are involved along every step of the way.

If we turn to man-made environments for living, the story is at least equally grave. Human beings and family units have become "components" to be stored away like carbon copies in the gigantic file cases that are today's tenements. When the cry of "urban renewal" is raised, the results are frequently less humane than the situation that originally gave cause for redesign. Thus, in a "renewed" ghetto area located in the southeastern part of Chicago, a series of more than thirty apartment buildings (each holding more than fifty family units) is strung out in a single four-mile-long chain, neatly placed between a twelve-lane superhighway (which cuts the development off neatly from the rest of the city) and, on the other side, a series of large manufacturing plants (with their perennially belching smokestacks) and a large municipal dump. In spite of all the old ghetto's faults, it did have a sense of community, and that has been destroyed completely.

The inhabitants have no park, green spaces, or even lone trees within walking distance. Each family is alienated from the rest; nights find them cowering in their cell-like apartments while the juvenile street gangs exchange gunfire down below. Crime is ever-present. The ghetto has been verticalized neatly and turned into a series of skyscrapers. Visually all the buildings are identical, a series of cement slabs into which have been carved an insufficient number of tiny windows. This area is also completely divorced from even the most basic shopping needs. A supermarket and a drugstore are located about 500 feet from the northernmost of the buildings, and public transport is lacking. An elderly woman living at the south end of the development has a five-mile walk (round trip) in order to do her shopping. A mother with small children is effectively removed from supervising her offspring for a period of nearly three hours when marketing. But the design of these barns for the storage of the poor is not all that different from similar developments for the well-to-do.

Years after building them, the federal government, in cooperation with local and state organizations, has finally decided to dynamite many of these housing developments, to the delight of their inhabitants and design critics (Peter Blake, *Form Follows Fiasco*, and Victor Papanek, *Design for Human Scale*).

Most designers (and not just in the areas of housing and community planning) also seem to have developed a set of blinkers. *This effectively keeps them from considering whether similar problems might not already have been solved intelligently somewhere else or at some other time.*

Say "Frank Lloyd Wright" to any shelter designer. He will immediately think of the Guggenheim Museum, Fallingwater, the Imperial Hotel in Tokyo, and some of the earlier Prairie Houses. He may even think of a certain mannerist, neo-Baroque interpenetration of space. But chances are that he will be totally unaware that Wright created an important "missing link" between individual homes and apartment dwellings.

In 1938 Frank Lloyd Wright designed the Sun Top Homes for Ardmore, Pennsylvania. Only one of the proposed four was actually built. It is really a cloverleaflike interpenetration of four individual homes. Each one consists of a one-and one-half-story living room and distributes a recreation room, bedrooms, kitchen, and so forth over a two-story area. Each individual quarter of the four-home construct is so defined that one is unaware of the other three units. The mechanical and plumbing core is in the center, but each individual unit has its own air-conditioning, plumbing, and lighting facilities, as well as its own kitchen garden and a recreational garden, screened through trees and plantings from the other units and from the street. The entire building was extremely low in cost and actually built (as a prototype) in 1941. In 1942 Mr. Wright further developed this concept for the Defense Housing

View of Frank Lloyd Wright's cloverleaf housing project that was to be built at Pittsfield, Massachusetts, in 1942. By permssion of the Frank Lloyd Wright Foundation. Copyright 1969 by Frank Lloyd Wright Foundation.

Cloverleaf housing plan. By permission of the Frank Lloyd Wright Foundation. Copyright 1969 by Frank Lloyd Wright Foundation.

Agency. One hundred of these cloverleaf homes (to house 400 families) were to be built at Pittsfield, Massachusetts. Incredible as it now sounds, both the Pennsylvania and Massachusetts legislatures agreed that it would be "wrong to give such a large job to a Wisconsin architect," so the projects were never built.

The original Sun Top Homes prototype still stands at Ardmore, Pennsylvania, nearly half a century later, mute testimony to the shortsightedness of the government.

The mix of heavy manufacturing offices, light industry, private homes, apartmentlike shelters, clinics, day nurseries, schools and universities, sports arenas, recreational facilities, bicycle paths, access roads, forested areas, parking lots, shopping communities, and linkages to public transport and high-speed road networks that Frank Lloyd Wright designed in 1935 as Broadacre City, still marks a high point of humane planning. With local variations, Wright envisioned Broadacre City as eventually spanning the entire North American continent. Again, this is not to suggest that either Broadacre City or the Ardmore Development is the ideal answer.

Tapiola, near Helsinki, is known as *the* prototypal housing development to designers. Together with Broadacre City and the Ardmore development they constitute only partial solutions, but solutions that are more concerned with the quality of life and human dignity than the nearly 30 million rabbit hutches that have been built for human habitation since.

According to Frank Lloyd Wright, *scale* was the greatest threat to social meaning. As early as the forties he wrote: "*Little* forms, *little* homes for industry, *little* factories, *little* schools, a *little* university going to the people mostly by way of their interest . . . *little* laboratories . . ." (Wright's italics.)

The whole concept of human scale has gone awry, not only with homes but in other areas as well. One would expect a system motivated only by self-interest and private profit making at least to spend some care in constructing its shopping places. This is not so, with notable exceptions. One such exception is *Strøget*, a "walking street" of shops in downtown Copenhagen, which is constructed for leisurely strolling and impulse buying. Two segments of it, *Frederiksberggade* and *Myhgade*, are together approximately 400 feet long and contain more than 180 shops. In my native Vienna the Kärntnerstrasse and, as of 1983, nearly all of the inner city, has become a pedestrian area.

In a contemporary American shopping center, a distance of 400 feet will frequently separate the entrances of two stores: the supermarket and, say, the drugstore. The intervening space consists of empty windows, bereft of displays, monotonous and uninteresting. Usually neither landscaping nor windbreaks is provided. The hot sun beats down mercilessly on the four acres of concrete in the summer; wind-whipped snow piles up in car-high drifts throughout the winter. Small wonder that, after finishing their shopping at the supermarket, people will walk back to their automobiles and drive 400 feet to the drugstore. There is nothing in the environment that prompts going for a stroll; it has been designed for the car alone. Most shopping plazas in the United States consist of a thin line of stores arranged along three sides of a huge square, the center of which is a parking lot. The large open side fronts on a superhighway. This may make shopping "efficient," but it also makes it something less than satisfying.

A notable exception is the Plaza Shopping Area in Kansas City, Missouri. Here distances are walkable; statuary, scores of fountains, planting areas, and benches compete for the attention of the casual stroller. A true street life has been retained. Buildings are, for the most part, no taller than three floors and embellished with tiles and sculpture. Why so human in scale? The Plaza was planned and built in 1923.

The problem of scale is especially dramatic in our suburbs and exurbs, which have become vast dormitory towns with a multiplicity of problems. Increasingly factories have moved away from large cities: cheap labor sources and large tax writeoffs have induced them to move to so-called Industrial Parks. As more factories congregate within each of these so-called park sites, clusters of service industries, shops, and tract housing have sprung up—without any plan, reason, or projection for future development. Transportation networks soon link these production centers to the old cities, and a whole new subculture of minor assembly plants, repair shops, and storage plants develops in the no man's land between city suburbs and satellite industrial centers. Without any rational plan, the city has just grown in area by a factor of twenty or thirty.

Even if we are willing to accept the psychological, social, and physical hazards of polluting our environment, there are other more immediate and weighty reasons for putting a stop to it. Recent information from weather satellites in space and the statistics provided to us by meteorological observation stations clearly point to a major change: it seems that a large area of permanently polluted warm air will actually *attract* bad weather. In the American Midwest and East Coast especially, more major storms, droughts, snowfalls, blizzards, and tornadoes have, over the last twenty years, hit large suburban centers. This phenomenon (by increasing the number of target areas on the world's surface) may in time have lasting climatic effects. This is the curse of scale, when not attended to. As Julian Huxley remarked: "Simply magnify an object without changing its shape, and, without meaning to, you have changed *all* its properties."

The most basic study of system design shows that a system made up of component parts will change eventually as each part is changed. By looking at some of the subsystems, we can locate some of the factors contributing to distortion. Hospitals and mental institutions are usually designed with greater care than other interior spaces. Architects, interior architects, and medical specialists routinely cooperate in the planning. In the floor plan, the rest-and-recuperation wing of a mental hospital will be well arranged for conversational grouping, relaxation, and games. But, once the wing is put into operation, hospital personnel quickly rearrange all seating. Chairs now are placed primly, neatly, and symmetrically. This has the virtue of bolstering the sense of security of the hospital personnel, cuts down the time needed to sweep and wash floors, and makes it far simpler for refreshment carts to be wheeled through the room. This furniture placement, however, creates barriers to interaction among patients and in some cases may help to drive them into autistic or catatonic states. The placement of chairs on the four sides of each pillar, facing in four different directions, makes conversation difficult for people seated adjacently and completely shuts off conversation with anyone else.

This example illustrates a cardinal error among designers: the failure to go back from time to time and see how the work has been implemented. To my knowledge, hospital or mental patients have never been "client-group representatives" working with a design team. Similar observations can be documented regarding prison populations, the arrangement of living spaces for military personnel, university students in dormitories, and other captive groups.

Edward T. Hall, in his studies of proximeters and human spacing, has shown that types and sizes of seating units used in contemporary airport terminals so strongly violate Western concepts of spacing that fully one-third of them are empty at any given time. This holds true even when the building is unusually crowded: many people prefer standing or pacing to being brought into too close proximity with strangers. Most Americans visiting Europe or Latin America demonstrate signs of minor strain when asked to share a restaurant table with strangers. And seldom has Thorstein Veblen's theory of conspicuous consumption been carried further than in the endless vestibules of motion-picture palaces, tenanted with gilt and scarlet chairs in which no one ever sits, or in similarly appointed waiting rooms to corporate offices (where teak and leather, steel and glass have replaced the simpering charm of fake French Empire).

Obviously, in each of these cases design decisions *have* been made, unfortunately the wrong ones. In each case the designer has "worked up" a combination between his personal aesthetic, the desires of his clients, and whatever has been considered good taste at the consumer level. By working with a design team, checking conclusions through our six-sided function complex, and working directly with members of the user group, such misdesign could be avoided.

We are beginning to understand that the main challenge for our society no longer lies in the production of goods. Rather, we have to make choices that deal with "how good?" instead of "how much?" But the changes, and our awareness of these changes, are becoming so highly accelerated that trying to make sense of change itself will become our basic industry. Moral, aesthetic, and ethical values will evolve along with the choices to which they will be applied. We may still consider religion, sex, morality, the family structure, or medical research to be remote from technology and design. But the margin is narrowing fast. With all these changes, the designer (as part of the multidisciplinary problem-solving team) can and must involve himself. He may *choose* to do so for humanitarian reasons. Regardless of this, he will be *forced* to do so by the simple desire for survival within the not-too-distant future. When you try to tell people in the West that

within a very short time millions may die of hunger, they simply do not hear. They give a little nervous laugh; embar-
rassed, they change the subject. But in many places in the
developing countries, thousands of bodies are being removed
by the sanitation squads each morning.

There was a time, only twenty years ago, when, as William
Paddock put it, "The stork passed the plough." And now people are increasing faster than the means of feeding them. Less
food is available per person in the world today than during
the Depression fifty years ago.

Stringent population control measures in China, India,
Thailand, and Indonesia are now finally beginning to halt this
trend. In Europe and the United States, population figures are
now arrested *below* replacement levels. But there are still millions that starve—and this must focus our attention on food.

Food production and the development of new food sources
have been of no interest to the design profession at all. Yet
designers *are* involved, like it or not, as human beings. All the
seeming concern in the northern half of the globe over the
population growth of the world's poor only thinly veils violent
and escapist feelings. It is no longer considered nice to be a
racist. But the specific words many of us use when we talk
about the people in developing countries, slums, and ghettoes
are bad. Their populations "explode," we say. They are a
"population bomb." They "breed like flies." We talk about
"uncontrolled fertility" and how we must "teach them to control population," and we talk (especially regarding Africa,
Asia, and Latin America) about "breeding swarms." Such
words reflect our thinking. And such thinking is our inheri-
tance of racism, prejudice, and colonialism. When we begin
to send "population control teams" to some country to "help,"
it is neocolonialism at its worst. Each country is responsible
for its own population.

Naturally, families should not have more children than they
can raise decently. *But birth-control measures prove effective
only after the living standards of the underprivileged have
been raised.* People begin to take interest in limiting the size

of their families only *after* they are secure, have achieved human dignity and purpose, and are no longer beset by the anxiety and fears of hunger, poverty, ignorance, and disease. A large number of children born are no more than genetic and economic insurance for people faced with the certainty of death for many of their children. For hundreds of years we assumed what we were pleased to consider laziness, languor, reduced energy, mental retardation, short life spans, and dullness to be racial characteristics in many underdeveloped countries. Today we know these are not races of lazy men; they are people chronically undernourished, to the point where they are no longer energetic and hopeful. Malnutrition causes high infant death rates, and often families have been made very large in the hopes of somehow compensating for this. But hunger and mental retardation go on, hand in hand.

> The brain grows more rapidly than the rest of the body, its cells proliferating so quickly that by the time a child is four, the circumference of its head is 90 percent as large as it ever will be. . . . This proliferation is almost entirely dependent on protein synthesis, which cannot take place in the absence of the essential amino acids which must be derived from food. (*Bioscience*, April 1967)

Around 1800 there were an estimated 180 million inhabitants in Europe. The amount of people had increased to 450 million around 1900. But this fantastically increased population had a much higher living standard, ate better, dressed better, and lived longer than their own great-grandparents. The Malthusian doctrine says food can *never* keep up with population growth. But this simple formula has just two factors: soil and population. Science, design, planning, research are completely left out. Malthus's theories may be applicable to animals (like laboratory rats), but the *one* function that is uniquely human, comprehensive anticipatory thinking and planning, changes his equation drastically. Only 100 years ago in the United States, a huge farm population (almost seventy-five percent of the people) struggled desperately to keep a population of eighty-five million people from hunger. Today, *only eight percent of the population is still farming*, the population has surpassed the 230-million mark, and the biggest agricultural problem is what to do with megatons of food surplus each year! Agricultural irrigation, scientific crop rotation, biological pest control, conservation, reforestation, selective breeding of stock animals—these are the fruits of science that modify mechanistic Malthusian thinking.

Producing basic agricultural implements for underdeveloped areas of the world brings less profit to industry than producing glittering consumer gadgets for abundant societies. Designing agricultural systems and tools is not thought of as a "glory job" or "fun" by most designers: how much more rewarding to scale down a 1931 Mercedes SS for fiberglass production than to improve a plough for Pakistan!

High-technology countries—especially the United States—live under the mistaken idea that, since they are the world's largest producers of food and have the most mechanized agriculture, this will guarantee the highest yield per acre. This is not true. Smaller countries, trying to reduce money for food imports, achieve significantly higher yields per acre than the United States. This is especially true of England, Austria, Holland, Belgium, and Japan. The *FAO Production Yearbook* (1977) reports that 1,660 pounds of grain per acre are achieved on U.S. wheat farms. The figure for Holland is 5,107 per acre. High-tech U.S. rice yields average 4,434 pounds per acre. Japan, with labor-intensive methods, averages 5,200 pounds per acre; Spain, 5,607. England and Belgium both produce more than 100,000 pounds of tomatoes per acre—this is three times the average of the United States. These high yields abroad are achieved by keeping farms small and by being labor intensive. Therefore the argument about the need for bigger and better farm machinery is not correct. What *is* needed is better small-scale agricultural machinery.

All five producers of large farm machinery in North America are hovering on the brink of bankruptcy—some others have already disappeared. The farmers who have millions of dollars of borrowed money invested in farm equipment that is too large in scale and too expensive to maintain and repair are seeing their farms repossessed.

In the early seventies my design studio developed the concept of a series of farm tractors and mechanized ploughs with power ranges between 1/2 horsepower and 24 horsepower. Presenting these ideas to the Big Seven farm machinery manufacturers, we were gently ushered out of their offices while their design directors tried to suppress their unbelieving giggles. We had explained that our tractor would perform in three separate areas:

1. It would be a highly profitable export item to developing countries, making the companies more competitive in the global marketplace.
2. It might be the one saving tool to maintain subsistence farms in the Appalachians, the South, northern New Mexico, and other marginal farmland in the Midwest and Pacific Northwest, and thus might reverse the trend of family farm collapse.
3. Our human scale "walking tractor" might be useful in part-time farming in suburbs, exurbs, or in difficult terrain.

But corporate intelligence (a contradiction in terms?) was not swayed. Now, ten years later, the Chinese People's Republic has developed a very similar "walking tractor." It comes in 1/2-, 3-, and 12-horsepower models. Shown is their top-of-the-line model, which has become the best-selling agricultural tool in the world. (It should be remembered that nearly three-quarters of the ploughs in the world are pulled by one woman power—considerably less than 1/2 horsepower.)

Fertilization and pesticides and their influence on the environment have been discussed elsewhere. But it is in the area

FOR SALE

**TWO WHEEL TRACTORS, MODEL "DONG FENG" 12 H.P.
MADE IN THE PEOPLE'S REPUBLIC OF CHINA – AVAILABLE
WITH ASSORTED ATTACHING IMPLEMENTS. IMMEDIATE
DELIVERY ! ! PRICE:- K1380.00 AND ONE TONNE TRAILER,
K300.00 (optional)**

AVAILABLE FROM:-

ANISA COMMODITY TRADERS PTY. LTD
RING LAE 42 3924 BHs FOR DETAILS

The "Dong-Feng" tractor. Advertisement courtesy: *The Lae News,*
Papua New Guinea.

of preservation and processing of foods that designers could
make a major contribution.

Food losses after harvest run as high as 80 percent in the
diet deficient countries, due largely to poor storage and processing. Microorganisms, insects and rodents are the main
cause of food loss after harvest. Rats consume 16 times more
food than humans per body weight; in India rats eat 30% of
stored grains; in some countries as much as 60%. One-third
of all harvested cereals in Africa is lost to rodents. Because of
poor and outdated equipment, lack of refrigeration and inefficient transport, 50% of marketed fruits and vegetables are
lost in the hungry nations, where most perishables must be
eaten within 24 hours of harvest.

In the 1970 edition of this book we showed a refrigerator-like bulk-food storage cooler. Designed by James Hennessey and myself, several years of field testing showed it to be not effective enough under tropical conditions. Since then I have developed a solar-powered version, run on lithium bromide, which works excellently and should make food storage easier in many poor countries.

It is criminal that design for agriculture forms not even a small part of any design curriculum taught at any school! Instead of addressing themselves to such environmental needs, design schools are making a concerted effort to teach design for settings far more exotic.

Design schools involve their students in competitions for housing and working environments on the ocean floor. The heavy publicity surrounding such an endeavor was nearly drowned out by another program, which dealt with the design of an entertainment center to be built on the moon. There is little doubt that soon men will have to harvest the protein-rich fields that are the world's oceans. Nor will it be long before we drill for minerals and oil on ocean floors and farm the fish and algae of the seas. And certainly soon mankind will look to the stars while living in semipermanent, domed

Solar-powered bulk-food cooler. Developed by the author and David Pennington.

settlements on the moon. But the necessities of today cannot be neglected for the expediencies of some uncertain tomorrow. Design competitions like the two mentioned are assigned because they are more glamorous, "glory jobs," more *fun* than coming to grips with real problems. It is also in the interest of the Establishment to provide science-fiction routes of escape for the young, lest they became aware of the harshness of that which is real.

Such design exercises, by exposing students to unfamiliar surroundings, also encourage new and creative responses, as we have seen in Chapters Seven and Eight. But *real* areas of need exist that are just as strange and unfamiliar to most students.

Design will be needed when man establishes himself on our ocean floors and on planets circling distant suns. But man's leap to the stars and his life beneath the seas is heavily conditioned by the environment we create here and now. There is something wrong when young people are less familiar with life on a southern Appalachian farm than with the construction of a gambling casino on Mars. They are taught a lie when they find themselves more at ease with atmospheric pressures in the Mindanao Deep than with atmospheric pollution over Detroit.

11

The Neon Blackboard:

Design Education and Design Teams

Telling lies to the young is wrong.
Proving to them that lies are true is wrong.
The young know what you mean. The young are people.
Tell them the difficulties can't be counted,
And let them see not only what will be
But see with clarity these present times.

YEVGENY YEVTUSHENKO

Education for designers (like nearly all education) is based on learning skills, nourishing talents, understanding the concepts and theories that inform the field, and, finally, acquiring a philosophy. It is unfortunate that our design schools proceed from wrong assumptions. The skills we teach are too often related to processes and working methods of an age that has ended. The philosophy is an equal mixture of self-indulgent and self-expressive bohemian individualism and a materialism both profit oriented and brutal. The method of teaching and transmitting this biased information is more than half a century out of date.

In 1929 Albert Langen Verlag of Munich published the book *Von Material zu Architektur* by László Moholy-Nagy as Volume 14 of the Bauhaus books. Moholy-Nagy tried to find new ways of involving young people with the interfaces between technology and design, design and the crafts, design and art. Possibly his most important idea was to have students experiment directly with tools, machines, and materials. When in 1938 Moholy-Nagy started the New Bauhaus (later the Institute of Design) in Chicago, the book was republished (by Norton) under the title *The New Vision*. An expanded and lavishly illustrated rehash was brought out shortly after his death under the title *Vision in Motion* in 1947. And now, almost forty years later, this 1947 rehash of a 1938 translation of a 1929 book describing design experiments carried on in 1919 still forms the introductory course of basic design curricula at nearly all architectural and design schools. Experiment turned into tradition marches stultifyingly into the last decades of the century. Can we wonder that students are bored? Surely a student entering a design school or university in September of 1984 must be educated to operate effectively in a professional world *starting* in 1989, and foreseeably he will reach the height of his professional competence sometime around the year 2009.

Playing with bandsaws or electric drills makes no sense for students today, nearly seventy years after the Bauhaus began—they are familiar with them. It is holography, microprocessors, computers, laser technology, and other tools at the leading edge of technology that can provide this learning function now.

Learning must be an ecstatic experience, as George B. Leonard maintains in *Education and Ecstasy*. At its best learning to drive a car is ecstasy (as any sixteen-year-old will tell you). To drive an automobile demands a fantastic combination of motor coordination, physiological, and psychological skills. Watch the thousands driving along the Los Angeles Freeway at 5 P.M. any day. People control two tons of steel and machinery, hurtling along at better than 55 miles per hour, with the distances between cars to be measured in inches. It is an impressive performance. It is a *learned* skill. And it just possibly may be the most highly structured non-instinctual activity these drivers have in their entire lives. They drive superbly; the clue to their performance lies in the original method of learning how to drive. For to learn is to change. Education is a process in which the environment changes the learner, and the learner changes the environment. In other words, both are *interactive*. Both learning driver and car, as well as road system, other cars, and the teacher, are locked into a self-regenerating system in which each slight perfection of every slight skill is immediately rewarded or positively reinforced. To return to George B. Leonard:

> No environment can strongly affect a person unless it is strongly interactive. To be interactive, the environment must be responsive, that is, must provide relevant feedback to the learner. For the feedback to be relevant, it must meet the learner *where he is*, then program (that is, change in appropriate steps at appropriate times) as he changes. The learner changes (that is, is educated) through his responses to the environment.

This constitutes a scale model of how mankind as a whole has learned to live. For through millions of years man was a hunter, a fisherman, a sailor-navigator. As a hunter, he roamed earth as a member of a small hunting party—a cross-disciplinary team, in a way. He evolved early (but elegantly functional) tools: evidence from Choukoutien in China shows that Peking Man (*Pithecanthropus pekinensis*) fashioned stone tools long before Homo sapiens appeared on earth and used fire as well.

Man as a hunter-fisherman-sailor was a nonspecialist or a generalist, whose brain furnished him with that social understanding and control of casual impulses needed in a hunting group or society. We are told that even language may have evolved in answer to group need in the hunting party.

As hunter, man was highly successful. Equipped with spear-thrower, slingshot, bow, and knives superbly crafted of obsidian, horn, or bone, he spread from Siberia to Spain and from the ice cliffs of Afghanistan to Mesopotamia. And adventuresome early hunters followed bison and mammoth across the frozen Bering Strait into North America, where they settled the Great Plains nearly 15,000 years ago. They were Homo sapiens, and they were hunters. *Farmers would never have survived.*

The art works of the Upper Paleolithic attest to a fairly leisurely existence. Such sculptures as the *Willendorf Venus* and the *Venus of Lespugue,* which originated in the Neanderthal in Bavaria and central France 35,000 years ago, and the cave paintings of Lascaux and Altamira provide evidence of significant amounts of leisure time. Whether or not these art productions were inspired by religious considerations is immaterial. The point is that nonspecialized hunters had lengthy rest periods in which to exercise their creative abilities.

I am not suggesting the hunter as a noble savage à la Rousseau. Compared with his farmer-descendant of the Neolithic, he may have been a rough, nearly savage fellow. Yet as we study Paleolithic archaeology or read about and live with the disappearing tribes still essentially Paleolithic today (the Bushman of the Kalahari, the Australian aborigine, or some of the Eskimo), we see much that is innovative, ingenious, and admirable.

To quote from Nigel Calder's *The Environment Game:*

> How do you deal with an angry bull elephant, when all you have is a sharpened stone? You nip aside, slip in behind, and cut the tendons of his heel. What can you do to lure a giraffe, the most timid of large animals? You play on its curiosity for bright objects by flashing a polished stone in its direction. The Bushmen, according to Laurens Van der Post, would use lions as hunting "dogs," letting them kill game and eat a little, before driving them off with fire. Franz Boas tells how Eskimo approach deer, two men together, one stooping behind like the back end of a pantomime horse, the other carrying his bow on his shoulders to resemble antlers and grunting like a deer. The despised Australian aborigine can "travel light" with only a

few wooden and stone implements and, by his knowledge of nature, survive indefinitely in the Great Sandy Desert. If we once let these echoes of our pre-history penetrate our sophisticated heads, they strike in us chords of excitement, if not of envy.

Traditionally we are taught to see farming as the prerequisite of civilization. An elaborate social life, we have been told, could not develop until man was freed from the daily chore of fishing or hunting. Since the seventies, however, this theory is being challenged by the view that early civilized settlements were based on highly organized food gathering rather than cultivation. The complex, structured societies of American Indians and the salmon-eaters of British Columbia were so well supplied with food that large settlements developed:

> Man's chief physical disadvantage as a hunter must have been the encumbrance of his family. The human infant is uniquely helpless and slow to mature. Accordingly, a fairly settled, well-defended domestic life was necessary from the outset. Women at home minding the children while the men were out hunting were well placed to develop arts like cooking, clothes-making, and pottery, to experiment with new foods, and to discover in their "gardens" the elementary principles of plant reproduction. Jacquetta Hawkes has remarked, "It is tempting to be convinced that the earliest Neolithic societies gave woman the highest status she has ever known." (*Pre-history*, UNESCO History of Mankind)

It was agriculture that made greater specialization not just possible but necessary. Mankind, heretofore dynamically moving through the environment as members of nonspecialized cross-disciplinary hunting parties, now settled down to a patient, millennia-long cultivation of the soil. Instead of learning through interaction with animals and rapidly changing environments, eons of boredom were substituted and tradition became elevated to wisdom. To be conservative was, and still is, the peasant's greatest virtue. New specialized classes began to emerge. Since natural disasters became major destructions in the social pattern of a settlement located permanently, zealous and vengeful gods had to be appeased through a priest class, which provided sacrifice and ritual. Weather changes, the time of the solstice, and other data had to be predicted, giving rise to astronomy, mathematics, and soil chemistry. Animal husbandry and the physics and engineering underlying mining and tool making or building also developed interspecialization. Records had to be kept, settlements had to be defended, so warrior classes began to appear. Man no longer stood and fought the surround alone, moving freely across the globe. Instead, territory became precious and war an extension of statecraft.

Most birds fly efficiently but find walking difficult. Fish swim beautifully and get along in their medium, but they can't walk and (with rare exceptions) can't survive on land. Man, by changing the environmental medium voluntarily—giving up forest, savannah, fishing stream, and ocean for arable farmland—had to lengthen his abilities, manufacture extensions to his hands in the form of tools, and become specialized. Buckminster Fuller has said that all living creatures are more specialized than man. Contrary to the highly specialized forms of life we find among fish, bird or insect, man has the unique ability to live in any environment.

For millions of years man's "little red schoolhouse" was earth itself. Mankind was taught to react and to behave by the environment, disasters, and predators. In early farming communities we tried to control catastrophes through religion and priestly craft, which later became organized yet highly specialized areas of knowledge. By driving us into ever-narrowing fields of specialization, schools and universities have made some of their greatest mistakes.

Modern technology (computers, automation, mass production, mass communication, high-speed travel) is giving mankind a chance to return to the interactive learning experience, the sensory awakening of the early hunter. Hydroponic farming, "fish-herding," and protein manufacture will also help.

Education can once again become relevant to a society of *generalists*, in other words, designer-planners. For the designer shapes the environments in which we all live, the tools we use. And from the more unpalatable manifestations of bad design, the design student cannot remain aloof for long.

The main trouble with design schools seems to be that they teach too much design and not enough about the ecological, social, economic, and political environment in which design takes place. It is impossible to teach anything *in vacuo*, least of all in a field as deeply involved with man's basic needs as we have seen design to be. To the problem of the dichotomy between the real world and the world of the school, there can be, understandably, many different answers.

What *is* the position of design in the West today? After sixty years of rather sterile Bauhaus-inspired anonymous and rational functionalism, design has splintered into many fragments. Research and engineering have brought about insistent advances that seemingly equate technological progress (especially when linked to consumer electronics) with good design. Increasing miniaturization and a continuous lowering of prices have brought such things as high-quality calculators, television sets, portable cassette players, and microprocessors to the mass market and could be credited with profits based on populism. The housing (or "shroud") for these products varies in style from a sort of industrial minimalism (Sony's Walkman-7 is nearly the same size as a cassette) to a sort of "World War III surplus" styling, where radios bristle with switches, dials, and exotic carrying straps. From opposite ends came the self-indulgent "antidesign" styling of the new wave of Italian design beginning around 1978. Best illustrated by furniture made of laminated chipboard, metal, plastics, and other materials, these productions of Alessandro Mendini and Studio Alchymia and the Memphis group started by Ettore Sottsass in 1981 are sold to a small international elite. These nearly unusable toys, camouflaged as 1920s kitsch furnishings, receive enormous publicity for their antirationalist appearance and their nonfunctional existence. They are an understandable salon-art reaction to the functional aesthetic that held sway from 1919 till the late seventies.

Objects are designed, made, and purchased in even more styles in the United States. A French Provincial television set, a Baroque refrigerator, or an Early American skyscraper—like Phillip Johnson's giant Duncan Phyfe *escretoire* built for the telephone company in New York—strikes few consumers, or even designers, as anachronistic or silly. Postmodernism has given new life to some of the more decadent stylistic extravaganzas of sixty-five years ago. The modern movement, which has seen a clear direction in the past, has changed into erratic and random fragmentation.

One cause of this fragmentation lies in our economic processes. Consumer goods of every sort, including houses, apartment buildings, civic centers, and motels, must appear continuously new. For we buy or rent only that which is changed and, moreover, *looks* changed. Industry, hand-in-hand with advertising and marketing, teaches us to look for and recognize these superficial changes, to expect them, and, ultimately, to demand them. Real changes—basic changes—mean retooling or rebuilding; the costs are prohibitively high. But to repaint and rearrange surfaces (interior or exterior) is just as exciting to a manipulated public and can be done on the cheap.

Thus, the vital working parts of a mechanism (the guts of a toaster, for instance) may remain unchanged for decades while surface finish, exterior embellishments, control mechanisms, skin color and texture undergo yearly mutations. This will be true even if the mechanism is faulty (as in the case of all too many automobiles, motorboats, air-conditioners, refrigerators, or washing machines). Automation also tends to make periodic reevaluation of the basic design approach prohibitively expensive. No wonder that the regional planner has become a landscape designer, the architect a decorator, and the designer a stylist or cosmetician. Mechanism and structure are frequently relegated to some product engineer, and the result lacks all unity or wholeness of purpose.

But even the stylist may accidentally strike some common associational or telesic chord that makes the consumer wish to hold onto the product, instead of trading it in for the latest version. (Examples of this are the 1961 Mustang and the 1954 Porsche.) To break down even this rare unwillingness on the part of consumers to throw things away, we have evolved materials that age badly. Throughout most of human history materials, being organic, have aged gracefully. Thatched roofs, wooden furniture, copper kettles, leather aprons, ceramic bowls, for example, would acquire small nicks, scratches, and dents, gently discolor, and acquire a thin patina as part of the natural process of oxidation. Ultimately, many would disintegrate into their organic components. Today we are taught that aging (of products or individuals) is wrong. We wear, use, enjoy things as long as they look as if they had just been bought. But once the plastic bucket deforms (however slightly), once the fake walnut tabletop melts under a cigarette, the anodizing on an aluminum tumbler slips, we get rid of the offending object.

This divorce between the working mechanism (which, because of tool- and die-making costs, remains unchanged) and the more evanescent skin surface has led to further specialization and to an aesthetic based on outward appearance only. The "skin" designers (Detroit's stylists) disdainfully avoid the "guts" designers (engineers and research people); form and function are artificially split. But neither a creature nor a product can survive for long when its skin and guts are separate.

A more durable kind of design thinking entails seeing the product (or tool, or transportation device, or building, or city) as a meaningful link between man and environment. We must see man, his tools, environment, and ways of thinking and planning, as a nonlinear, simultaneous, integrated, comprehensive whole.

This approach is *integrated design*. It deals with the *specialized* extensions of man that make it possible for him to remain a *generalist*. All man's functions—breathing, balancing, walking, perceiving, consuming, symbol-making, society-generating—are interrelated and interdependent. If we wish to relate the human environment to the psychophysical wholeness of the human being, our goal will be to replan and redesign both function and structure of all the tools, products, shelters, and settlements of man into an integrated living environment, an environment capable of growth, change, mutation, adaptation, regeneration, in response to man's needs.

Integrated design will concern itself, for the first time since the Late Paleolithic, with *unity*. This must include locally autonomous planning, as well as regional and city planning, architecture (both interior and exterior), industrial design (including systems analysis, transportation, and bionic research), product design (including clothing), packaging, and all the graphic, video and film-making skills that can be generally subsumed under the phrase visual design. Dividing lines exist between these areas at present, but the lunacy of these divisions is apparent even on the most basic level. To use one example: what is architecture? Assuredly it is more than the skill of building arches. Consider today's mix of civil engineering, speculative building, contracting, interior decoration, federally subsidized mass housing, landscaping, regional planning, rural and urban sociology, sculpture, and industrial design: what is left?

Architecture can hardly still be considered an area of its own (it lacks definition), and it overlaps with dozens of different fields. In view of all this, what is architecture? Could this be the reason so many architects have moved toward research, self-indulgent paper fantasies, heroic but ecologically unsound monumentalism, planning, and industrial design during the last decade? And during that same time, industrial designers have concerned themselves increasingly with the development of prefabricated houses and building components. Interior designers have developed furniture and tools and got caught up in such fads as supergraphics, nostalgia, brutalism, and so forth, while visual designers develop products and make films.

There is a sort of Brownian motion going on throughout all the separate areas of design, and I believe this to be an intuitive response to dynamically changing times. Within design many different levels of complexity exist. These might concern themselves with the relationship of human and structural factors in a material (or a set of materials) that provides shelter, with a transportation device, a road network, or the landscape.

If we speak of integrated design, of design-as-a-whole, of unity, we need designers able to deal with the design process comprehensively. Lamentably, designers so equipped are not yet turned out by any school. Their education would need to be less specialized and include many disciplines now considered to be only distantly related to design, if related at all.

Integrated design is not a set of skills, techniques, or rules but should be thought of as a series of functions occurring simultaneously rather than in a linear sequence. These simultaneous "events" can be thought of (in biological terms) as initial fertilization, developmental growth, production (or mimesis), and evaluation, the latter leading to reinitiation or regeneration or both, thus forming a closed feedback loop. Integrated design (a general unified design system) demands that we establish at what level of complexity the problem belongs. Are we, for instance, dealing with a tool that must be redesigned, or are we dealing with a manufacturing method in which this tool has been used, or should we rethink the product itself in relation to its ultimate purpose? Questions like these do not yield to a "seat-of-the-pants" examination.

A second area of investigation (unavoidably entwined with the previous one) is the historical perspective of the problem. All that we design is an extension of the human being (usually from generalization to specialization). Although a high-fidelity system, for instance, may be loaded with associational values and hence carry a great deal of status, it is basically an extension of the human ear. As we have seen in our six-sided function complex (Chapter One), all design must fill a human need. The history of man's emphasizing or deemphasizing

Experimental configuration of high-fidelity speakers, based on the dodecahedron. "Ideal" sound cones happen to follow the continuation of planes ex-
tending the edges of a dodecahedron. This design uses twelve 93-cent speakers;
two such speaker clusters give the stereo equivalent of a system costing ten
times as much. Author's design.

particular needs and how they have been met is vital to the understanding and initiation of new products or systems. Furthermore, such needs must be re-examined and regrouped as the culture changes. Thus when the human, historical coordinates of an idea are found, we must determine what particular phase of the idea we are dealing with.

Another consideration must be that of human and humane factors. If we assume that all design is an extension of man (either good or bad), the relevance of humane values is obvious. Any design, on this level of consideration, is an organic substitute (much like a transplanted heart, an artificial kidney, contact lenses, or a prosthetic hand). It must be recognizable and usable not only by the so-called five senses but also by the inner senses, both psychological and kinesthetic. Furthermore we must recognize the artificiality of this divorce between outer perceptions and the inner responses in man, for it gravely jeopardizes any unified human and humane factors study.

Next, integrated design must place the problem in its social perspective. Factory system and automation (both are, as of this writing, supreme extensions of man) may result in making all that we fancy we need available without effort to all people, in all places, and at all times. But as our living patterns and needs change radically, the ultimate consumer values may no longer be "availability" and "effortlessness." Taking the long view, we see that our attempts to move all of our activities from the manual to the mechanical and then to the automatic indiscriminately may be quite wrong, as we have seen in examining the automobile *vis-à-vis* our Triad of Limitations. Chronically, we have failed to distinguish the means from the end, and we have made mechanical what should have remained manual and have made automatic that which might have been more rationally replaced with an entirely different system. A good example of such wasted energy is the automatic gear shift. The energy used by a driver when shifting gears is incomparably smaller than the energy expended in manufacturing the automatic shift, not to mention the energy required to supply the factory and the automobile with the additional raw materials and man-hours required to make it. To quote Bob Malone:

> Is the automatic gear shift then a true advance in humane design or not? Since it tends to *remove* man from a basic and relatively simple use of his motor responses, rather than to simplify and integrate the processes, we can see that the validity of the automatic gear shift is illusory. When a true need or desire is satisified for a passive human being without effort, the result is not gratification but rather a more complex level of dissatisfaction. The man caught helplessly in a natural catastrophe has good reasons to think about human dignity and to wish that the material necessities of his life could be met more simply.

Finally integrated design must consider social groups, classes, and societies. Much design must be re-examined to see how far it may perpetuate existing class systems and social status.

An excellent example are *tratöfflor*, leather and wood slipper-shoes made in Angelholm, Sweden. This footwear can be worn both at home and (with casual dress) on the street. They sell for about $10 a pair in Sweden. The upper part is made of cowhide; the last and heel are shaped of wood. The soles are rubber. All three materials age well. These slipper-shoes are orthopedically so beneficial to the foot that they are required to be worn by surgeons and nurses in operating theaters. They are also very comfortable. They have a life expectancy of at least four years, can be worn in every kind of weather and, being nearly identical, cut completely across social and income classes, conveying no idea of status. (It is interesting to note in this connection that of late *tratöfflor* are being made in a variety of textures, colors, and artificial materials. This makes them tend to wear out faster; repairs are more difficult and sometimes impossible.) They constitute, *in their original form*, a superb example of indigenous, non-manipulated design. Several brands of *tratöfflor* became pop-

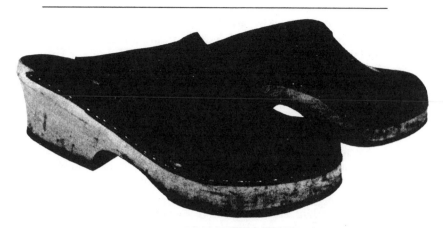

Trätofflor, still made in Ängelholm, Sweden, are a superb example of rational, vernacular design.

ular in the United States in the seventies. Known as Swedish clogs, they sell for as much as $45 in the United States in 1984.

Turning back to education, we find that part of the philosophical and moral bankruptcy of many design schools and universities lies in the ever-increasing trend to train students to become narrowly vertical specialists, whereas the real need is for broad, horizontal generalists or synthesists. Nearly everything in today's university milieu militates against educating for general synthesis. Prerequisite courses, corequired courses, required "electives," and empire-building by deans and professors with their own vested interests make a broader education nearly impossible. With students worrying more and more about jobs and job security, specialization has increased even more during the early eighties. But, whereas students increasingly feel that greater specialization will help to get that job, they are wrong in the long run. Industry and the professions tell us every day that they need students with a broader general background. The highly specialized student will often get that first job fairly easily. But over the next five or ten years he or she will fall by the wayside as those with the ability to synthesize and bring wider experiences to bear on the social dimensions of design and architecture are continually promoted. The academic desperation toward speciality becomes worrisome when we remember that the price a species pays for specialization usually turns out to be extinction.

Ideally, of course, groups of concerned people of all ages would meet together to engage in design. This would mean to learn, study, teach one another, experiment, engage in research and discussion, and interact with one another and with people from disciplines not generally considered design. Such a group would be small (thirty to fifty in number), and its members might stay together for weeks, months, or even years. Individual team members or small groups might detach themselves from the group, traveling or working directly with other groups or with manufacturing systems. Computer-assisted learning programs, as well as computer-assisted data acquisition, storage, and retrieval, would of course be available to all members of the team.

But it is probably more meaningful to determine what can be done right now and in the immediate future.

In establishing five-year undergraduate curricula for industrial and environmental design in 1964, 1971, 1972, 1977, and 1982, each student's program of studies was as broad a mix as possible. We attempted to break down the false dividing lines between various specialized fields of design, such as visual design, interior design, and industrial design. This was helped by training with twentieth-century tools of communication and expression: computer sciences, photography, kinetics, cybernetics, electronics, and filmmaking. In addition to exploring verbal, visual, and technological methods of transmitting information, students were encouraged to participate in other disciplines of concern to integrated comprehensive design. Thus sociology, anthropology, psychology (perception, human engineering factors, ergonomics), and the behavioral sciences were stressed. Because both individual human beings and social groups are biologically functional, the so-called life sciences became a keystone in the study of systems, forms, structures, and processes. Hence, a study of chemistry, physics, statics, and dynamics was more than augmented by work in structural biology, ecology, and ethology. This led to courses in theoretical and applied bionics and biomechanics (cf. Chapter Eight). Finally, nearly one-third of all undergraduate time was left open for entirely free electives, which meant in practice that a student could assemble a "minor" in some area that was of concern to him, such as anthropology or political science.

It is unfortunate that almost all schools or departments of design in the United States require an undergraduate degree in the same field as that in which the student hopes to do graduate work. We chose a different way, because of our passionate belief that the true design needs of the world must be carried out by cross-disciplinary teams. Hence, for graduate work we did not require four or five previous years of study in industrial design, architecture, or some other design area but preferred taking our young people from the field of behavioral sciences. This added meaning to their work.

I have had almost twenty years of excellent results with such a cross-disciplinary mix. Since coming to the School of Architecture and Urban Design at the University of Kansas, I have helped to start a new postgraduate option leading to a Master's Degree in Architecture. Under the title *Built Form & Culture*, research is carried out into vernacular building and indigenous shelter in many different countries. Students from eleven different countries work at their research and design, but *no undergraduate degree in architecture is required for entry*. Consequently students with a background in physical geography, anthropology, fine arts, law, or design work with others whose training is more orthodoxly in architecture.

Today's student (born into the electronic age) brings many differing skills to school before the first lesson has been taught. He may have more recent, more accurate, or more relevant information in some fields than his professors: a class of ten students and one professor is really an interacting group of eleven teachers, eleven researchers in search of knowledge, whose differing backgrounds complement each other. In schools where I have taught, we encourage students to teach one another. If we are lucky enough to have a student who worked in the electronics industry or who draws exceedingly well, he is asked to take over the relevant teaching. For it has become abundantly clear by now that there is much the school can learn from the students.

Students help us write our ever-changing curriculum and frequently initiate courses they feel are needed. In order to experience different working conditions, students work on individual projects as well as in "buddy teams" (two students). Often larger teams are formed encompassing students and professors from different disciplines. The problems to be solved may vary in time from simple two-hour exercises to problems lasting a month or two. In some cases, a larger team may work on a more formidable problem for a full year. Since each student, to learn the meaning of integrated comprehensive design, is encouraged to analyse each problem thoroughly for social and human content, students have the right to refuse work on some particular task and to substitute a self-chosen problem with the same learning content. Students can also challenge whether a problem should be undertaken at all. Such topics are settled in free and open discussion, and sometimes problems are changed or dropped.

Students are urged to travel widely and to work in many jobs—not necessarily in design. They may work in offices, industry, or factories and farms. Such work forms a required part of their study during summer vacations; a full year of internship is enormously helpful.

It is the experience of working as part of multidisciplinary teams that is essential—although this may be one of the hardest things to teach. Young designers have been propagandized into the concept of the lonely, struggling genius, the individual problem-solver. Reality does not bear this out. Most working designers today find themselves part of a team (like it or not). A typical marketing enterprise will consist of manage-

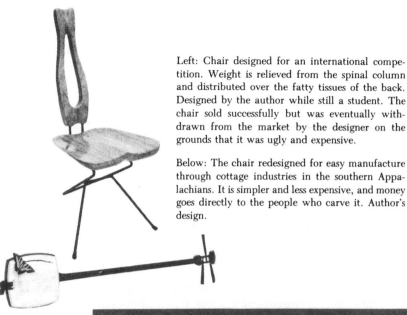

Left: Chair designed for an international competition. Weight is relieved from the spinal column and distributed over the fatty tissues of the back. Designed by the author while still a student. The chair sold successfully but was eventually withdrawn from the market by the designer on the grounds that it was ugly and expensive.

Below: The chair redesigned for easy manufacture through cottage industries in the southern Appalachians. It is simpler and less expensive, and money goes directly to the people who carve it. Author's design.

ment personnel, market and motivation research experts, advertising people, production engineers, and, often as not, consumer psychologists. Some of these people make decisions; others may work as consultants; still others may have broad advisory powers. In many cases the designer finds himself just a sort of vermiform appendix to the marketing-cum-advertising brigade.

Integrated design teams may need specialists too—specialists whose orientation may be not only profit making but rather a human and humane concern for man and his environment. Typically such a team might consist of a designer, an anthropologist, a sociologist, and people in some specialized area of engineering. A biologist (or someone versed in bionics and biomechanics) and medical doctors and psychologists might complete the team. Most importantly, the people for whom the design team works must be represented on the team itself. Without the help of the eventual end-users, no socially acceptable design can be done. Students, first faced with this concept, often try to escape direct confrontation with some client groups, assuming that there will be communication difficulties or that the members of the group might be too ignorant to realize their own needs fully. Such lack of faith in the people can never be justified.

I have worked on design teams that included rural poor people without formal education, small children, or mentally disturbed patients. While communication was slow and difficult, we ultimately succeeded in every case and were made directly aware of needs that professional opinion-takers didn't suspect or considered unimportant.

Such a team, whose only aim lies in designing-planning, may not only *solve* problems, but also search for, isolate, and identify problems that need solving. It is in this last area—locating, isolating, and identifying problems—that schools fall lamentably short and often provide no practice for the student at all. In most learning situations students are asked to solve problems. This means that a "special-case" situation is presented; after a certain amount of time the student is expected

Candlesticks specifically designed to be made through home-cottage industries in southern Appalachia where these candles are also made. Author's design.

to regurgitate a "special-case" answer to the teacher. He may be asked to make a ceramic teapot for six cups of tea, and this (embellished in his own particular way) is precisely what he will return to the teacher. Instead of the concept of a ceramic teapot, we could just as easily have asked for the design of a better chair, housing project, or a magazine cover. It really does not matter what specific design problem is assigned—in each instance it is a special-case situation, and that is *not* how things work. Even if *all* the problems are socially relevant, the general-case learning experience of the student would still be nil. The human mind continuously moves from generalizations to particulars and then broadens out to generalizations again. It is a never-ending pendulum swing between special case and general case.

A problem can be assigned either way: as a special or general case. What is important is the functional processing of the idea by the student, the designer, the team, or the class, and their understanding of this process and its links to other similar processes. For example, a problem may be assigned as special case: "Design a chair!" The student will then move from this special case out toward the generalization "chair." He will review alternative design strategies and, from these, develop a number of so-called sets. These sets are various directions, general and often mutually exclusive, in which the problem could be solved. Some sets the student may discover in a general case could include a disposable chair, a chair for people with injured backs, a chair for children in primary schools, a method of sitting in a boat, a chair for performing some specific technical task, such as playing in a string quartet, or a "fun" chair that will appeal to a particular subgroup. The student now selects his particular set out of the general case and proceeds to work toward his own special-case solution. This is shown schematically in Figure A.

Figure A
One design "Event"
Special case to general case to
special case.

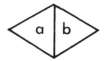

By contrast, a general-case statement might be: "Design something to help in developing countries!" The student now has to do a good deal of research from various sources and disciplines. Eventually he may narrow down the choices to the special-case concept "bicyclelike power source." But to get this far he will unavoidably find out much about the whole field of research with many spinoffs and spillovers and thus again find many general-case solutions and applications. (It is specifically this type of problem that is almost never set in school, since it is slow and—without strong guidance—can become frustrating.) This process—looking somewhat like a butterfly or a bow tie—is illustrated in Figure B.

Figure B
One design "Event"
General case to special case to
general case.
(Or Team problem)

In any team design problem, the flow diagram will always be as in Figure B. Many different students are assembling general-case information through research and bringing together an information package to be commonly shared under special case. From here they will again fan out to many general-case solutions.

It will be useful to remember that both Figure A and Figure B can be thought of as single links in continuous, cyclic chains, as in Figure C.

Figure C
A series of design
"Events", cyclic
in nature.

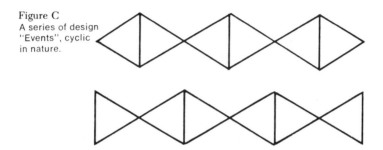

A series of possible design "events" (Figures A and B) will yield an omnidirectional, two-dimensional net of equilateral triangles organized into closely packed hexagons, with no wasted space. This is shown in Figure D.

Figure D
The omni-directional net of
several design "Events."

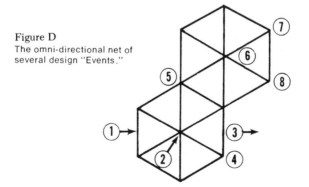

By study of the schematic function of Figure D, its use can be understood. Conventionally, designer or student may start with a general-case idea input at *1*, expecting to routinely reach special case at *2*, and hopefully plan to derive an answer at *3*. However, *2* is a locus for at least six different disciplines, and he may in fact eventually emerge at either general- or special-case points *4*, *5*, *6*, *7*, *8*, . . . or *n*. Figure D then becomes a schematic representation of a series of interlinking events, each one of which can be represented by a flow chart, each flow chart carrying within the bias or set of its own particular discipline.

Now let us examine the flow of a real design problem through our schematic. An illustration of this will be found as Figure E: At *1* (triangle *a*) the designer enters the picture with a special case problem: "Design a chair." Triangle *a* represents his normal data-gathering phase, bringing him to point *2*, the general-case collection of ideas. He is still acting independently as a designer; if left to his own resources he would eventually emerge at *3* (triangle *b*) with, say, a low-cost desk chair for secretaries. Still left to his own resources, he might now, still at *3*, start on some design job (a radio, a tool, or whatever). This would carry him through triangles *c* and *d*. (In fact the undisturbed activity of a typical designer-specialist of today can be read as the cyclic axis: *a*, *b*, *c*, *d*, *e*, and so forth.) However, our designer friend is *not* a specialist but rather a member of a multidisciplinary team. When he reaches *2*, he has reached general-case data but also the intersection of several other lines of thought. For there the kinesiologist or medical doctor will provide information regarding sitting postures (normally the doctor's own specialized cyclic axis would continue towards triangle *w* as well as *x*, *y*, *z*—the treatment of work-induced diseases). Here at *2* the sociologist (axis: *p*, *q*, *r*, *s*) and some secretaries as representatives of the client group (axis: *g*, *h*, *i*, *j*) also intersect. Our designer, through meeting and working with many other team members, may finally emerge at, say, *7* (triangle *m*), which might unexpectedly be a systems design for computer terminals that permits secretaries to work in their homes.

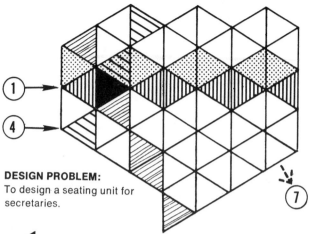

Figure E

Schematic representation of the behavior of a multi-disciplinary team. Only a small section of the hexagonal net is shown.

DESIGN PROBLEM:
To design a seating unit for secretaries.

 Designer's cyclic path (triangles a, b, c, d, e, etc.) if uninterrupted by other disciplines.

 Doctor's cyclic path (triangles u, v, w, x, y, z): the treatment of work-induced diseases.

 Sociologist's cyclic path (triangles p, q, r, s): work habits and attitudes of secretaries in offices.

 "Client" group's cyclic path (triangles g, h, i, j, k): in *this* case, office secretaries, doing their work.

 Intersection of various disciplines' paths.

 Cyclic paths of other groups not concerned in this particular problem.

1: Entry point of designer.

4: Interface between sociologist's path (near point of his emergence) and consultation with some other discipline, say, engineering.

7: One of many possible, unpredictable emergence points by the team.

To understand all the ramifications of integrated comprehensive design fully, it is necessary to try to become aware of as many influences as possible that have bearing on the design process. Since so many factors and variables are involved (more than can possibly be kept in mind), the simplest solution is to *externalize* it by constructing a flow chart. A flow chart (as my students and I use it) may be a large roll of brown wrapping paper pinned across an entire wall, listing all the various aspects needed in analysing the design.

During the primary design stage of a playground for a slum area, some of the factors appearing on a chart were as follows: Psychological and physiological needs for participation, exercise, and group-needs of children at various age levels. What kind of supervisory personnel would be needed, their availability locally. What kinds of playground equipment could be designed and built and with what resources, tools and processes. How could money be raised for this. What materials could be used for constructing equipment and toys, and what were the characteristics of these materials under (a) extremely hard wear and use; (b) frost, ice, snow, storms, and hard rain; (c) prolonged use over a period of five to fifteen years; (d) dangers of shearing, splintering, torque, or fracture while being used by a child; (e) toxic characteristics of the various materials and coloring agents; (f) perceptual and psychological responses of children (at various age levels) to the colors used; (g) relative ease of care, maintenance, repair, and replacement of equipment. Questions regarding the setting of the playground within the neighborhood area with such determinants as (a) location of playground entrances in relation to main traffic arteries; (b) number of streets to be crossed by children hoping to use the playground; (c) illumination of the playground at night; (d) accessibility to homes and other neighborhood centers, such as nursery schools, kindergartens, day-care centers, were also included. Possible ancillary services, such as toilets, drinking fountains, a swimming pool, a wading pool for small children, telephone facilities, first-aid equipment, a rain shelter, benches for older people, landscaping (grass, bushes, trees, and flowers), were listed together with activities other than play that might occur on the site, such as outdoor concerts, motion-picture showings, street theater for older people, "story-time" and sing-alongs for small children, dances and athletics for teenagers. Climate also had to be considered: could parts of the playground be flooded for ice-skating during the winter? Could some of the hills (which we were to create with bulldozers) be used for bobsleds, sleds, and skis? What about drainage problems during rainstorms and after the melting of permafrost in the spring?

A flow chart works quite simply: We listed all the parameters we could think of (some are mentioned above), putting each under the classification that seemed to make most sense. Under activities, we might list climbing, jumping, running, sliding, singing, and talking. We then began to establish *relationships* where none seemed to exist before. For example, under "materials" we listed sailcloth or heavy canvas. Its characteristics are (when stretched and supported like a membrane) buoyancy and comparatively resilient softness. This could now be brought into a direct relationship with "jumping" and suggest a trampolinelike structure. One of the important functions of a flow chart is that new relationships can be read directly off the wall, and that solutions, or at least directions for solutions, emerge without their ever having been consciously listed. A flow chart can, by definition, *never be complete*. That is: new concepts and entire new categories can be added almost indefinitely; hence new relationships will constantly emerge.

At this point, half of the flow chart (or triangle *a* in Figure A) has been completed. The second half of the flow chart (triangle *b*) will consist of implementation. That is, who does what, when, how, and by what date. Here again, alterations and additions can be continuously performed. The design team keeps the flow chart going until *after* the design job is completed.

We are now able to establish the work flow of any design job:

1. Assembling a design team representing all relevant disciplines, as well as members of the client group.
2. Establishment of a primary flow chart (triangle *a* part only).
3. Research and fact-finding phase.
4. Completion of the first half of the flow chart (triangle *a*).
5. Establishment of the second half of the flow chart (triangle *b*): what to do.
6. Individual, buddy-team, or team design, and development of ideas.
7. Checking these designs against the goals established in the flow chart, and correcting both designs and flow chart in the light of these experiences.
8. Building of models, prototypes, test models, or working models.
9. Testing these by the relevant user-group.
10. Test results are now fed into the flow chart.
11. Redesign, retesting, and completion of the design job, together with whatever written reports, graphic communication, statistical support data, or working drawings are necessary.
12. The flow chart is then preserved, to be used as a follow-up guide in checking actual in-use performance characteristics of the designed objects. After this the flow chart is filed; it is to be used as a guide for future design work.

In actual practice, the design process can never follow a path quite as linear and sequential as is suggested (for one thing, new research data emerge continuously).

While participating in a design conference held by the Scandinavian Student Design Organization (SDO) at Copenhagen in 1969, it was my job to construct a general-case portion of a flow chart, concerned with the social and moral responsibility of the designer and his position in a profit-oriented society. This is so large a job that this entire book

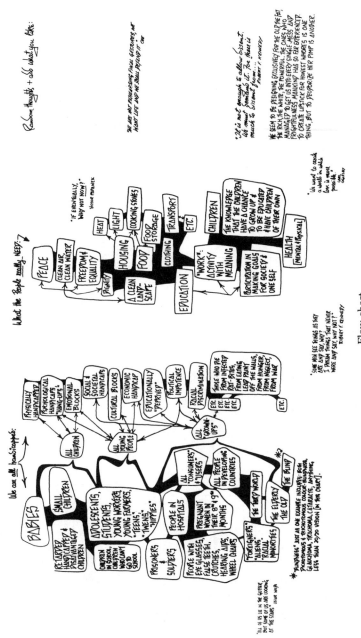

Flow chart

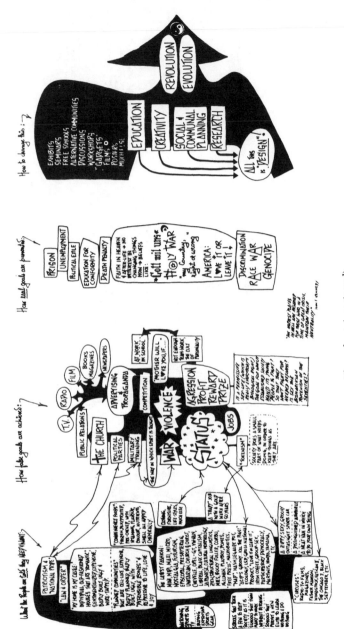

Flow chart (continued)

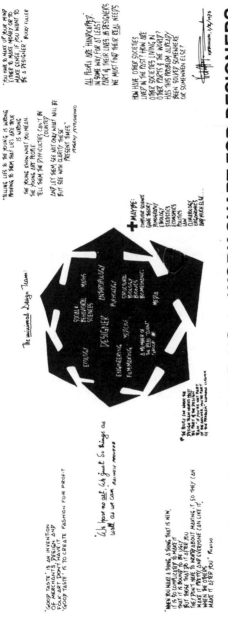

"BIG CHARACTER" POSTER NO.1: WORK CHART FOR DESIGNERS.

Flow chart (continued)

attempts to address itself to precisely that same question. Nonetheless, a revised version of the flow chart is reproduced here. Study it, and note especially its nonlinear character. The reader is encouraged to play with the flow chart, to add to it, and discover his own relationships. Parts have been purposely left open for your own comments. It could be argued that the subject of this particular chart is too broad. But flow charts are, by their very nature, general-case statements. A very narrow subject would be too technical for a simple explanation.

All this, however, is merely a broad philosophical background. What about specifics? In what real world situations can students learn best?

During the summer of 1968 a multidisciplinary team of design students (under the guidance of Yrjö Sotamaa, Zoltan Popovic, Barbro Kulvik-Siltavuori, and Jorma Vennola) worked with me on a small island in Finland. We invented, designed, and built a foldable, movable environment for children with cerebral palsy. This environment included toys, exercising devices, and other pieces of equipment. We met in Helsinki after the team members had played with and interviewed the children. We had also spoken to parents, visited clinics, playgrounds, and homes, finding that little or no equipment had been specifically invented or provided for children with cerebral palsy and that some of the toys in use to train children in specific motor skills were inhumane and barbaric. (CP children must be trained to use their thumb and index finger in grasping. Their natural tendency is to use the other three fingers instead. Until now this had been done by strapping these three fingers together, thus forcing them to use thumb and index finger alone. We designed and made several toys that provided reward sequences and enjoyment to the child when he used thumb and first finger. In this way the medieval practice of forced restraints could be abandoned.) The students also found that most clinics and hospitals were drab and unexciting.

We made a flow chart and met as a team, together with

An exercising and play environment built on Suomenlinna in Finland. Designed and built by a cross-disciplinary team of students under the direction of Zoltan Popovic, Yrjö Sotamaa, and Victor Papanek.

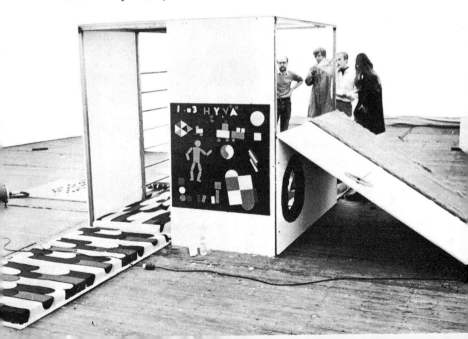

two experts in child psychology and neurophysiology from Sweden. As a team we spent a total of twelve hours developing a two-meter cube that knocked down into two sections, each 6½ by 6½ by 3 feet in size. This module permits the two parts of the cube to be moved easily from clinic to clinic, to be carried through doors and transported on small trucks. Once erected at the clinic (indoors or outdoors), the cube unfolds into a play environment that is 6½ feet high, with equipment covering an area of about 66 square feet. It is bright and colorful and includes slides, climbing, a crawling surface, and many individual activity areas and toys. It is easy to build and low in cost. Our first prototype cube was built and completed (including toys) in thirty hours of teamwork and then tested with children. We called it CP-1 to suggest that it was merely the first of a generation of similar cubes, each one of which would be modified by testing and experiences with children. We assumed that other cubes (for hydrotherapy, for autistic and retarded children) would eventually be built. During the following fourteen years, CP-2 was designed and built—a do-it-yourself exercise environment for children with cerebral palsy—to be built by a group of parents. This was published in *Cerebral Palsy Crusader*, a U.S. self-help magazine, in 1969. Yrjö Sotamaa has built further environments in Finland (CP-3 and CP-4). In 1981 students at the Kansas City Art Institute developed and built under my direction XCP-5: a plug-together environment for severely retarded children at a clinic in Kansas City.

At Purdue University we concerned ourselves with problems of paraplegic, quadriplegic, spastic, and palsied children. We designed and built a series of vehicles with built-in motivational factors that provide healthy exercise and training for these children. A study showed that the nature and extent of their handicaps and abilities varied greatly (some could use only their arms, some only their legs; with others the entire right or left side was useless; a few had only one usable limb). In many of these cases it is healthy to exercise the useless-seeming limbs. One thing all these children have

Above: An exercising vehicle for disabled or retarded children. Designed by Robert Worrell, as a student at Purdue University.

Below: Vehicle for exercising children with weak arms and shoulders. Designed by Charles Schreiner, as a student at Purdue University.

A least-effort vehicle designed for children with cerebral palsy. Both the pedals and the arm move the vehicle. Whatever limb the child can use propels him, while the other limbs are exercised. Designed by Charles Lanius, as a student at Purdue University.

in common is a great enjoyment of speed. The vehicles illustrated were designed so that they can be operated with one or more limbs; the rest are exercised in the process. The harder the child exercises, the faster he goes. Hence, enjoyment and exercise go hand-in-hand. The vehicles were tested with handicapped children and were turned over to local clinics.

In this brief discussion, we should also concern ourselves with what the student has gained. Obviously he or she has engaged in research, worked with a team, met the needs of people, used a flow chart, and gained new skills and new insights. But the actual learning content of these problems is far greater, going from the immediate to the lasting. A series of educational steps and learning experiences have taken place, all on an interactive level:

1. The student has located, identified, and isolated a problem. In so doing he or she has interacted with other members of a multidisciplinary team and engaged in a meaningful work experience directly with a group of clients whose very existence and needs were previously unknown to him.
2. Through his work he has made the client people aware of the promise that design (applied intelligently) can hold out for them. He has satisfied their needs at least partially.
3. By working with and helping the group, he has exposed
    a. the needs of the group to society;
    b. the lack of knowledge on the part of society regarding the needs of the group, or the very existence of the group;
    c. the cynical indifference of many governmental and industrial power structures to genuine needs of people;
    d. the inability of traditional design as it is taught to cope with genuine social problems;
    e. the existence of methods and disciplines to work intelligently for these needs;
    f. the lack of training or discussion in school of *applied design ethics.*
4. He has completed deeply satisfying work; never again will it be possible to engage in design directed *only* toward "good taste." Having experienced this kind of work, he will forever after feel a little ashamed when he designs a pretty, sexy toaster.

He will forever after feel a little ashamed when he designs a pretty, sexy toaster. . . .

12

Design for Survival and Survival through Design: A Summation

Some men see things as they are and say, why?
I dream things that never were and say, why not?
ROBERT F. KENNEDY

Again: design is basic to all human activities. The planning and patterning of any act toward a desired, foreseeable end constitutes the design process. Any attempt to separate design, to make it a thing-by-itself, works counter to the inherent value of design as the primary, underlying matrix of life.

Integrated design is comprehensive: it attempts to take into consideration all the factors and modulations necessary to a decision-making process. Integrated, comprehensive design is anticipatory. It attempts to look at existing data and trends and to continuously extrapolate, as well as interpolate, from the scenarios of the future it constructs.

Integrated, comprehensive, anticipatory design is the act of planning and shaping carried on across the various disciplines, an act continuously carried on at interfaces between them.

In metallurgy it is at the boundary layers (the interfaces between crystals in metals) that action takes place under force. The very imperfections make it possible for us to shape and deform metals mechanically. Geologists tell us that the great changes on earth take place where forces meet along boundary lines. Here surf meets shore, fault blocks move in different directions. Diamond cutters cut along flaw lines, the sculptor's chisel follows the grain, and naturalists study the edge of the forest meeting the meadow. The architect's main concern is with the juncture between building and ground; the industrial designer is concerned with the smooth transition from working edge to tool handle, as well as with a secondary interface: the "fit" of tool and hand. Passengers relax visibly after that split second when the aircraft finally leaves the ground, and, for each single navigational map of the ocean, there are a thousand showing reefs and shorelines. We fight our wars over those symbolic boundaries we draw across our maps and find life's most shatteringly poignant experiences in crossing the boundary lines of birth and death; the apotheosis is the sex act: ultimate encounter between interfaces.

It is at the border between different techniques or disciplines that most new discoveries are made and most action is inaugurated. It is when two differing areas of knowledge are forcefully brought in contact with one another that, as we have seen in a previous chapter on bionics, a new science may come into being. Frederick J. Teggart, the historian, says that "the great advances of mankind have been due, not to the mere aggregation, assemblage, or acquisition of disparate ideas, but to the emergence of a certain type of mental activity which is set up by the opposition of different idea systems." Sociobiology, biomechanics, extraterrestrial medicine, and ethnomusicology are a few examples that come readily to mind.

Acceleration, change, and the acceleration of change itself arise from the meeting of structures or systems along their edges. Intuitively, young people in the early seventies sensed this; their repeated use of confrontations was a symbolic, externalized illustration of this fact.

By its very nature the design team thrives on confrontations, being itself born of interfaces. The design team is structured to bring many different disciplines to bear upon problems that need solving, as well as to search for those problems that need to be rethought. The task is to research our true needs and to reshape environments, tools, and the way in which we think about them.

Although computers have been with us for nearly forty years, the introduction of microprocessors into offices and especially homes is still fairly recent. Understandably many people are concerned over the changes caused by the advent of microcprocessors and computers. Unfortunately several groups still take a hostile or negative viewpoint. One group sees computers as a threat to organized labor, to the standard forty-hour work week, and to the Puritan work ethic, and find much to fear in that. Others, while realizing that microprocessors and computers help to phase out monotonous, routine intellectual labor, still take a negative view of the future: they fear the leisure they envision. Piet Mondrian, painting as though he himself were a computer, did this work with a sense of fun and adventure. However, some artists feel a particular angst when faced by data-processing machines. But certainly there are many of us who see the microprocessor, and computers in general, as an enormous liberating force that is ridding us of an enormous amount of busywork, freeing us to address the aesthetic, philosophical, and conceptual underpinnings of what we do.

Between 1976 and 1983 the people working on images and backgrounds for such films as *Star Wars*, *The Empire Strikes Back*, and *Close Encounters of the Third Kind* attempted to find painters and watercolorists in England who were willing to work with graphic computer modeling. In August 1983, I shared the speaker's platform at the twentieth world congress of ICOGRADA (International Congress of Graphic Artists and Designers) in Dublin. My cospeaker explained that *all* the artists hired disliked what they were going to do at first. Within weeks, as they became conversant with "Colorbox" as a graphic working tool they changed their minds; artistic and human curiosity were aroused. Now, two years later, many of these artists work with graphic computers and "Colorbox" exclusively and by their own choice.

As computers and other data-processing equipment are coming into more general use, a new but beguiling division and redefinition of our activities comes into being. A greater share of those activities that we have heretofore considered as exclusively intellectual—but which in fact are sheer monotony—are assigned to the computer, permitting us to restate the *truly* cerebral component of our intellectuality. It is precisely here, at the juncture between computerized work and human work and leisure, that the design team is located.

In a world in which much work increasingly will be done through automation and in which most routine supervision, quality control, and computation are performed by word and data processors, the work of the design team (research, social planning, creative innovation) *is one of the few meaningful and crucial activities left to man.* Inescapably, designers will be needed to help set goals for all of society.

Social historians tell us that the predicament of twentieth-century man can be traced unerringly to the discoveries of five men: Copernicus, Malthus, Darwin, Marx, and Freud. But during just the last fifteen years the interfaces between sociology and biology, psychology and anthropology, and archaeology and medicine have generated wide new insights into the human condition. A dozen and a half books—Robert Ardrey's *The Territorial Imperative* and *Hunting Hypothesis;* Gregory Bateson's *Mind and Nature;* Buckminster Fuller's *Operating Manual for Spaceship Earth;* Edward T. Hall's *The Hidden Dimension* and *The Dance of Life;* Ivan Illich's *Tools for Conviviality;* Arthur Koestler's *The Ghost in the Machine* and *Bricks to Babel;* Konrad Lorenz's *On Aggression* and *Civilized Man's Eight Deadly Sins;* J. E. Lovelock's *Gaia: A New Look At Life On Earth;* Desmond Morris's *The Naked Ape;* Jonathan Schell's *The Fate of the Earth;* Peter Singer's *The Expanding Circle;* Rattray Taylor's *The Biological Time Bomb* and *How to Avoid the Future;* and Edward Wilson's *Sociobiology*—have redefined man's relation to man and to his en-

vironment in new and profound ways. The interdependence
of various disciplines can best be illustrated by a story Fuller
liked to tell:

> In the last decade, two important papers were presented to
> learned societies, one on anthropology and the other on biol-
> ogy. And both these researchers were working completely in-
> dependently. But it happened by chance that I saw both
> papers. The biological one was looking into all the biological
> species that have become extinct. The anthropological one was
> looking into all the human tribes that had become extinct. Both
> researchers were trying to find a commonality of causes for
> extinction. Both of them found the same cause indepen-
> dently—extinction is a consequence of over-specialization. As
> you get more and more over-specialized, you inbreed special-
> ization. It's organic. As you do, you outbreed general adapt-
> ability.
> So here we have the warning that specialization is a way to
> extinction, and our whole society is thus organized . . . .

Man is a generalist. It is his extensions (tools and environments) that are designed, that help him to achieve specialization. But by misdesigning such tools or environments, we
often achieve a closed feedback loop, the tools and environments in turn affect men and groups in a way that turns them
into permanent specialists themselves. But the potential consequences of any device, tool, or environment can be studied
before it is structured or manufactured. Computers now make
it possible to generate mathematical models of processes, in-
teractions, and systems, and to study them beforehand. Recent strides made in the social sciences are providing greater
insights into that which is socially and societally valuable.

For thousands of years philosophers, artists, and designers
have argued about the need for beauty and aesthetic value in
the things we use and live with. Designers and engineers have
insisted on optimal function. One only has to look out the window or into one's own room to see where this schizoid preoccupation with function and the look of things has led us: *the*

world is ugly, but it doesn't work well either! In a world of abject want, a preoccupation with *only* making things pretty is a crime against humanity. But to design things that work well but fail otherwise is an equally fundamental error. As we have seen in our function complex in Chapter One, man needs structures and tools that are enriched beyond the severely utilitarian. Delight, balance, and that pleasing harmony of proportions that we project outward into the world (and are told to regard as the eidetic image) are psychological necessities for us. And not only a creature as sophisticated as man, but lower species as well, seem to need this aesthetic and associational enrichment. Here is a description of this mechanism among birds, as quoted by a philosopher-naturalist:

> Everyone knows that most birds build houses, and very efficiently, too. Although not usually artistic, their nests are careful and often ingenious. The tailorbird puts nesting material inside a large leaf, then sews up the edges in a curve so that the leaf cannot unroll. The South American ovenbird, which weighs less than three ounces, makes a nest weighing between seven and nine *pounds*, out of a hollow ball of earth fixed to a branch. In Australia the rock warbler makes a long hanging nest and attaches it to the roof of a cave by spiders' webs; the reaction of the spiders is not described. On the Malay Peninsula the megapodes build artificial incubators: piles of vegetation mixed with sand, which gradually decay and keep the eggs warm. The birds themselves are not as big as ordinary fowl, but the nests can be eight feet high and twenty-four feet across, composed of five tons of material scratched together from a radius of several hundred yards. The house martin builds a neat little house of clay with a front door. A simple nest, like that of the redstart, means six hundred separate flights for material.
>
> Some birds, however, go further, and build simply for aesthetic effect. These are the bowerbirds of Australia and New Guinea. They are perching birds, between eight and fifteen inches long, which look rather like our own woodpeckers, but are more handsomely costumed. Their specialty is unique. The males make clearings in the forest, and at their edges build

elaborate arbors of grass and leaves. On the clearings and in the arbors they set out decorations, carefully chosen and grouped: the heads of blue flowers, shells or brilliant objects such as pieces of glass, cartridge cases, and even glass eyes (though these are harder to come by). The scientist who has studied them most closely, A. J. Marshall, shows pretty clearly that this is simply a variation of sexual display intended to attract the little female, to mark off each particular male's own territory, and to allow him a proper stage on which to display his plumage and his masterful poses. And yet Marshall is bound to admit that the birds seem to enjoy their arbors; that their building goes beyond mere functionalism; and that they display very marked discrimination, which can only be called aesthetic choice, in decorating their bowers. An American collector in New Guinea was making his way through the jungle without thinking of bowerbirds or ever having seen one of their structures, when he suddenly came on a place where the undergrowth had been neatly cleared away from an area some four feet square, and a hutshaped bower had been built beside it, about three feet tall and five feet broad, with an opening a foot high. "This curious structure fronted on the cleared area. The impression of a front lawn was heightened by several beds of flowers or fruit. Just under the door there was a neat bed of yellow fruit. Further out on the lawn there was a bed of blue fruit. Off to one side there were ten freshly picked flowers." Later this explorer saw the architect returning to its bower. The first thing it did was to notice a match that had been carelessly thrown into the middle of its clearing. It hopped over, picked up the match and, with a toss of its head, threw it out of the clearing. So the explorer collected some pink and yellow flowers and one red orchid, and put these in the clearing. Soon the bird came back and flew straight to the new flowers. It took all the yellow ones and threw them away. Then, after some hesitation, it removed the pink ones. Finally it picked up the orchid, decided not to throw it away with the rest, and spent some time carrying it from one pile to another of its own decorations, until it found one where it would fit in with advantage.

Does that sound incredible? There are other facts about the bowerbirds which far surpass it. After one male has completed his arbor he must guard it, for if he flies off in search of food, a rival male will wreck his bower and steal his decorations. Some species not only decorate their bowers but paint them, with coloured fruit pulp, charcoal powder from burnt logs, and (near homes in Australia) stolen bluing. If a flower in the display fades, it is removed at once; and if a human being interferes, the result of this interference is rectified. One observer took some moss out of a bower and hung it some distance away in the forest. Time and again a radiantly colored male bird angrily put the moss back. And then the same observer conducted an experiment which I can only call brutal. He set fire to three of the bowers. In each case, a male bird flew out of the trees and perched close by the burning arbor, "his beautiful head bowed and wings dropped, as though sorrowing over a funeral pyre." O Science, what crimes are committed in thy name!*

More controlled experiments have been carried on to prove the importance of aesthetically enriched environments. Work done by Professor David Krech at the University of California at Berkeley has provided a multitude of insights. Krech assembled two groups of laboratory rats. One group was brought up in a "deprived" environment, similar to conditions existing for people in slums, *barrios*, *favelas*, and ghettoes. The rats were crowded, sanitary controls were absent or nearly absent, food was uninteresting and meager. The cages were in perpetual gloom, and shrill, unstructured sounds of a decibel level far too high interrupted the occupants during both waking and sleeping. The second group of animals were brought up in an "enriched" environment. Here colors, textures, and materials had been chosen with great care. Food and water were

*The difficulty with writing a book in many parts of the world is that source material sometimes disappears. This charming study of bowerbirds quoted above just had to be included. But the book from which it came is gone irretrievably. Whether it gently floated from Viken towards Denmark or was left behind after a shadow-puppet play in Ubud (Bali), the fact remains that I would like to acknowledge and request permission to quote it, but, knowing neither author nor title, this is impossible.

plentiful, vitamin enriched, and plenty of space was set aside for family grouping. Soft and pleasant music was piped into their habitat, and slowly changing lights and colors further enhanced the environment.

The result of this experiment showed that members of the "enriched" group had greater learning capacity, faster mental development, greater flexibility and adaptability to new stimuli, and far better memories. They also maintained their greater mental capacity into old age. Even their offspring, brought up under normal laboratory conditions, maintained a sizeable lead over those offspring of the "deprived" rats that were brought up in standard ways. Dissection showed that the size and weight of the cerebral cortex of the enriched rats (the part of the brain responsible for a rich flow of associations) was larger, heavier, and more convoluted.

When the experiment was repeated, retaining the differences in environment, *but feeding identical amounts of water and identical food* to both groups of rats, results were nearly identical to the first experiment. In both cases the environment-enriched rats developed a high concentration of an important brain enzyme responsible for the growth of brain tissue. The experiment showed that just the environment and its relationship to the rats can modify the basic brain chemistry. This is not to claim that people and rats are alike, but many child-care centers, kindergartens, nursery schools, and schools manage to recapitulate the deprived rats' environment. Too many parents (considering schools to be merely permanent baby-sitting agencies) never ask *whether the schools are robbing their children of potential brain tissue!*

Unfortunately, the rats' deprived environment can be said to exist for people in over ninety percent of the world. During the last fifty years or so, man-made environments have begun taking on the characteristics of a natural ecology: they are interlocking, user-responsive, and self-regenerating. All of humanity is fed into this new ecology, with little forethought as to how a biological mechanism responds to being ripped out of one habitat and compelled to exist in another. But we have only to look at our zoos. . . .

Apologists for both schools as they are and for slums (and they often tend to be the same people) explain that life is grim and earnest, that existence is a continuous battle where the strong reap victory, and that the young are merely being taught to be tough in order to survive more easily in a difficult world. And in many countries life is tough indeed, with survival the only goal. In the first chapter we defined design. Under *Need* we listed three components in hierarchical order: Survival, Identity, and Goals. (This is my simplification of Abraham Maslow's classic, five-tiered description: Physical Needs, Security, Social Acceptance, Love, and Self-actualization.) The first imperative is always survival; only after that do we care to explore who we are. And only when the questions of our survival and our identity have come clear do we begin to establish goals. Beyond this lie extensions of these three basic imperatives: self-actualization, uniqueness, awareness, empathy, love, ecstasy, joy, and passion. The concept that the strong will perpetually triumph over the weak ("a boot stamping on your head, forever") is partially based on Social Darwinism—survival of the fittest, as consciously misinterpreted by the rising capitalist class in late nineteenth-century England and America. Partially it arises from the concept that there "is just not enough to go around," until recently a historical fact. But in 1983 there is more than enough to go around for everyone if only it is properly planned, distributed, and frugally used. The amounts spent preparing for a nuclear terracide alone would feed, educate, and heal all people everywhere.

But a second fallacy is inherent in viewing schools as toughening-up experiences. According to Dr. M. W. Sullivan, during World War II members of the United States Marine Corps fighting in the South Pacific were exposed to some of the most insufferable conditions in history. Climate, vegetation, and wildlife made life nearly unbearable; the added hazards of battle and disease were staggering. A study showed that those men coming from deprived environments (in other words, those who had been "toughened up for life") *were the first to crack up.* The Marines whose background had been both an enriched and a more tranquil one more easily withstood the ravages of environment and enemy action. The same experience also has been documented by Dr. Bruno Bettelheim for the inmates of Nazi extermination camps and held especially true for those Americans captured during the Korean War (Eugene Kincaid. *In Every War But One.* New York: Norton, 1959).

In a dramatically changing world that is (tremblingly) afraid of change and that educates its young into ever-narrowing areas of specialization, the integrated, comprehensive, anticipatory designer is a dedicated synthesist. Much of the hope lies in the fact that a society grown too large and complex to understand itself or to respond to new events is often unaware of the changes taking place within it. Thus by the year 2000 more than half of all people will be less than twenty years old—at the same time the proportion of the elderly and extremely old will be greater than ever before. Today there are more college students in the United States than there are farmers. Yet enormously generous subsidies provided for American farmers (implemented at a time when agricultural workers accounted for ninety-eight percent of the population, rather than today's eight percent) are still enforced and pay farmers *not* to grow food while millions starve. Buckminster Fuller observes, "Each child today is born in the presence of less misinformation." The accelerated up-grading of so sizeable a part of the population in schools and universities everywhere will inescapably affect all our systems.

Much is done both inside and outside the schools to keep young people from realizing their abilities or fulfilling their potential. One answer is war. "*Every twenty years or so we scrap a generation by violent and expensive means, and very soon it is the expense and not the scrapping that bothers us*" (Michael Innes). And in the universities we teach narrow, specialized vocational skills (with the emphasis on earning a living made more important by economic recessions) while paying lip service to "educating the whole man."

Nearly all of us are so victimized by the propaganda of the profit system that we are no longer able to think straight.

In 1971 the Swedish government acquired a ten percent slice of the pharmaceutical industry. Immediately a leading paper in Stockholm pushed the panic button, saying that if Sweden's entire drug industry were to be socialized, then "*they would only produce what is needed*"! Sociopathic and ridiculous, their point is well taken: in industrial circles today, most major research concerns itself not with producing for actual needs, but rather propagandizes people to only desire what has been produced. *If industry in all countries were to produce only what is needed, the future would look bright indeed.*

The industrial design profession still largely continues to heavily support the worst excesses of a profit-seeking system. David Chapman, owner and director of one of the largest design firms in the United States, is a member of the Board of the Industrial Designers Society of America and has been elected a Fellow of both the Royal Society of Arts in England and the International Institute of Arts and Letters in Lindau, Germany. Here is what he said about his concept of true market needs:

> The gift market is another enormous area. In 1966, exclusive of Christmas presents, 90 million people received 107 million gifts. Over 40 percent of table appliances are gifts, even though nobody packs or designs them as gifts. They're designed with some stubborn suspicion that they're meant to *work*. Well, they are—but who *needs* a blender? (In *Design Seminar*. Report. American Iron and Steel Institute, 1970, pp. 4–5.)

He continues, somewhat dejected over a market that does not, alas, yet exist:

> There are 35 million pets in the United States. The owners of those pets spend $300 million a year on pet food, but *only $35 million each year on pet "things." No one has offered the owner a thing to buy for Rover.* It is probably possible to get mink collars at Neiman-Marcus, *but no such merchandise crosses America.* (Italics by Chapman.)

Mr. Chapman also talks about food needs in the United States. After explaining that "the kitchen is as dead as a dodo" and that "the kitchen business—just as the buggy whip—is on its way out," he says that we shall all eat TV dinners. However, he adds reassuringly, "Mamma may give the food a pinch of oregano or shot of sherry for womanly, psychological reasons."

"Designers must learn a lot more about the effect of social factors on products and markets," he continues. "There are 75 million Americans over 45—25 million of them over 65. *They have dentures, stomach trouble and things like that. It's a whole new market,* and they have lots of money to spend on the things they want." Having thus explored the problems of nutrition, the elderly, the sick, and the needy, Mr. Chapman triumphantly concludes:

> On a new car, for instance, the list price was recently $2,500, but with the extras the car cost $4,200. Who *needs* whitewalls? They don't last longer, *they look cuter.* It is possible to mis-recognize the kind of animal we are all dealing with. Basically, it is a creature seeking total indulgence.

When Mr. Chapman uses words like "animal" and "creature," he is talking about you and me: consumers, clients, his public.

Note: When the first edition of this book appeared, outraged letters, telephone calls, and even one telegram accused me of inventing both Mr. Chapman and the quotes given above. It is a question still asked in letters from time to time. I should like to confirm that David Chapman exists and is an esteemed spokesman of the design establishment. Moreover,

Mr. Chapman was definitely not sarcastic in any of his comments; in fact, he went to the trouble of having them printed up in a pamphlet and had his office mail hundreds of copies to fellow designers and students. His remarks were, if anything, a great deal more moderate than those of others in his field. More extreme viewpoints dominated designers' societies, professional meetings, and, what is most disturbing, most design schools in North America. Unblushingly, industrial design in America elected to serve as pimp for the excesses of big business interests.

Ironically, many "glamour jobs" the majority of industrial design students in the United States are educated to deal with and delighted to have just happen to be with firms whose policies and practices are far from enlightened in terms of the public interest or people's desire for well-made, ecologically responsible, and aesthetically pleasing products. Many American corporate giants have been involved in litigation with the government on charges of price-fixing, criminal or civil conspiracies, fraud, antitrust violations, or product liability suits. In other words, in teaching industrial design as we do, we prepare young people to aid and abet those who fail to measure up to even the prevailing minimal standards of ethics or morality—feebly enforced by our judicial agencies.

Here is one example from the seventies: The big three automobile firms were accused before the Supreme Court of having conspired for seventeen years to keep antipollution devices off the market. The three firms freely admitted this. They begged the courts, however, not to prosecute in exchange for their promise that they would "try harder," presumably during the next seventeen years.*

---

*On 30 June 1971, when firms that pollute were to file statements with the federal government, only 50 out of an estimated 80,000 had bothered to do so. More recently (November 1983), we have seen the operators of Three Mile Island indicted on criminal charges by the federal government for destroying data that demonstrated their collusion in refusing to live up to safety standards, to follow clean-up orders, or to cease polluting (ABC *Evening News*, 8 November 1983).

One gratifying fact is that many young designers or students studying design today are unwilling to go on in this same malign way, being fed the pap that the schools dispense so readily. The role of such destructive old-fashioned design is slowly coming to an end. If we list a few of the new generation of products to be expected within the next ten years at most, and if we furthermore restrict this listing to products serving *only the Western world*, we will find:

Tools and artifacts that promote greater autonomy and decentralization

Better and smaller communication devices

Alternative energy sources

Autodiagnostic medical tools

Monorail systems

Ultracompact electric or alternatively powered cars

Personal, battery-driven mobility devices, which can easily be hand-carried

High-quality home appliances (low in energy use, easy to repair)

Mass-produced multiple-use buildings

Modular components for mass housing (informed by vernacular styles of the region)

Automated traffic

High-speed rail networks

Computerized medical diagnostic devices

Television-phones

Education aided through television and teaching machines

Depolluted manufacturing systems

Wide use of biodegradable materials

The effect of these new products would be to leave us with completely obsolete roads, automobile factories, schools, universities, housing, factories, hospitals, newspapers, stores, farms, and railroad systems. It is not difficult to see why big business is afraid of changes that may phase out its plants and

Table service for use by the severely handicapped. The knife blade adjusts to various angles; fork and spoon have extra-heavy handles. The second set of cutlery is for minimally handicapped or "normal" people so that the handicapped feel less conspicuous at meals. The water or wine glasses are plastic (nonbreakable) and have a heavier handle but are otherwise like standard Swedish drinking glasses. Note that the plates (sitting in rubber footing to prevent slipping) have one side raised so that people can more easily push against one edge. Designed for RFSU Rehab, Stockholm, Sweden. Photo by John Charlton.

Experimental light shades. An exercise in "alternative style," designed by Jochen Gros. Photo courtesy: Jochen Gros, Offenbach and International Design Center, Berlin.

products. As factories and industrial combines grow in size, complexity, and investment capital, their opposition to innovation grows. Changes in the system, replacements of the system itself or parts of it become more costly to contemplate and more difficult to institute. Directions of change therefore cannot be expected to be initiated by big business or the military-industrial complex (or the tame, captive designers working for them) but will be initiated by independent design teams.

But before we begin to design smaller and safer things, I

feel that consumers need their own bill of rights—guidelines
that might serve them, as well as designers and industry:

A MANIFESTO OF CONSUMER RIGHTS

1. The *right to safety*, to be protected from hazardous goods.
2. The *right to information*, the right not to be misled by
   lack of information or manipulated misinformation.
3. The *right to basic services, fair prices, and choice*—to
   have access to a variety of products and services and,
   where monopolies do exist, a minimum guaranteed quality at reasonable prices.
4. The *right to representation*, to be consulted and to participate in decisions affecting consumers.
5. The *right to be heard*, to have access to an ombudsman,
   to channels for complaint, and to fair and speedy com-
   pensation procedures.
6. The *right to consumer education*, lifelong consumer education from the viewpoint of users themselves.
7. Finally, and of increasing importance, the *right to a
   healthy and safe environment.* *

Before we can address ourselves to the questions raised by
this Manifesto of Consumer Rights and before we can intelligently think about the more profound issues we face, an
enormous amount of research into the human condition is
necessary. We must explore how human cultures exist in many
times and many places. This will mean assembling diverse
cultural, religious, and structural knowledge, as well as information on social organizational behavior in groups. We
would need facts on countless groups and social structures: the
American Plains Indians; the Mundugumor of the Lower Se-
pik River basin; the priest cultures of the Inca, Maya, Toltec,
and Aztec; the Pueblo cultures of the Hopi; the priest-goddess

---

*These seven points are loosely based on the paper "Striking Out for the
Consumer" by Anwar Fazal (Government of Malaysia Seminar on Consumerism and Society, Kuala Lumpur, December, 1977).

in Crete; the mountain-dwelling Arapesh; Periclean Greece; Samoa of the late nineteenth century; Nazi Germany; modern-day Sweden; Australian aborigines, Bantu, and Eskimo; the place of authority and decision-making in China, imperial Rome, slums, and ghettos; the Loyalist Regime in Spain; delegation of authority in armies, the Catholic Church, modern industrial networks; and so forth.

What are optimal conditions for human society on earth? An inquiry into living patterns, sexual mores, world mobility, codes of behavior, primitive and sophisticated religions and philosophies, and moral issues will be necessary to answer this question.

What are the parameters of the global ecological and ethological systems? Here new insights from such diverse disciplines as sociobiology, meteorology, climatology, physics, chemistry, geology, Von Neumann's Game Theory, cybernetics, oceanography, biology, and all the behavioral sciences will be urgently required, as well as ways of establishing new links between these disciplines.

What are the limits of our resources? Studies comparable to those carried on by Buckminster Fuller's World Resources Inventory Center at Southern Illinois University from 1960 to 1978 will have to be brought into continuous contact with changing technologies and new discoveries.

What are the human limits?

What are the basic housekeeping rules for human life on the planet earth? (Or, in Fuller's phrase: *An Operating Manual for Spaceship Earth.*)

And, finally, what don't we know?

There are very few answers to any of these questions as yet. But the first beginnings have been made in creating tools that may help to begin giving us answers. The International Geophysical Year, the International Years of the Quiet Sun, and the International Upper Mantle Project were all scientific data-gathering attempts of a transnational character. Agencies already exist. UNESCO, UNICEF, the World Health Organization, the International Labor Organization, the

Scientific Committee of Water Research, the International Council of Scientific Unions, the Intergovernmental Oceanographic Commission, and the International Committee of Manpower Resources are just a few of the organizations now in existence who gather, store, and retrieve data of global importance.

In 1970 I felt that there was no question but that an International Council of Anticipatory Comprehensive Design should be established at the earliest moment. It might well be partially funded by and work with UNESCO. Since then there have been a number of approaches made to me to establish such a council, usually in the form of a postgraduate school. What has gone awry so far has to do with a sense of scale. Both Nigeria and Tanzania have tried to interest me in starting such an organization, saying: "It will be the biggest group of its kind in all of black Africa." A similar proposal has been extended to me with the promise that it would "become the largest in Europe." My own feeling is that such a council must be small in scale. The question of scale is more fully discussed in the following pages of this book.

But doing the gigantic research task is only one-third of the job that needs to be done to come to grips with the needs of the world.

The second part is the immediate preempting of presently wasted design efforts and the redirection of these efforts toward short-range practical design needs. One way of achieving this at once has been suggested in Chapter Four as *kymmenykset*. It suggests that designers and design offices immediately begin turning at least one-tenth of their talents and working time toward the solving of those social problems that may yield to design solutions. Furthermore, it means (as suggested in Chapter Ten) that designers refuse to participate in work that is biologically or socially destructive (whether directly or indirectly).

Just this alone would be a gigantic step toward the common good. We have marveled together, in an earlier chapter, that merely by eliminating the rotting of food and by stopping the destruction of food by vermin, the total protein intake of billions would be raised from starvation to nutritionally acceptable levels. The same can be done in design. Merely by eliminating the social and moral irresponsibility still prevalent in all too many design offices and schools, the needs of the neglected southern half of the world could be met.

Finally, and as my third point, completely new directions must be explored in the education of young designers. While this topic has been given an entire chapter to itself, some further observations are in order.

The unchecked growth of schools, colleges, and universities has created an environment that is harmful to innovation or, for that matter, education. The problem of scale alone (the university at which I used to teach has 27,000 students, and there are universities more than three times as large) works against education. It tends to make students feel like cogs in a machine, reduces them to numbers, and alienates them. This fragments their efforts, and a true learning situation cannot arise. At the other end of the scale there are private schools, which are considered small, with between 500 to 3,000 students. These institutions substitute exclusiveness and the atmosphere of a country club for the giantism of state universities. The third type of school is usually a highly specialized one, dealing with the specific problems of the arts, crafts, or what have you. These schools suffer from a lack of broad general resources and subject matter and tend to perpetuate the exclusivity of artists-craftsmen and the formation of little cliques. The fourth possibility, as set up in England nearly two decades ago, is a university open to all, where courses are taken via correspondence, radio, and television.

The last-mentioned model is the Open University program on television in England, now in its twentieth year. By tying viewers together through books, quizzes, television programs, and small discussion groups—as well as by requiring participants to engage in correspondence with the scholars that organize it—Open University classes have been enormously effective, especially in product design, graphics, and environmental design. This, in spite of the fact that it precludes the design team, does away with open ended communication and leaves the nub of the learning process in design, synthesis, up to each individual student.

In all likelihood there are reasons and needs in our society that can be used to justify all four of these methods of teaching. But we are too often forced to make a choice between size and exclusiveness.

Some intensive hands-on design education has come from the crafts. In today's renaissance of crafts, weaving, silversmithing, glassblowing, ceramics, and sculpture are all practiced and taught in small centers that are directed primarily toward the summer vacation trade. Such centers exist in Maine, California, New Mexico, Michigan, Wisconsin, and North Carolina. Through its summer tuition, such craft centers support a group of resident craftsmen throughout the other nine months of the year. Penland in North Carolina is dedicated to a free mix of professional craftsmen, craft teachers, college students, retired couples, little old ladies in tennis shoes, and world-renowned designers. It is a seminal force in re-establishing a cottage industry based on the crafts among nearly inaccessible small farms in southern Appalachia.

Frank Lloyd Wright tried to create a milieu that would be conducive to the study of architecture and planning at Taliesin and Taliesin West. Unfortunately this experiment, lasting fifty years, was too strongly overshadowed by Mr. Wright's own powerful personality. With this architectural exception, the study, research, and practice of design and planning as socially and morally responsible activities has rarely been attempted.

It seems crucial that such an experimental design milieu be established somewhere in the world now. I envision it less as a school than as a working environment. Here, young people would learn through working on real design problems rather than artificially constructed exercises. Such a working environment would, of necessity, be small in size, at no time accepting more than thirty students. It would serve as a prototype for similar environmental design workshops to be set up as parts of an interacting global network. Ultimately, students might then have the choice between one school with 30,000 students and 1,000 environments of thirty students each.

The young people coming to this first, prototypal school would come from all parts of the world. They would stay for a year or longer and participate in the simultaneous learning and practicing of integrated design. These young men and women would be of varied backgrounds, differing age groups, with study and work experiences in many different fields. At all times they would operate as a multidisciplinary design team. Their work would be socially relevant. Rather than setting to work on theoretical problems chosen only for their similarities to problems dealt with in professional design offices (as is done in present-day schools), members of the team would direct their attention to the actual needs of society. All the work carried on in this milieu would be anticipatory.

Such an environment would satisfy a major social need not filled today: the creation of a body of designers trained in the skills that the future will demand of them. Just as astronauts and cosmonauts are taught skills that may be demanded of them months or years hence on the moon or Mars, the design team too will have to prepare itself for the social challenges of integrated comprehensive design that the future will bring. The solutions of design problems will be turned over to concerned individuals, social groups, governments, or transnational organizations.

This entire concept of an experimental design environment is thought of as nonprofit. Any money earned through solving such real problems would be directly returned to the work group as tools, machinery, devices, structures, and land. We only have to examine learning situations that people find rewarding, fun, and in which they learn optimally, to see why the small scale of this group is important.

There is no question that teachers (especially in design) must be constantly involved in its practice. But only a system such as the one proposed here will eliminate the false divorce between practice and teaching.

All members of this team might live and work communally. Their existence would be eased through communal sharing: that is, consuming more, but owning less. A representative group of thirty present-day university students will serve as one small example: they own, on the average, twenty-six automobiles, thirty-one radios, and fifteen high-fidelity systems. Without belaboring the obvious, such a capital investment in transient consumer goods would eliminate itself. While expediency would demand the starting of such a "school" in a series of old buildings, a farm, or the like, the eventual buildings would be the responsibility of the team. Temporary domes, information-input cubes (à la Ken Isaacs), and the constructing of more permanent working rooms, sleeping spaces, and social spaces would provide team members with valuable experiences in a living-working environment—one that is constantly changing, constantly being questioned, and experimentally restructured through their own thinking and their own labor.

Their "curriculum" would be a loosely woven mesh of those activities and skills needed for creative problem-solving. There could be no separation between their work and their leisure-time activities. The newest methods of data-processing, film-making, and so forth would be available to the team. Such a center of design research and planning would have to be able to offer its hospitality to workers from many disciplines. Such concerned workers could then be drawn into the working and living experiences of the team for a few days, weeks, or even a year. Because of the experimental nature of the various structures making up the environment, such a center would best be located in the country but close enough to major urban centers to participate in studies, internship work, and experiences in the city environment. What is studied, and how, would evolve organically out of the needs of society. There could never be a static "plan of study."

Within two or three years some members would leave, their

minds full of ideas for a better way of running such an environment. The students' leaving would be actively encouraged to bring about dynamic changes. For it is my belief that if such a center were to be established, soon other similar centers would begin to "spin off." These new centers would be able to address themselves to local and regional problems around the world. They would form the links in a network of such environments. At each center, young people would be encouraged to travel widely. Such travel could well include a few months' or years' stay and participation in the work at another center. Two things are proposed here: the establishment of a learning-working environment for thirty young people and, ideally, a network of learning centers for the world.

In the preceding chapter I explored the dynamics of the integrated designer's methods of problem solving and diagramed them. By now, it will be obvious that I have written this entire book according to this same diagram. It has been derived from the input of many flow charts. That is why it must lack a smooth, linear sequence. The task at hand has been to present you, the reader, with a collection of jigsaw puzzle pieces, which I urge you to put together in whatever pattern seems to make sense. There is no other way of presenting the simultaneity of events.

Books like this are expected to end with a dazzling view of the future, and ordinarily this would be the place to speak about vast cities under the ocean, colonies on Mars and Proxima Centauri, machines that will provide us with an everlasting cornucopia of electronic gadgets. But that would clearly be insane.

Design, if it is to be ecologically responsible and socially responsive, must be revolutionary and radical in the truest sense. It must dedicate itself to nature's principle of least effort, in other words, maximum diversity with minimum inventory (to use Peter Pearce's good phrase) or doing the most with the least. That means consuming less, using things longer, and being frugal about recycling materials.

The insights, the broad, nonspecialized, interactive over-view of a team (heritage of early man, the hunter) that the designer can bring to the world must now be combined with a sense of social responsibility. In many areas designers must learn how to redesign. In this way we may yet have survival through design.

BIBLIOGRAPHY

Bibliography

Nearly 500 titles appeared in the bibliography to the first edition of this book. More than 200 more have been added. Having just written a book on design as a multidisciplinary approach, I have tried to make the bibliography multidisciplinary as well. Consequently books (and, occasionally, journals, catalogs, and pamphlets) dealing with ecology, ethology, economics, biology, planning, psychology, literature, anthropology, politics, and the behavioral sciences are listed together with books on the future, the environment, popular culture, and design.

The function of this bibliography is to suggest some titles that would make a good start for a designer or design student wishing to read in other areas in order to see the interrelation of design with other disciplines.

From the linear thinking of the Renaissance (that great setting of the sun, which man mistook for the dawn), when men still thought all their knowledge classifiable, we have inherited our graphs, divisions, classifications, and lists. Typically when we wish to classify areas of knowledge too vast to be so comprehended, we make the crowning mistake: we educate *specialists*.

But as we go toward the year 2000, as we see divisions that the last few generations have painstakingly erected out of the quicksand of their statisticians' minds crumble away, we find no need for more such distinct areas but for unity. Not the *specialist* then, but the *synthesist*.

This is the way in which a meaningful organic pattern, unity, synthesis, will grow between you and each book you read. Out of all the battles you have with the author, the enlightenments and insights his book gives you, the mistakes and confusions you will discover in his work, there *will grow a new entity*, and it will be your gain.

In the preface to the first edition I wrote, ". . . the one book I wanted to read, the one book I most wanted to hand to my fellow students and designers, was missing . . . . So I decided to write the kind of book that I'd like to read." Nearly a dozen books on design have been published since then. Several of these are excellent.

Mayal, W.H. *Principles in Design*. New York: Van Nostrand Reinhold, 1979.

Nelson, George. *How to See*. Boston: Little Brown & Co., 1977.

———. *On Design*. New York: Whitney Publications, 1979.

Pile, John F. *Design: Purpose, Form, and Meaning*. Amherst: University of Massachusetts Press, 1979.

Potter, Norman. *What is a Designer: Things, Places, Messages*. Reading, England: Hyphen Press, 1980.

Pye, David. *The Nature and Aesthetics of Design*. New York: Van Nostrand Reinhold, 1978.

Williams, Christopher. *Origins of Form*. New York: Architectural Book Publishing Co., 1981.

Unfortunately none of these books addresses itself to the social and human dimensions of design.

Critchlow, Keith. *Time Stands Still*. London: Gordon Fraser, 1979.

Doczi, Gyorgy. *The Power of Limits*. Boulder, Colorado: Shambhala Publications, 1981.

Lawlor, Robert. *Sacred Geometry*. London: Thames & Hudson, 1982.

These three excellent volumes deal with the relationship between design, biology, and geometry.

Finally I have found two books that deal with the relationship between culture and design, design and society.

Keller, Goroslav. *Dizajn.* Zagreb: Vjesnik, 1975.
Selle, Gert. *Ideologie und Utopie des Design: zur Gesellschaftlichen Theorie der Industriellen Formgebung.* Cologne: DuMont, 1975.

Both are difficult to read in the original language and have not been translated.

STRUCTURE, NATURE, AND DESIGN

Alexander, Christopher. *The Linz Cafe/Das Linz Cafe.* New York: Oxford University Press, 1981.
_____. *Notes on the Synthesis of Form.* Cambridge, Massachusetts: Harvard University Press, 1964.
_____. "Systems Generating Systems," in *Systemat.* Inland Steel Co., 1967.
_____. *A Timeless Way of Building.* New York: Oxford University Press, 1979.
Alexander, Christopher; Ishikawa, Sara; and Silverstein, Murray. *A Pattern Language.* New York: Oxford University Press, 1977.
Alexander, R. McNeill. *Animal Mechanics.* Sidgwick & Jackson, 1968.
Architectural Research Laboratory. *Structural Potential of Foam Plastics for Housing in Underdeveloped Areas.* Ann Arbor, Michigan, 1966.
Baer, Steve. *Dome Cookbook.* Corrales, New Mexico: Lama Foundation, 1969.
Bager, Bertel. *Nature as Designer.* Frederick Sarne, 1971.
"Bionik." Special number of *Urania* magazine. Leipzig, Germany, August, 1969.
Blake, Peter. *Form Follows Fiasco.* Boston: Atlantic, Little, Brown, 1977.
Bootzin, D., and Muffley, H.C. (eds.). *Biomechanics.* New York: Plenum Press, 1969.
Borrego, John. *Space Grid Structures.* Cambridge, Massachusetts: M.I.T. Press, 1968.
Boys, C. V. *Soap-Bubbles.* London: Heinemann Educational Books, 1960.
Brand, Stewart (ed.). *The Whole Earth Catalog* (all issues). Menlo Park, California, 1968–1970.
Burkhardt, Dietrich; Schleidt, Wolfgang; and Altner, Helmut. *Signals in the Animal World.* London: Allen & Unwin, 1967.
Clark, Sir Kenneth. *The Nude.* Middlesex: Penguin, 1970.

Cook, Theodore Andrea. *The Curves of Life.* London: Constable & Co., 1940.

Critchlow, Keith. *Order in Space.* London: Thames & Hudson, 1969.

Cundy, M. Martyn, and Rollet, A.P. *Mathematical Models.* (2d ed.). New York: Oxford University Press, 1962.

Doczi, Gyorgy. *The Power of Limits: Proportional Harmonies in Nature, Art and Architecture.* Boulder, Colorado: Shambhala Publications, 1981.

Fathy, Hassan. *Architecture for the Poor.* Chicago: University of Chicago Press, 1973.

Ganich, Rolf. *Konstruktion, Design, Aesthetik.* Germany: Esslingen am Neckar, 1968.

Gerardin, Lucien. *Bionics.* London: Weidenfeld & Nicolson, 1968.

Grillo, Paul Jacques. *What Is Design?* Chicago: Paul Theobald, 1962.

Hertel, Heinrich. *Structure, Form and Movement: Biology and Engineering.* New York: Van Nostrand Reinhold, 1966.

Heythum, Antonin. *On Art, Beauty and the Useful.* Stierstadt im Taunus, Germany: Verlag Eremiten-Presse, 1955.

Hoenich, P.K. *Robot Art.* Haifa, Israel: Technion, 1962.

Holden, Alan, and Singer, Phyllis. *Crystals and Crystal Growing.* London: Heinemann Educational Books, 1961.

Huntley, H.E. *The Divine Proportion.* New York: Dover, 1970.

Jenny, Hans. *Cymatics: The Structure and Dynamics of Waves and Vibrations.* Basel: Basilius Presse, 1967.

Kare, Morley, and Bernard, E.E. (eds.). *Biological Prototypes and Manmade Systems.* New York: Plenum Press, 1962.

Katavolos, William. *Organics.* Hilversum, Holland: De Jong & Co., 1961.

Keller, Goroslav. *Dizajn.* Zagreb: Vjesnik, 1975.

———. *Ergonomija za Dizajnere.* Belgrade: "Ergonomija," 1978.

Lawlor, Robert. *Sacred Geometry.* New York: Crossroad, 1982.

Negroponte, Nicholas. *The Architecture Machine.* Cambridge, Massachusetts: M.I.T. Press, 1970.

Oliver, Paul. *Shelter and Society.* London: Barrie & Jenkins, 1970.

———. *Shelter in Africa.* New York: Praeger, 1971.

———. *Shelter, Sign and Symbol.* New York: The Overlook Press, 1977.

Otto, Frei (ed.). *Pneumatic Structures,* Vol. 1 of *Tensile Structures.* Cambridge, Massachusetts: M.I.T. Press, 1967.

———. *Cables, Nets and Membranes,* Vol. 2 of *Tensile Structures.* Cambridge, Massachusetts: M.I.T. Press, 1969.

Pawlowski, Andrzej. *Fragmenty Prac Naukowo-Badawczych.* Krakau, Poland, 1966.

Pearce, Peter. *Structure in Nature is a Strategy for Design*. Cambridge, Massachusetts: M.I.T. Press, 1978.

Pearce, Peter, and Pearce, Susan. *Experiments in Form*. New York: Van Nostrand Reinhold, 1978.

_____. *Polyhedra Primer*. New York: Van Nostrand Reinhold, 1978.

Popko, Edward. *Geodesics*. Detroit: University of Detroit Press, 1968.

Ritterbush, Philip C. *The Art of Organic Forms*. Washington, D.C.: Smithsonian Press, 1968.

Schillinger, Joseph. *The Mathematical Basis of the Arts*. New York: Philosophical Library, 1948.

Schwenk, Theodor. *Sensitive Chaos: The Creation of Flowing Forms in Water and Air*. Rudolf Steiner Press, 1965.

Selle, Gert. *Ideologie und Utopie des Design*. Cologne: DuMont, 1973.

Sinnott, Edmund W. *The Problem of Organic Form*. New Haven, Connecticut: Yale University Press, 1963.

Thompson, Sir D'Arcy Wentworth. *On Growth and Form* (2 vols.). Cambridge: Cambridge University Press, 1952.

Turner, John F. C. *Housing by People: Towards Autonomy in Building Environments*. London: Marion Boyars Ltd., 1976.

Watkin, David. *Morality and Architecture*. Oxford: Clarendon Press, 1977.

Wedd, Dunkin. *Pattern & Texture*. New York: Studio Books, 1956.

Weyl, Hermann. *Symmetry*. Princeton, New Jersey: Princeton University Press, 1952.

Whyte, Lancelot Law. *Accent on Form*. New York: Harper, 1954.

_____. *Aspects of Form*. London: Lund Humphries, 1951.

_____. *The Next Development in Man.* New York: Mentor, 1950.

Williams, Christopher. *Origins of Form*. New York: Architectural Book Publishing Company, 1981.

Zodiac (magazine). Vol. 19. Milan, Italy, 1969.

DESIGN AND THE ENVIRONMENT

Arvill, Robert. *Man and Environment*. Middlesex: Penguin, 1967.

Baer, Steve. *Sunspots*. Seattle: Cloudburst Press, 1979.

Boughey, Arthur S. *Ecology of Populations*. New York: Macmillan, 1968.

Calder, Ritchie. *After the Seventh Day*. New York: Mentor, 1967.

Commoner, Barry. *Science and Survival*. London: Gollancz, 1966.

Consumer's Association of Penang. *Development and the Environmental Crisis: A Malaysian Case*. Penang: Consumer's Association of Penang, 1982.

Curtis, Richard, and Hogan, Elizabeth. *Perils of the Peaceful Atom*. London: Gollancz, 1970.

DeBell, Garrett (ed.). *The Environmental Handbook*. New York: Ballantine, 1970.

Dubos, Rene. *Celebrations of Life*. New York: McGraw-Hill, 1981.

––––––. *Man, Medicine, and Environment*. Middlesex: Penguin, 1970.

––––––. *The Wooing of Earth*. New York: Charles Scribner, 1980.

Ehrlich, Paul. "Eco-Catastrophe!" *Ramparts*, September, 1968.

––––––. *The Population Bomb*. New York: Ballantine, 1970.

Giedion, Siegfried. *Mechanization Takes Command*. New York: Oxford University Press, 1948.

––––––. *Space, Time and Architecture*. Cambridge, Massachusetts: Harvard University Press, 1949.

––––––. *The Beginnings of Architecture*. Vol. 2. Princeton, New Jersey: Bollingen Series, Princeton University Press, 1964.

––––––. *The Eternal Present: The Beginnings of Art*. Vol. 1. Princeton, New Jersey: Bollingen Series, Princeton University Press, 1962.

Johnson, Warren. *Muddling Toward Frugality*. San Francisco: Sierra Club Books, 1978.

Kaprow, Allan. *Assemblage, Environments and Happenings*. New York: Abrams, 1966.

Kouwenhoen, John A. *The Beer Can by the Highway*. New York: Doubleday, 1961.

––––––. *Half a Truth is Better than None*. Chicago: University of Chicago Press, 1982.

––––––. *Made in America*. New York: Doubleday, 1948.

Kuhns, William. *Environmental Man*. New York: Harper & Row, 1969.

Linton, Ron. *Terracide: America's Destruction of Her Living Environment*. Boston: Little, Brown, 1970.

Lippard, Lucy R. *Overlay: Contemporary Art and the Art of Pre-History*. New York: Pantheon, 1983.

Lovelock, J. E. *Gaia: A New Look at Life on Earth*. New York: Oxford University Press, 1979.

Lynes, Russell. *The Tastemakers*. New York: Harper, 1954.

––––––. *Confessions of a Dilettante*. New York: Harper & Row, 1967.

––––––. *The Domesticated Americans*. New York: Harper & Row, 1963.

McHarg, Ian L. *Design with Nature*. New York: Natural History Press, 1969.

Marine, Gene. *America the Raped: The Engineering Mentality and the Devastation of a Continent.* New York: Simon & Schuster, 1969.

Marx, Wesley. *The Frail Ocean.* New York: Ballantine, 1970.

Mitchell, John G. (ed.). *Ecotactics.* New York: Pocketbooks, 1970.

Mollison, Bill. *Perma-Culture One.* Melbourne: Transworld, 1978.

————. *Perma-Culture Two.* Stanley, Tazmania: Tagari Books, 1979.

Mumford, Lewis. *Technics and Civilization.* New York: Harcourt, Brace, 1934.

————. *The Brown Decades.* New York: Dover, 1955.

————. *The City in History.* Middlesex: Penguin, 1966.

————. *The Condition of Man.* New York: Harcourt, Brace, 1944.

————. *The Conduct of Life.* New York: Harcourt, Brace, 1951.

————. *The Culture of Cities.* New York: Harcourt, Brace, 1938.

————. *From the Ground Up.* New York: Harcourt, Brace, 1956.

————. *Sticks and Stones.* New York: Dover, 1955.

Paddock, William, and Paddock, Paul. *Famine 1975!* Boston: Little, Brown, 1967.

Palmstierna, Hans. *Plundring, Svält, Forgiftning.* Orebro, Sweden: Rabén & Sjögren, 1969.

Ramo, Simon. *Cure for Chaos.* New York: David McKay, 1969.

Rienow, Robert, and Train, Leona. *Moment in the Sun.* New York: Ballantine, 1970.

Shepard, Paul. *Man in the Landscape.* New York: Knopf, 1967.

Shepard, Paul, and McKinley, Daniel. *The Subversive Science: Essays Toward an Ecology of Man.* Boston: Houghton Mifflin, 1969.

Shurcliff, William A. *S/S/T and Sonic Boom Handbook.* New York: Ballantine, 1970.

Smithsonian Institution. *The Fitness of Man's Environment.* Washington, D.C.: Smithsonian Press, 1967.

Sommer, Robert. *Big Art.* Philadelphia: Running Press, 1977.

————. *Design Awareness.* San Francisco: Rinehart Press, 1972.

————. *Personal Space: The Behavioral Basis of Design.* Englewood Cliffs, New Jersey: Prentice-Hall, 1969.

————. *Street Art.* New York: Links Books, 1975.

————. *Tight Spaces.* Englewood Cliffs, New Jersey: Prentice-Hall, 1974.

Sotamaa, Yrjö (ed.). *Teollisuus, Ymparisto, Tuotesuunnittelu [Industry, design, environment]* (4 vols., trilingual). Helsinki, Finland, 1969.

Still, Henry. *The Dirty Animal.* New York: Hawthorn, 1967.

Taylor, Gordon Rattray. *The Biological Time Bomb.* London: Panther, 1969.

Todd, John, and Todd, Nancy. *Tomorrow is our Permanent Address*. New York: Harper & Row, 1979.

United Nations. *Chemical and Bacteriological (Biological) Weapons and the Effects of Their Possible Use*. New York: Ballantine, 1970.

Whiteside, Thomas. *Defoliation*. New York: Ballantine, 1970.

DESIGN AND THE FUTURE

Allaby, Michael. *Inventing Tomorrow*. London: Abacus Books, 1977.

Allen, Edward. *Stone Shelters*. Cambridge, Massachusetts: M.I.T. Press, 1969.

Calder, Nigel. *The Environment Game*. London: Panther, 1968.

———(ed.). *The World in 1984*. 2 vols. Middlesex: Penguin, 1965.

Chase, Stuart. *The Most Probable World*. New York: Harper & Row, 1968.

Clarke, Arthur C. *Profiles of the Future*. London: Gollancz, 1962.

Cole, Dandridge M. *Beyond Tomorrow*. Madison, Wisconsin: Amherst Press, 1965.

Cook, Peter. *Experimental Architecture*. New York: Universe Books, 1970.

Ellul, Jacques. *The Betrayal of the West*. New York: The Seabury Press, 1978.

———. *The Technological Society*. New York: Vintage, 1967.

———. *The Technological System*. New York: Continuum, 1980.

Ewald, William R. Jr. *Environment and Change. The Next Fifty Years*. all: Bloomington, Ind.: Indiana University Press, 1968.

———. *Environment and Policy. The Next Fifty Years*.

———(ed.). *Environment for Man. The Next Fifty Years*.

Fuller, R. Buckminster. *Education Automation*. Carbondale, Illinois: Southern Illinois University Press, 1964.

———. *Ideas and Integrities*. Englewood Cliffs, New Jersey: Prentice-Hall, 1963.

———. *Nine Chains to the Moon*. Philadelphia: J.B. Lippincott, 1938.

———. *No More Secondhand God*. Carbondale, Illinois: Southern Illinois University Press, 1963.

———. *Operating Manual for Spaceship Earth*. Carbondale, Illinois: Southern Illinois University Press, 1969.

———. *Untitled Epic Poem on the History of Industrialization*. Highlands, North Carolina: Jonathan Williams Press, 1962.

———. *Utopia or Oblivion*. London: Allen Lane, 1970.

———(ed.). *Inventory of World Resources, Human Trends and Needs* (World Science Decade 1965–75: Phase I, Document 1).

_____. *The Design Initiative* (Phase I, Doc. 2).
_____. *Comprehensive Thinking* (Phase I, Doc. 3).
_____(ed.). *The Ten Year Program* (Phase I, Doc. 4).
_____. *Comprehensive Design Strategy* (Phase I, Doc. 5).
_____. *The Ecological Context: Energy and Materials* (Phase II, Doc. 6).
_____. *Synergetics*. New York: Macmillan, 1975.
_____. *Synergetics 2*. New York: Macmillan, 1979.
_____. *Critical Path*. New York: St. Martin's Press, 1981.
Hellman, Hal. *Transportation in the World of the Future*. New York: J.B. Lippincott, 1968.
Kahn, Herman, and Wiener, Anthony J. *The Year 2000: Scenarios for the Future*. New York: Macmillan, 1967.
Krampen, Martin (ed.). *Design and Planning*. New York: Hastings House, 1965.
_____. *Design and Planning 2*. New York: Hastings House, 1967.
McHale, John. *The Future of the Future*. New York: George Braziller, 1969.
Marek, Kurt W. *Yestermorrow*. New York: Knopf, 1961.
Marks, Robert W. *The Dymaxion World of Buckminster Fuller*. New York: Reinhold, 1960.
Morgan, Chris. *Future Man?* London: David & Charles, 1980.
Prehoda, Robert W. *Designing the Future*. New York: Chilton, 1967.
Ribeiro, Darcy. *The Civilizational Process*. Washington, D.C.: Smithsonian Press, 1968.
Schell, Jonathon. *The Fate of the Earth*. London: Pan Books, 1982.
Skinner, B.F. *Walden Two*. New York: Macmillan, 1948.
Toward the Year 2000: Work in Progress. *Daedalus*, summer 1967.

AGGRESSION, TERRITORIALITY, BIOLOGICAL SYSTEMS, AND DESIGN

Ardrey, Robert. *African Genesis*. London: Collins, 1961
_____. *The Hunting Hypothesis*. New York: Atheneum, 1976.
_____. *The Social Contract*. London: Collins, 1970.
_____. *The Territorial Imperative*. London: Collins, 1967.
Bates, Marston. *The Forest and the Sea*. New York: Vintage, 1965.
Bateson, Gregory. *Mind and Nature: A Necessary Unity*. New York: E.P. Dutton, 1979.
Birdsal, Derek. *The Living Treasures of Japan*. London: Wildwood House, 1973.
Bliebtreu, John N. *The Parable of the Beast*. London: Paladin, 1970.
Blond, Georges. *The Great Migration of Animals*. New York: Collier, Macmillan, 1962.

Broadhurst, P. L. *The Science of Animal Behavior*. Middlesex: Penguin, 1963.

Brooks, John. *Showing Off in America: From Conspicuous Consumption to Parody Display*. Boston: Little, Brown, 1981.

Brunwald, Jan Harold. *The Vanishing Hitchhiker: American Urban Legends and Their Meanings*. New York: W.W. Norton, 1981.

Burton, John. *The Oxford Book of Insects*. Oxford: Oxford University Press, 1981.

Buxton, Jean. *Religion and Healing in Mandari*. Oxford: The Clarendon Press, 1973.

Callan, Hilary. *Ethology and Society: Towards an Anthropological View*. Oxford: The Clarendon Press, 1970.

Charter, S.P.R. *For Unto Us a Child is Born: A Human Ecological Overview of Population Pressures*. San Francisco: Applegate, 1968.

————. *Man on Earth*. San Francisco: Applegate, 1965.

Cohen, Abner. *Custom and Politics in Urban Africa*. London: Routledge & Kegan Paul, 1969.

————. *Two-Dimensional Man*. London: Routledge & Kegan Paul, 1974.

Critchfield, Richard. *Villages*. New York: Doubleday, 1981.

Darling, F. Fraser. *A Herd of Red Deer*. Oxford University Press, 1937.

Douglas, Mary. *Implicit Meanings*. London: Routledge & Kegan Paul, 1975.

————. *Natural Symbols*. New York: Pantheon, 1982.

————. *Purity and Danger*. London: Routledge & Kegan Paul, 1966.

————. *Risk and Culture: An Essay on the Selection of Technical and Environmental Dangers*. Berkeley: University of California Press, 1982.

————. *The World of Goods*. New York: Basic Books, 1979.

Dowdeswell, W.H. *Animal Ecology*. London: Methuen, 1966.

Eiseley, Loren. *The Firmament of Time*. New York: Atheneum, 1966.

————. *The Immense Journey*. New York: Vintage, 1957.

Elgin, Duane. *Voluntary Simplicity*. New York: William Morrow, 1981.

Evans-Pritchard, E. E. *Essays in Social Anthropology*. London: Faber and Faber, 1962.

————. *A History of Anthropological Thought*. London: Faber and Faber, 1981.

————. *The Nuer*. Oxford: The Clarendon Press, 1940.

————. *Nuer Religion*. Oxford: The Clarendon Press, 1956.

————. *The Position of Women in Primitive Societies and Other Essays in Social Anthropology.* London: Faber and Faber, 1965.

————. *The Sanusi of Cyrenaica.* London: Faber and Faber, 1949.

————. *Social Anthropology.* London: Routledge & Kegan Paul, 1951.

————. *Theories of Primitive Religion.* London: Faber and Faber, 1965.

————. *Witchcraft Oracles and Magic Among the Azande.* London: Faber and Faber, 1937.

————(ed.). *Man and Woman Among the Azande.* London: Faber and Faber, 1974.

————(ed.). *The Zande Trickster.* London: Faber and Faber, 1967.

Evans-Pritchard, E. E., and Fortes, M. *African Political Systems.* London: Oxford University Press, 1940.

Farb, Peter, and Armelagos, George. *Consuming Passions: The Anthropology of Eating.* Boston: Houghton Mifflin, 1980.

Fogg, William. *The Living Arts of Nigeria.* London: Studio Vista, 1971.

Ford, E. B. *Moths.* London: Collins, 1955.

Fox, Robin. *Encounter with Anthropology.* New York: Harcourt Brace Jovanovich, 1973.

Gabus, Jean. *Au Sahara: Arts et Symboles.* Neuchâtel: La Baconniere, 1958.

Gray, James. *How Animals Move.* Middlesex: Penguin, 1959.

Grey, Walter W. *The Living Brain.* Middlesex: Penguin, 1961.

Hall, Edward T. *Beyond Culture.* New York: Doubleday, 1976.

————. *The Dance of Life.* New York: Doubleday, 1976.

————. *The Hidden Dimension.* London: Bodley Head, 1969.

————. *The Silent Language.* New York: Doubleday, 1959.

Hill, Polly. *Rural Hausa.* Cambridge: Cambridge University Press, 1972.

Ingle, Clyde. *From Village to State in Tanzania.* Ithaca: Cornell University Press, 1973.

Koenig, Lilli. *Studies in Animal Behavior.* New York: Apollo Editions, 1967.

Koestler, Arthur. *Bricks to Babel.* New York: Random House, 1980.

————. *The Case of the Midwife Toad.* New York: Random House, 1971.

————. *The Ghost in the Machine.* London: Hutchinson, 1967.

————. *Insight and Outlook.* New York: Macmillan, 1949.

————. *Janus: A Summing Up.* New York: Random House, 1972.

————. *Kaleidoscope.* London: Hutchinson, 1959.

————. *The Roots of Coincidence.* New York: Random House, 1972.

————. *The Sleepwalkers.* London: Hutchinson, 1959.

Kohr, Leopold. *The Breakdown of Nations.* New York: E. P. Dutton, 1978.

————. *Development Without Aid.* New York: Schocken Books, 1979.

————. *The Overdeveloped Nations.* New York: Schocken Books, 1979.

Lévi-Strauss, Claude. *The Raw and the Cooked. Vol. 1. of Introduction to a Science of Mythology.* London: Jonathan Cape, 1970.

————*From Honey to Ashes. Vol. 2 of Introduction to a Science of Mythology.* New York: Harper & Row, 1973.

————. *The Origin of Table Manners. Vol. 3 of Introduction to a Science of Mythology.* New York: Harper & Row, 1978.

————. *The Naked Man. Vol. 4 of Introduction to a Science of Mythology.* New York: Harper & Row, 1981.

————. *Tristes tropiques.* Paris: Plon, 1955.

————. *The Way of the Masks.* Seattle: University of Washington Press, 1982.

LeVine, Robert A. *Culture, Behaviour, and Personality.* London: Hutchinson, 1973.

Lienhardt, Godfrey. *Divinity and Experience: The Religion of the Dinka.* Oxford: The Clarendon Press, 1961.

Lindauer, Martin. *Binas Sprak.* Stockholm: Bonniers, 1964.

Lorenz, Konrad. *Behind the Mirror.* New York: Harcourt Brace Jovanovich, 1977.

————. *Civilized Man's Eight Deadly Sins.* London: Metheun, 1974.

————. *Darwin hat recht Gesehen.* Pfullingen, Germany: Guenther Neske, 1965.

————. *Der Vogelflug.* Pfullingen, Germany: Guenther Neske, 1965.

————. *Er redete mit dem Vieh, den Vögeln, and den Fischen.* Vienna, Austria: Borotha-Schoeler, 1949.

————. *Man Meets Dog.* London: Methuen, 1955.

————. *On Aggression.* London: Methuen, 1966.

————. *Studies in Animal and Human Behavior. Volume I.* Methuen, 1970.

————. *Ueber tierisches und menschliches Verhalten.* 2 vols. Munich, Germany: Piper, 1966.

————. *The Year of the Greylag Goose.* New York: Harcourt Brace Jovanovich, 1978.

Marais, Eugene. *The Soul of the Ape.* New York: Atheneum, 1969.

Morris, Desmond. *The Biology of Art.* London: Methuen, 1966.

————. *The Naked Ape.* London: Jonathan Cape, 1967.

Mumford, Lewis. *Technics and Human Development. Vol. 1 of The Myth of the Machine.* London: Secker & Warburg, 1967.

————. *The Pentagon of Power*. Vol. 2 *of The Myth of the Machine*. London: Secker & Warburg, 1971.

National Museum of Chad. *L'Art Sao*. N'djamena: Debroisse, 1960.

Paturi, Felix R. *Nature, Mother of Invention: The Engineering of Plant Life*. Middlesex: Pelican, 1978.

Riefenstahl, Leni. *The Last of the Nuba*. New York: Harper & Row, 1974.

————. *The People of Kau*. New York: Harper & Row, 1976.

————. *Vanishing Africa*. New York: Harmony Books, 1982.

Rifkin, Jeremy. *Entropy*. New York: The Viking Press, 1980.

Shepard, Paul. *The Tender Carnivore and the Sacred Game*. New York: Charles Scribner, 1973.

————. *Thinking Animals*. New York: Viking Press, 1978.

Sheppard, Mubin. *Living Crafts of Malaysia*. Singapore: Times Books International, 1978.

Siebert, Erna and Forman, Werner. *L'Art des Indiens d'Amerique*. Paris: Editiones Cercle d'Art, 1967.

Sikes, Sylvia K. *Lake Chad*. London: Eyre Methuen, 1972.

Singer, Peter. *The Expanding Circle: Ethics and Sociobiology*. New York: Farrar, Straus & Giroux, 1981.

Stavrianos, L. S. *Global Rift: The Third World Comes of Age*. New York: William Morrow & Co., 1981.

————. *The Promise of the Coming Dark Age*. San Francisco: W. H. Freeman & Co., 1976.

Storr, Anthony. *Human Aggression*. Middlesex: Allen Lane, Penguin Press, 1968.

Taylor, Gordon Rattray. *The Biological Time Bomb*. London: Panther, 1969.

Telfer, William, et al. (eds.). *The Biology of Organisms*. New York: Wiley, 1965.

————. *The Biology of Populations*. New York: Wiley, 1966.

Thompson, William Irwin. *At the Edge of History*. New York: Harper & Row, 1971.

————. *Darkness and Scattered Light*. New York: Doubleday, 1978.

————. *Evil and World Order*. New York: Harper & Row, 1976.

————. *Passages About Earth*. New York: Harper & Row, 1974.

Thurow, Lester C. *The Zero-Sum Society*. New York: Basic Books, 1980.

Tiger, Lionel. *Optimism: The Biology of Hope*. New York: Simon & Schuster, 1979.

Tinbergen, Nicolaas. *The Herring Gull's World*. London: Collins, 1967.

————. *Social Behavior in Animals*. London: Methuen, 1953.

————. *The Study of Instinct*. London: Oxford University Press, 1951.

von Frisch, Karl. *Animal Architecture*. New York: Harcourt Brace Jovanovich, 1978.

―――. *Bees, Their Vision, Chemical Senses and Language*. London: Jonathan Cape, 1968.

―――. *The Dancing Bees*. London: Methuen, 1966.

―――. *Man and the Living World*. New York: Harvest, 1963.

Wickler, Wolfgang. *Mimicry in Plants and Animals*. London: Wiedenfeld and Nicholson, 1968.

Wilson, Edward O. *Sociobiology*. Cambridge, Massachusetts: Harvard University Press, 1974.

―――and Lumsden, Charles J. *Promethian Fire*. Cambridge, Massachusetts: Harvard University Press, 1974.

Wilson-Hoffenden, J. R. *The Red Men of Nigeria*. London: Frank Cass Ltd., 1967.

Wylie, Philip. *The Magic Animal*. New York: Doubleday, 1968.

Zipf, George K. *Human Behavior and the Principle of Least Effort: An Introduction to Human Ecology*. Boston: Addison-Wesley Press, 1949.

ERGONOMICS, HUMAN ENGINEERING, AND HUMAN FACTORS DESIGN

Alger, John R.M., and Hays, Carl V. *Creative Synthesis in Design*. New York: Prentice-Hall, 1962.

Anthropometry and Human Engineering. London: Butterworth's, 1955.

Asimov, Morris. *Introduction to Design*. New York: Prentice-Hall, 1962.

Banham, Reyner. *Theory and Design in the First Machine Age*. London: Architectural Press, 1960.

Buhl, Harold R. *Creative Engineering Design*. Ames, Iowa: Iowa State University Press, 1960.

Consumers' Union (ed.). *Passenger Car Design and Highway Safety*. Mount Vernon, New York: Consumers Union, 1963.

Diffrient, Niels; Tilley, Alvin; and Bardagjy, Joan. *Humanscale 1/2/3*. Cambridge: M.I.T. Press, 1974.

―――. *Humanscale 4/5/6*. Cambridge: M.I.T. Press, 1981.

―――. *Humanscale 7/8/9*. Cambridge: M.I.T. Press, 1981.

Glegg, Gordon L. *The Design of Design*. Cambridge: Cambridge University Press, 1969.

Goss, Charles Mayo (ed.). *Gray's Anatomy*. (27th ed.) Philadelphia: Lea & Febiger, 1959.

Jones, J. Christopher, and Thronley, D.G. *Conference on Design Methods*. New York: Permagon Press, 1963.

McCormick, Ernest Jr. *Human Engineering*. New York: McGraw-Hill, 1957.

Nader, Ralph. *Unsafe at any Speed*. New York: Grossman, 1965.

Schroeder, Francis. *Anatomy for Interior Designers*. (2d ed.) New York: Whitney Publications, 1948.

Starr, Martin Kenneth. *Product Design and Decision Theory*. New York: Prentice-Hall, 1963.

U.S. Navy (ed.). *Handbook of Human Engineering Data (Second Edition) U.S. Navy Office of Naval Research, Special Devices Center*, by NAVEXOS P-643, Report SDC 199-1-2 (NR-783-001. N6onr-199. TOI PDSCDCHE Project 20-6-1). Tufts University, Medford, Mass., n.d.

Woodson, Wesley, E. *Human Engineering Guide for Equipment Designers*. Berkeley: University of California Press, 1954.

GESTALT, PERCEPTION, CREATIVITY, AND RELATED FIELDS

Adorno, T.W. *et al. The Authoritarian Personality*. New York: Harper, 1950.

Allport, Floyd. *Theories of Perception and the Concept of Structure*. New York: Wiley, 1955.

Berne, Dr. Eric. *Games People Play*. London: Penguin, 1970.

———. *Principles of Group Treatment*. London: Oxford University Press, 1966.

———. *The Structure and Dynamics of Organizations and Groups*. New York: J.B. Lippincott, 1963.

———. *Transactional Analysis in Psychotherapy*. New York: Grove Press, 1961.

Bettelheim, Bruno. *The Empty Fortress: Infantile Autism and the Birth of the Self*. New York: Free Press, 1967.

———. *The Informed Heart: Autonomy in a Mass Age*. London: Paladin, 1970.

DeBono, Edward. *New Think*. New York: Basic Books, 1968.

Freud, Sigmund. *Beyond the Principle*. Translated by Strachey. London: Hogarth Press, 1961.

———. *Moses and Monotheism*. Translated by Jones. London: Hogarth Press, 1951.

———. *On Creativity and the Unconscious*. New York: Torchbooks, n.d.

———. *Totem and Taboo*. Translated by Brill. London: Routledge & Kegan Paul, 1950.

Fromm, Erich. *The Art of Loving*. London: Allen & Unwin, 1957.

———. *The Revolution of Hope*. New York: Harper, 1968.

Ghiselin, Brewster (ed.). *The Creative Process*. New York: Mentor Books.

Gibson, James J. *The Perception of the Visual World*. Boston: Houghton Mifflin, 1950.

Gordon, William J.J. *Synectics*. New York: Harper, 1961.

Gregory, R.L. *The Intelligent Eye*. London: Wiedenfield & Nicholson, 1970.

Gregory, R.L., and Gombrich, E. H. (eds.). *Illusion in Nature and Art*. London: Duckworth, 1973.

Grotjahn, Martin. *Beyond Laughter*. New York: McGraw-Hill, 1957.

Gunther, Bernard. *Sense Relaxation*. London: MacDonald, 1969.

Jung, C.G. *Archetypes and the Collective Unconscious*. 2 vols. London: Routledge & Kegan Paul, 1922.

———. *Psychology of the Unconscious*. London: Routledge & Kegan Paul, 1922.

Katz, David. *Gestalt Psychology*. New York: Ronald Press, 1950.

Koehler, Wolfgang. *Gestalt Psychology*. rev. ed. New York: Liveright, 1970.

Koestler, Arthur. *The Act of Creation*. London: Hutchinson, 1969.

Kofka, K. *Principles of Gestalt Psychology*. London: Routledge & Kegan Paul, 1935.

Korzybski, Alfred. *The Manhood of Humanity*. Chicago: Library of General Semantics, 1950.

———. *Science and Sanity*. Chicago: Library of General Semantics, 1948.

Kubie, Lawrence S. *The Neurotic Distortion of the Creative Process*. Lawrence, Kansas: The University of Kansas Press, 1958.

Leonard, George B. *Education and Ecstasy*. London: John Murray, 1970.

Lindner, Robert. *Must You Conform?* New York: Rinehart, 1956.

———. *Prescription for Rebellion*. New York: Rinehart, 1952.

Neumann, Erich. *The Archetypal World of Henry Moore*. London: Routledge & Kegan Paul, 1959.

Parnes, Sidney, and Harding, H. *A Source Book of Creative Thinking*. New York: Scribner, 1962.

Perls, F.S. *Ego, Hunger and Aggression*. New York: Random House, 1969.

———. *Gestalt Therapy Verbatim*. Edited by J. Stephens. Lafayette, California: Real People Press, 1969.

———. *In and Out of the Garbage Pail*. Lafayette, California: Real People Press, 1969.

Petermann, Bruno. *The Gestalt Theory and the Problem of Configuration*. New York: Harcourt, Brace, 1932.

Rawlins, Ian. *Aesthetics and the Gestalt*. London: Nelson, 1953.

Reich, Wilhelm. *The Cancer Biopathy*. New York: Orgone Institute Press, n.d.

———. *The Function of the Orgasm*. London: Panther, 1968.

———. *The Mass Psychology of Fascism*. New York: Orgone Institute Press, 1946.

———. *Selected Writings: An Introduction to Orgonomy*. New York: Vision Press, 1972.

———. *The Sexual Revolution*. New York: Vision Press, 1969.

Rolf, Dr. Ida P. *Structural Integration*. Santa Monica, California: Esalen Press, 1962.

Ruesch, Jurgen. *Communication*. New York: Norton, 1951.

———. *Disturbed Communication*. New York: Norton, 1957.

———. *Non-Verbal Communication*. Berkeley: University of California Press, 1956.

Shanks, Michael. *The Innovators*. Middlesex: Penguin, 1967.

Smith, Paul. *Creativity*. New York: Hastings House, 1959.

Spence, Lewis. *Myth and Ritual in Dance, Game and Rhyme*. London: Watts Ltd., 1947.

Vernon, Magdalen D. *A Further Study of Visual Perception*. Cambridge: Cambridge University Press, 1952.

Wertham, Fredric. *Dark Legend*. New York: Paperback Library, 1966.

———. *Seduction of the Innocent*. New York: Macmillan, 1954.

———. *The Show of Violence*. New York: Paperback Library, 1966.

———. *A Sign for Cain: An Exploration of Human Violence*. New York: Macmillan, 1966.

Wiener, Norbert. *Cybernetics*. New York: Wiley, 1948.

———. *The Human Use of Human Beings*. London: Sphere, 1969.

POPULAR CULTURE, SOCIAL PRESSURES, AND DESIGN

Adams, Brooks. *The Law of Civilization and Decay*. New York: Vintage, n.d.

Arensberg, Conrad M., and Niehoff, Arthur H. *Introducing Social Change*. Chicago: Aldine, 1964.

Boorstin, Daniel J. *The Image: A Guide to Pseudo-Events in America*. New York: Harper & Row, 1964.

Brightbill, Charles K. *The Challenge of Leisure*. New York: Spectrum, 1960.

Brown, James A.C. *Techniques of Persuasion*. Middlesex: Penguin, 1963.

Cassirer, Ernst. *An Essay on Man.* New Haven, Connecticut: Yale University Press, 1944.

———. *Language and Myth.* New York: Harper & Brothers, 1946.

———. *The Myth of the State.* London: Oxford University Press, 1946.

Galbraith, John Kenneth. *The Voice of the Poor.* Cambridge, Massachusetts: Harvard University Press, 1983.

Goodman, Paul. *Art and Social Nature.* New York: Arts and Science Press, 1946.

———. *Compulsory Mis-education.* Middlesex: Penguin, 1971.

———. *Drawing the Line.* New York: Random House, 1962.

———. *Growing Up Absurd.* London: Sphere, 1970.

———. *Like a Conquered Province: The Moral Ambiguity of America.* New York: Random House, 1967.

———. *Notes of a Neolithic Conservative.* New York: Random House, 1970.

———. *Utopian Essays and Practical Proposals.* New York: Vintage, 1964.

Gorer, Geoffrey. *Hot Strip Tease.* London: Graywells Press, 1934.

Gurko, Leo. *Heros, Highbrows and the Popular Mind.* New York: Charter Books, 1962.

Hofstadter, Richard. *Anti-intellectualism in American Life.* London: Jonathan Cape, 1964.

Hofstadter, Richard, and Wallace, Michael. *American Violence.* New York: Knopf, 1970.

Jacobs, Norman (ed.). *Culture for the Millions?* Boston: Beacon, 1964.

Joad, C.E.M. *Decadence.* London: Faber, 1948.

Kefauver, Estes. *In a Few Hands: Monopoly Power in America.* Middlesex: Penguin, 1966.

Kerr, Walter. *The Decline of Pleasure.* New York: Simon & Schuster, 1964.

Kronhausen, Dr. Phyllis, and Kronhausen, Dr. Eberhard. *Erotic Art.* London: W.H. Allen, 1971.

———. *The First International Exhibition of Erotic Art.* Catalogue. Copenhagen, Denmark: Uniprint, 1968.

———. *The Second International Exhibition of Erotic Art.* Catalogue. Copenhagen, Denmark: Uniprint, 1969.

Künen, James Simon. *The Strawberry Statement: Notes of a College Revolutionary.* New York: Random House, 1969.

Larrabee, Eric, and Meyersohn, Rolf (eds.). *Mass Leisure.* New York: Free Press, 1958.

Legman, Gershon. *The Fake Revolt.* New York: The Breaking Point Press, 1966.

————. *Love and Death: A Study in Censorship*. New York: The Breaking Point Press, 1949.

————(ed.). *Neurotica: 1948–1951*. New York: Hacker, 1963.

————. *Rationale of the Dirty Joke: An Analysis of Sexual Humour*. London: Panther, 1972.

Levy, Mervyn. *The Moons of Paradise: Reflections on the Female Breast in Art*. New York: Citadel, 1965.

MacDonald, Dwight. *Masscult and Midcult*. New York: Random House, 1961.

McLuhan, Marshall. *Culture is Our Business*. New York: McGraw-Hill, 1970.

————. *The Gutenberg Galaxy*. London: Routledge & Kegan Paul, 1962.

————. *The Mechanical Bride*. London: Routledge & Kegan Paul, 1967.

————. *Understanding Media*. London: Routledge & Kegan Paul, 1964.

————and Carpenter, Edmund. *Explorations in Communication*. London: Jonathan Cape, 1970.

————and Watson, Wilfred. *From Cliché to Archetype*. New York: Viking, 1970.

————and Fiore, Quentin. *The Medium Is the Message*. Middlesex: Penguin, 1971.

————and Parker, Harley. *Through the Vanishing Point*. New York: Harper & Row, 1968.

————and Papanek, Victor J. *Verbi-voco-Visual Explorations*. New York: Something Else Press, 1967.

————and Fiore, Quentin. *War and Peace in the Global Village*. New York: Bantam, 1968.

Mannheim, Karl. *Ideology and Utopia*. London: Routledge & Kegan Paul, 1966.

Mehling, Harold. *The Great Time Killer*. New York: World, 1962.

Mesthene, Emmanuel G. *Technological Change*. Cambridge, Massachusetts: Harvard University Press, 1970.

Molnar, Thomas. *The Decline of the Intellectual*. New York: Meridian, 1961.

Myrdal, Jan and Kessle, Gun. *Angkor: An Essay on Art and Imperialism*. London: Chatto & Windus, 1971.

O'Brian, Edward J. *The Dance of the Machines*. New York: Macaulay, 1929.

Packard, Vance. *The Hidden Persuaders*. Middlesex: Penguin, 1970.

————. *The Status Seekers*. Middlesex: Penguin, 1971.

————. *The Wastemakers*. Middlesex: Penguin, 1970.

Palm, Goran. *As Others See Us*. Indianapolis: Bobbs-Merrill, 1968.

Reich, Charles A. *The Greening of America*. Middlesex: Penguin, 1972.

Repo, Satu (ed.). *This Book is About Schools*. New York: Pantheon Books, 1970.

Riesman, David. *Faces in the Crowd*. New Haven, Connecticut: Yale University Press, 1952.

———. *Individualism Reconsidered*. New York: Free Press, 1954.

———. *The Lonely Crowd*. rev. ed. New Haven, Connecticut: Yale University Press, 1950.

Rosenberg, Bernard, and White, David M. *Mass Culture*. New York: Free Press, 1957.

Roszak, Theodore. *The Making of a Counter Culture*. London: Faber, 1971.

Ryan, Willima. *Blaming the Victim*. Orbach & Chambers, 1971.

Snow, C.P. *The Two Cultures: And a Second Look*. Cambridge: Cambridge University Press, 1963.

Thompson, Denys. *Discrimination and Popular Culture*. Middlesex: Penguin, 1970.

Toffler, Alvin. *The Culture Consumers*. New York: St. Martin's, 1964.

Veblen, Thorstein. *The Theory of the Leisure Class*. London: Allen & Unwin, 1971.

Wagner, Geoffrey. *Parade of Pleasure: A Study of Popular Iconography in the USA*. London: Derek & Verschoyle, 1954.

Walker, Edward L., and Heyns, Roger W. *An Anatomy for Conformity*. London: Brooks-Cole, 1968.

Warshow, Robert. *The Immediate Experience*. New York: Doubleday, 1963.

Young, Wayland. *Eros Denied: Sex in Western Society*. London: Corgi, 1968.

DESIGN AND OTHER CULTURES

Austin, Robert, and Ueda, Koichiro. *Bamboo*. Tokyo: Weatherhill, 1978.

Belo, Jane. *Traditional Balinese Culture*. New York: Columbia University Press, 1970.

Benrimo, Dorothy. *Camposantos*. Fort Worth, Texas: Amon Carter Museum, 1966.

Beurdeley, Jean-Michel. *Thai Forms*. Freiburg: Office du Livre, 1979.

Bhagwati, Jagdish. *The Economics of Underdeveloped Countries*. London: Weidenfeld & Nicholson, 1966.

Carpenter, Edmund. *Eskimo*. Toronto: University of Toronto Press, 1959.

Cavarrubias, Miguel. *Bali*. New York: Knopf, 1940.

———. *Mexico South*. New York: Knopf, 1946.

Cordry, Donald, and Cordry, Dorothy. *Mexican Indian Costumes*. Austin: University of Texas Press, 1968.

Cushing, Frank Hamilton. *Zuni Fetishes*. Flagstaff, Arizona: KC Editions, 1966.

de Bermudez, Graciela Samper (ed.). *Artesanias de Colombia*. Bogota: Litografia Arco, 1978.

Dennis, Wayne. *The Hopi Child*. New York: Science Editions, 1965.

DePoncins, Contran. *Eskimos*. New York: Hastings House, 1949.

Eliade, Mircea. *Shamanism: Archaic Techniques of Ecstasy*. London: Routledge & Kegan Paul, 1964.

Gardi, René. *African Crafts and Craftsmen*. New York: Van Nostrand Reinhold, 1969.

———. *Architecture sans Architecte*. Bern: Buchler & Co., 1974.

Glynn, Prudence. *Skin to Skin: Eroticism in Dress*. London: George Allen & Unwin, 1982.

Grass, Antonio. *Animales mitologicos*. Bogota: Litografia Arco, 1979.

———. *Diseno Precolumbina Colombiano*. Bogota: Museo del Oro, 1972.

Harris, Marvin. *Cultural Materialism*. New York: Random House, 1979.

Harrison, Paul. *Inside the Third World*. Middlesex: Penguin, 1979.

———. *The Third World Tomorrow*. Middlesex: Penguin, 1980.

Heineken, Ty, and Heineken, Kyoko. *Tansu: Traditional Japanese Cabinetry*. Tokyo: Weatherhill, 1981.

Herrigel, Eugen. *Zen in the Art of Archery*. London: Routledge & Kegan Paul, 1953.

Hiler, Hilaire. *From Nudity to Raiment*. London: W. & G. Foyle Ltd., 1930.

Hokusai. *One Hundred Views of Mount Fuji*. New York: Frederik Publications, 1958.

Kasba 64 Study Group. *Living on the Edge of the Sahara*. The Hague: Government Publishing Office, 1973.

Kwamiys, Takeji. *Katachi: Japanese Pattern and Design in Wood, Paper and Clay*. New York: Abrams, 1967.

Jenness, Diamond. *The People of the Twilight*. Chicago: University of Chicago Press, Phoenix, 1959.

Kakuzo, Okakura. *The Book of Tea*. Tokyo: Tuttle, 1963.

Kitzo, Harumichi. *Cha-No-Yu*. Tokyo: Shokokusha, 1953.

———. *Formation of Bamboo*. Tokyo: Shokokusha, 1958.

———. *Formation of Stone*. Tokyo: Shokokusha, 1958.

Kubler, George. *The Shape of Time*. New Haven, Connecticut: Yale University Press, 1962.

Lee, Sherman E. *The Genius of Japanese Design*. Tokyo: Kodansha, 1981.

Leppe, Markus. *Vaivaisukot*. Helsinki, Finland: Werner Soderstrom, 1967.

Liebow, Elliot. *Tally's Corner*. Boston: Little, Brown, 1967.

Linton, Ralph. *The Tree of Culture*. New York: Knopf, 1955.

Lip, Evelyn. *Chinese Geomancy*. Singapore: Times Books International, 1979.

Lopez, Oscar Hidalgo. *Manual de construcción con bambú*. Bogotá: National University of Colombia, 1981.

McPhee, Collin. *A House in Bali*. New York: John Day, 1946.

––––––. *Music in Bali*. New Haven, Connecticut: Yale University Press, 1966.

Malinowski, Bronislaw. *Magic, Science and Religion*. New York: Anchor, 1954.

––––––. *Sex and Repression in Savage Society*. London: Routledge & Kegan Paul, 1927.

Manker, Ernst. *People of Eight Seasons: The Story of the Lapps*. New York: Viking, 1964.

Mead, Margaret. *Coming of Age in Samoa*. Middlesex: Penguin, 1971.

––––––. *Cultural Patterns and Technological Change*. New York: Mentor, n.d.

––––––. *Growing up in New Guinea*. Middlesex: Penguin, 1970.

––––––. *Male and Female*. Middlesex: Penguin, 1970.

––––––. *Sex and Temperament*. New York: Morrow, 1935.

Meyer, Karl. *Teotihuacan*. Milan: Mondadori, 1973.

Michener, James A. *Hokusai Sketchbooks*. Tokyo: Tuttle, 1958.

Mookerjee, Ajit. *Tantra Art*. New Delhi, India: Kumar Gallery, 1967.

Mowat, Farley. *People of the Deer*. New York: Pyramid, 1968.

Nicolaisen, Johannes. *Ecology and Culture of the Pastoral Tuareg*. Copenhagen: National Museum of Copenhagen, 1963.

Oka, Hideyuki. *How to Wrap Five Eggs*. New York: Harper & Row, 1967.

Ortega y Gasset, José. *The Dehumanization of Art*. Translated by Weyl. Princeton, New Jersey: Princeton University Press, 1948.

Ortiz, Alfonso. *The Tewa World: Space, Time, Being, & Becoming in a Pueblo Society*. Chicago: University of Chicago Press, 1969.

Page, Susanne, and Page, Jake. *Hopi*. New York: Abrams, 1982.

Pianzola, Maurice. *Brasil Barroco*. Rio de Janeiro: Edicao Funarte, 1980.

Ramseyer, Urs. *The Art and Culture of Bali*. Oxford: Oxford University Press, 1977.

Reichard, Gladys A. *Navajo Religion: A Study of Symbolism.* Princeton, New Jersey: Bollingen Series, Princeton University Press, 1950.

Richards, Audrey I. *Hunger and Work in a Savage Tribe.* New York: Meridian, 1964.

Rodman, Selven. *Popular Artists of Brazil.* Old Greenwich: Devin-Adair, 1977.

Roediger, Virginia More. *Ceremonial Costumes of the Pueblo Indians.* Berkeley: University of California Press, 1961.

Rudofsky, Bernard. *Architecture without Architects.* New York: Museum of Modern Art, 1964.

──────. *Are Our Clothes Modern?* Chicago: Paul Theobald, 1949.

──────. *Behind the Picture Window.* New York: Oxford University Press, 1954.

──────. *The Kimono Mind.* London: Gollancz, 1965.

──────. *The Prodigious Builders.* New York: Harcourt Brace Jovanovich, 1977.

──────. *Streets for People.* New York: Doubleday, 1969.

──────. *The Unfashionable Human Body.* New York: Doubleday, 1971.

Saunders, E. Dale. *Mudra: A Study of Symbolic Gestures in Japanese Buddhist Sculpture.* London: Routledge & Kegan Paul, 1960.

Schafer, Edward H. *The Golden Peaches of Samarkand: A Study of T'ang Exotics.* Berkeley: University of California Press, 1963.

──────. *Tu Wan's Stone Catalogue of Cloudy Forest.* Berkeley: University of California Press, 1961.

Scully, Vincent. *Pueblo: Mountain, Village, Dance.* New York: Viking Press, 1975.

Sesoko, Tsune. *The I-Ro-Ha of Japan.* Tokyo: Cosmo Corporation, 1979.

Spencer, Robert F. *The North Alaskan Eskimo: A Study in Ecology and Society.* Washington, D.C.: Smithsonian Institution Press, 1969.

Spies, Walter, and de Zote, Beryl. *Dance and Drama in Bali.* London: Faber, 1938.

Suzuki, Daisetz T. *Zen and Japanese Culture.* London: Routledge & Kegan Paul, 1959.

Sze, Mai-Mai. *The Tao of Painting.* 2 vols. London: Routledge & Kegan Paul, 1957.

Tange, Kenzo, and Gropius, Walter. *Katsura: Tradition and Creation in Japanese Architecture.* New Haven, Connecticut: Yale University Press, 1960.

Tange, Kenzo, and Kawazoe, Noboru. *Ise: Prototype of Japanese Architecture.* Cambridge, Massachusetts: M.I.T. Press, 1965.

Thiry, Paul and Mary. *Eskimo Artifacts: Designed for Use.* Seattle: Superior Publishing Co., 1977.

Valladares, Clarival and do Prado. *Artesanato brasileiro.* Rio de Janeiro: Edição Funarte, 1980.

Vazquez, Ramirez. *Mexico: The National Museum of Anthropology.* Lausanne: Helvetica Press, 1968.

Viezzer, Moema. *Si me permiten hablar . . . .* Bolivia: underground pamphlet, 1977.

Wagley, Charles. *Welcome of Tears: The Tapirape Indians of Central Brazil.* New York: Oxford University Press, 1977.

Watts, Alan R. *Beat Zen, Square Zen and Zen.* San Francisco: City Lights, 1959.

————. *The Joyous Cosmology.* New York: Pantheon Books, 1962.

————. *Nature, Man and Woman.* New York: Pantheon Books, 1958.

Wichmann, Siegfried. *Japonisme.* New York: Harmony Books, 1981.

Wyman, Leland C. (ed.). *Beautyway: A Navajo Ceremonial.* Princeton, New Jersey: Bollingen Series, Princeton University Press, 1957.

Yee, Chiang. *The Chinese Eye.* New York: Norton, 1950.

————. *Chinese Calligraphy.* London: Methuen, 1954.

Yoshida, Mitsukuni, et al. *Japan Style.* Tokyo: Kondansha, 1981.

PERSONAL STATEMENTS BY DESIGNERS AND OTHERS

Åkerman, Nordal. *Kan Vi Krympa Sverige?* Stockholm: Rabén & Sjögren, 1980.

Brecht, Bertolt. *Gesammelte Werke.* Frankfurt, Germany: Suhrkamp Verlag, 1967.

Cleaver, Eldridge. *Soul on Ice.* London: Jonathan Cape, 1969.

————. *Eldridge Cleaver: Post-Prison Writings and Speeches.* London: Jonathan Cape, 1969.

Debray, Régis. *Revolution in the Revolution.* Middlesex: Penguin, 1968.

Deshusses, Jerome. *The Eighth Night of Creation.* New York: The Dial Press, 1982.

Dow, Alden B. *Reflections.* Midland, Michigan: Northwood Institute, 1970.

Fanon, Frantz. *The Wretched of the Earth.* Middlesex: Penguin, 1967.

Fischer, Ernst. *The Necessity of Art: A Marxist Approach.* Middlesex: Pelican, 1964.

Freire, Paulo. *Cultural Action for Freedom.* Middlesex: Penguin, 1972.

————. *Educacão como Prática da Liberdade*. São Paulo: P. P. C., 1967.
————. *Pedagogy of the Oppressed*. Middlesex: Penguin, 1972.
Frisch, Bruno. *Die Vierte Welt: Modell einer neuen Wirklichkeit*. Stuttgart: DVA, 1970.
Gardner, John. *On Moral Fiction*. New York: Basic Books, 1977.
Gonzales, Xavier. *Notes About Painting*. New York: World, 1955.
Greene, Herb. *Mind & Image: An Essay on Art and Architecture*. Lexington: University Press of Kentucky, 1976.
Greenough, Horatio. *Form and Function*. Washington, D.C.: privately published, 1811.
Guevara, Ché. *Bolivian Diary*. London: Cape & Lorrimer, 1968.
————. *Guerrilla Warfare*. Middlesex: Penguin, 1969.
Harris, Marvin. *Cultural Materialism: The Struggle for a Science of Culture*. New York: Random House, 1979.
Kennedy, Robert F. *To Seek a Newer World*. London: Michael Joseph, 1968.
Koestler, Arthur. *Arrow in the Blue*. London: Hutchinson, 1969.
————. *Dialogue with Death*. London: Hutchinson, 1966.
————. *The Invisible Writing*. London: Hutchinson, 1969.
————. *Scum of the Earth*. London: Hutchinson, 1968.
Laing, R.D. *The Politics of Experience*. Middlesex: Penguin, 1970.
Mailer, Norman. *The Armies of the Night*. Middlesex: Penguin, 1970.
————. *Miami and the Siege of Chicago*. Middlesex: Penguin, 1971.
Mao Tse-tung. *Collected Writings*. 5 vols. Peking: Foreign Language Press, 1964.
————. *On Art and Literature*. Peking: Foreign Language Press, 1954.
————. *On Contradiction*. Peking: Foreign Language Press.
————. *On the Correct Handling of Contradictions among the People*. Peking: Foreign Language Press, 1957.
Marcuse, Herbert. *Das Ende der Utopie*. Berlin: Maikowski, 1967.
————. *One-Dimensional Man*. London: Routledge & Kegan Paul, 1964.
Marin, John. *The Collected Letters of John Marin*. New York: Abelard-Schuman, n.d.
Miller, Henry. *My Bike and Other Friends*. Santa Barbara, California: Capra Press, 1978.
Myrdal, Jan. *Confessions of a Disloyal European*. London: Chatto & Windus, 1968.
————. *Report from a Chinese Village*. Middlesex: Penguin, 1967.
————. *Samtida*. Stockholm: Norstedt, 1967.
Perlman, Janice E. *The Myth of Marginality: Urban Poverty and Politics in Rio de Janeiro*. Berkeley: University of California Press, 1976.

Richards, M.C. *Centering: In Pottery, Poetry and the Person*. Middletown, Connecticut: Wesleyan University Press, 1964.

Saarinen, Eliel. *Search for Form*. Detroit: Kennikat Press, 1970.

Safdie, Moshe. *Beyond Habitat*. Cambridge, Massachusetts: M.I.T. Press, 1970.

————. *For Everyone a Garden*. Cambridge, Massachusetts: M.I.T. Press, 1974.

————. *Form and Purpose*. Boston: Houghton Mifflin Co., 1982.

St. Exupéry, Antoine de. *Bekenntnis einer Freundschaft*. Düsseldorf, Germany: Karl Rauch, 1955.

————. *Carnets*. Paris: Gallimard, 1953.

————. *Flight to Arras*. Middlesex: Penguin, 1967.

————. *Freiden Oder Krieg?* Düsseldorf, Germany: Karl Rauch, 1957.

————. *Gebete der Einsamkeit*. Düsseldorf, Germany: Karl Rauch, 1956.

————. *Lettres a l'amie inventee*. Paris: Plon, 1953.

————. *Lettres a sa mere*. Paris: Gallimard, 1955.

————. *Lettres de jeunesse*. Paris: Gallimard, 1953.

————. *The Little Prince*. Middlesex: Penguin, 1970.

————. *Night Flight*. Middlesex: Penguin, 1939.

————. *A Sense of Life*. New York: Funk & Wagnalls, 1965.

————. *Wind, Sand and Stars*. Middlesex: Penguin, 1971.

————. *The Wisdom of the Sands*. New York: Harcourt, Brace, 1952.

Servan-Schreiber, Jean Jacques. *The American Challenge*. London: Hamish Hamilton, 1968.

————. *The World Challenge*. New York: Simon & Schuster, 1981.

Shahn, Ben. *The Shape of Content*. Cambridge, Massachusetts: Harvard University Press, 1957.

Soleri, Paolo. *Arcology: The City in the Image of Man*. Cambridge, Massachusetts: M.I.T. Press, 1970.

Sontag, Susan. *On Photography*. New York: Farrar, Straus and Giroux, 1977.

Sullivan, Louis H. *The Autobiography of an Idea*. Chicago: Peter Smith, 1924.

————. *Kindergarten Chats*. Chicago: Scarab Fraternity, 1934.

Thoreau, Henry David. *Walden* and *Essay on Civil Disobedience*. London: Dent.

Van Gogh, Vincent. *The Complete Letters of Vincent Van Gogh in Three Volumes*. London: Thames & Hudson, 1958.

Weiss, Peter. *Notizen zum Kulterellen Leben in der Demokratischen Republik Viet Nam*. Frankfurt, Germany: Suhrkamp Verlag, 1968.

Wills, Philip. *Free as a Bird*. London: John Murray, 1973.
_____. *On Being a Bird*. London: David & Charles, 1977.
_____. *Where No Birds Fly*. London: Newnes, 1961.
Wright, Frank Lloyd. *Autobiography*. New York: Duel, Sloane & Pearce, 1943.
_____. *The Disappearing City*. New York: William Farquhar Payson, 1932.
_____. *The Living City*. New York: Horizon, 1958.
_____. *The New Frontier: Broadacre City*. Springreen, Wisconsin: Taliesin Fellowship Publication, vol. 1, no. 1, October, 1940.
_____. *A Testament*. New York: Horizon, 1957.
_____. *When Democracy Builds*. Chicago: University of Chicago Press, 1945.
Wright, Olgivanna Lloyd. *The Shining Brow*. New York: Horizon, 1958.
Yevtushenko, Yevgeny. *Collected Poems*. London: Calder & Boyars, 1969.
_____. *A Precocious Autobiography*. New York: Dutton, 1963.

THE BACKGROUND OF DESIGN

Arnheim, Rudolf. *Art and Visual Perception*. London: Faber, 1967.
_____. *Film as Art*. London: Faber, 1967.
_____. *Toward A Psychology of Art*. London: Faber, 1967.
Bayer, Herbert, and Gropius, Walter. *Bauhaus 1919–1928*. Boston: Branford, 1952.
Berenson, Bernard. *Aesthetics and History*. New York: Pantheon Books, 1948.
Biederman, Charles. *Art as the Evolution of Visual Knowledge*. Red Wing, Minnesota: Charles Biederman, 1948.
Boas, Franz. *Primitive Art*. New York: Dover, 1955.
Burckhardt, Lucius. *Der Werkbund*. Stuttgart: DVA, 1978.
Conrads, Ulrich, and Sperlich, Hans G. *The Architecture of Fantasy*. New York: Praeger, 1962.
Danz, Louis. *Dynamic Dissonance in Nature and the Arts*. New York: Longmans Green, 1952.
_____. *It is Still the Morning*. New York: Morrow, 1943.
_____. *Personal Revolution and Picasso*. New York: Longmans Green, 1941.
_____. *The Psychologist Looks at Art*. New York: Longmans Green, 1937.
_____. *Zarathustra Jr.*. New York: Brentano, 1934.
Dorfles, Gillo. *Kitsch: An Anthology of Bad Taste*. London: Studio Vista, 1970.

Ehrenzweig, Anton. *The Hidden Order of Art*. London: Paladin, 1970.

Feldman, Edmund B. (ed.). *Art in American Higher Institutions*. Washington, D.C.: The National Art Education Association, 1970.

Friedmann, Herbert. *The Symbolic Goldfinch: Its History and Significance in European Devotional Art*. Princeton, New Jersey: Bollingen Series, Princeton University Press, 1946.

Gamow, George. *One, Two, Three . . . Infinity*. rev. ed. New York: Viking, 1961.

Gerstner, Karl. *Kalte Kunst?* Basel, Switzerland: Arthur Niggli, 1957.

Gilson, Étienne. *Painting and Reality*. Princeton, New Jersey: Bollingen Series, Princeton University Press, 1957.

Gombrich, E.H. *Art and Illusion*. Oxford: Phaidon, 1962.

———. *Ideals and Idols*. New York: E. P. Dutton, 1979.

———. *The Image and the Eye*. Ithaca: Cornell University Press, 1979.

———. *Meditations on a Hobbyhorse*. Oxford: Phaidon, 1963.

———. *The Sense of Order*. Ithaca: Cornell University Press, 1979.

Graves, Robert. *The White Goddess*. London: Faber, 1952.

Hatterer, Lawrence J. *The Artist in Society: Problems and Treatment of the Creative Personality*. New York: Grove Press, 1965.

Hauser, Arnold. *The Social History of Art*. 4 vols. London: Routledge & Kegan Paul, 1951.

Hinz, Berthold. *Art in the Third Reich*. New York: Pantheon, 1979.

Hogben, Lancelot. *From Cave Painting to Comic Strip*. New York: Chanticleer Press, 1949.

Hon-En Historia. Catalogue. Stockholm: Moderna Museet, 1967.

Huizinga, Johan. *Homo Ludens: A Study of the Play-element in Human Culture*. London: Paladin, 1970.

Hulten, K.G. Pontus. *The Machine as Seen at the End of the Mechanical Age*. New York: Museum of Modern Art, 1968.

Illich, Ivan. *Energy and Equity*. London: Calder & Boyars, 1974.

———. *Tools for Conviviality*. London: Calder & Boyars, 1973.

Keats, John. *The Insolent Chariots*. New York: Crest Books, n.d.

Klingender, Francis D. *Art and the Industrial Revolution*. London: Paladin, 1972.

Kracauer, Siegfried. *From Caligari to Hitler*. Princeton, New Jersey: Princeton University Press, 1947.

Kranz, Kurt. *Variationen über ein geometrisches Thema*. Munich, Germany: Prestel, 1956.

Langer, Susanne K. *Feeling and Form*. London: Routledge & Kegan Paul, 1953.

_____. *Philosophy in a New Key*. New York: Scribner, 1942.

_____. *Problems of Art*. New York: Scribner, 1957.

Le Corbusier. *The Modulor*. London: Faber, 1954.

_____. *Modulor 2*. London: Faber, 1958.

Lethaby, W.R. *Architecture, Nature and Magic*. New York: George Braziller, 1956.

Malraux, André. *The Metamorphosis of the Gods*. New York: Doubleday, 1960.

_____. *The Voices of Silence*. New York: Doubleday, 1952.

Maritain, Jacques. *Creative Intuition in Art and Poetry*. Princeton, New Jersey: Bollingen Series, Princeton University Press, 1953.

Middleton, Michael. *Group Practice in Design*. London: Architectural Press, 1968.

Moholy-Nagy, Sibyl. *Native Genius in Anonymous Architecture*. New York: Horizon, 1957.

Neumann, Erich. *The Great Mother: An Analysis of the Archetype*. London: Routledge & Kegan Paul, 1955.

Neutra, Richard. *Survival through Design*. New York: Oxford University Press, 1954.

Nielsen, Vladimir. *The Cinema as Graphic Art*. New York: Hill & Wang, 1959.

Okaley, Kenneth P. *Man the Tool-maker*. London: British Museum, 1963.

Ozenfant, Amedee. *Foundations of Modern Art*. New York: Dover, 1952.

Panofsky, Erwin. *Gothic Architecture and Scholasticism*. Latrobe, Pennsylvania: Archabbey Press, 1951.

_____. *Meaning in the Visual Arts*. Middlesex: Penguin, 1970.

Rapoport, Amos. *House, Form and Culture*. Englewood Cliffs, New Jersey: Prentice-Hall, 1969.

Read, Sir Herbert. *The Grass Roots of Art*. New York: Wittenborn, 1955.

_____. *Icon and Idea?* London: Faber, 1955.

_____. *The Philosophy of Modern Art*. London: Faber, 1965.

Rosenberg, Harold. *The Tradition of the New*. London: Paladin, 1970.

Sahlins, Marshall. *Stone Age Economics*. London: Tavistock Publications, 1974.

Scheidig, Walther. *Crafts of the Weimar Bauhaus*. London: Studio Vista, 1967.

Sempter, Gottfried. *Wissenschaft, Industrie und Kunst*. Mainz, Germany: Florian Kupferberg, 1966.

Singer, Charles (ed.). *A History of Technology*. 5 vols. Oxford University Press, 1954–1958.

Snaith, William. *The Irresponsible Arts*. New York: Atheneum, 1964.

Thompson, E. P. *William Morris: Romantic to Revolutionary*. New York: Pantheon, 1977.

Von Neumann. *Game Theory*. Cambridge, Massachusetts: M.I.T. Press, 1953.

Willett, John. *Art & Politics in the Weimar Period*. New York: Pantheon, 1978.

Wingler, Hans M. *The Bauhaus*. Cambridge, Massachusetts: M.I.T. Press, 1969.

Youngblood, Gene. *The Expanded Cinema*. London: Studio Vista, 1971.

THE PRACTICE OF DESIGN AND ITS PHILOSOPHY

Albers, Anni. *On Designing*. New Haven, Connecticut: Pellango Press, 1959.

Anderson, Donald M. *Elements of Design*. New York: Holt, Rinehart & Winston, 1961.

Art Directors' Club of New York. *Symbology*. New York: Hastings House, 1960.

———. *Visual Communication: International*. New York: Hastings House, 1961.

Baker, Stephen. *Visual Persuasion*. New York: McGraw-Hill, 1961.

Bayer, Herbert. *Visual Communication, Architecture, Painting*. New York: Reinhold, 1967.

Bill, Max. *Form*. Basel, Switzerland: Karl Werner, 1952. Text in German, English, French.

Doxiadis, Constantinos. *Architecture in Transition*. London: Hutchinson, 1965.

———. *Between Dystopia and Utopia*. London: Faber, 1966.

———. *Ekistics*. London: Hutchinson, 1968.

Gropius, Walter. *Scope of Total Architecture*. New York: Harper, 1955.

Itten, Johannes. *The Art of Color*. New York: Reinhold, 1961.

———. *Design and Form*. New York: Reinhold, 1963.

Kandinsky, Wassily. *On the Spiritual in Art*. New York: Wittenborn, 1948.

———. *Point to Line to Plane*. New York: Guggenheim Museum, 1947.

Kepes, Gyorgy. *Language of Vision*. Chicago: Paul Theobald, 1949.

———. *The New Landscape in Art and Science*. Chicago: Paul Theobald, 1956.

———. *Vision-Value Series*. Vol. 1, *Education of Vision*. Vol. 2, *Structure in Art and Science*. Vol. 3, *The Nature and Art of*

Motion. Vol. 4, *Module Proportion Symmetry Rhythm.* Vol. 5, *The Man-made Object.* Vol. 6, *Sign, Image, Symbol.* New York: George Braziller, 1966.

_____(ed.). *The Visual Arts Today.* Middletown, Connecticut: Wesleyan University Press, 1960.

Klee, Paul. *Pedagogical Sketch Book.* London: Faber, 1968.

_____. *The Thinking Eye.* London: Lund Humphries, 1961.

Kranz, Stewart, and Fisher, Robert. *The Design Continuum.* New York: Reinhold, 1966.

Kuebler, George. *The Shape of Time.* New York: Schocken, 1967.

Kumar, Satish (ed.). *The Schumacher Lectures.* London: Blond & Briggs, 1980.

Larrabee, Eric, and Vignelli, Massimo. *Knoll Design.* New York: Abrams, 1981.

Lethaby, W. R. *A Continuing Presence: Essays from Form in Civilization.* Manchester, England: British Thornton Ltd., 1982.

_____. *Architecture, Mysticism and Myth.* New York: George Braziller, 1975.

_____. *Architecture, Nature & Magic.* New York: George Braziller, 1956.

Lovins, Amory B. *Soft Energy Paths.* New York: Harper & Row, 1979.

Malevich, Kasimir. *The Non-objective World.* Chicago: Paul Theobald, 1959.

Mayall, W. A. *Principles in Design.* New York: Van Nostrand Reinhold, 1979.

Moholy-Nagy, László. *The New Vision.* 4th ed. New York: Wittenborn, 1947.

_____. *Telehor.* Bratislava, Czechoslovakia: 1968.

_____. *Vision in Motion.* Chicago: Paul Theobald, 1947.

Moholy-Nagy, Sibyl. *Moholy-Nagy: Experiment in Totality.* New York: Harper, 1950.

Mondrian, Piet. *Plastic and Pure Plastic Art.* New York: Wittenborn, 1947.

Mundt, Ernest. *Art, Form & Civilization.* Berkeley: University of California Press, 1952.

Nelson, George. *How to See.* Boston: Little, Brown, 1977.

_____. *On Design.* New York: Watson-Guptill, 1979.

_____. *Problems of Design.* New York: Whitney Publications, 1957.

Newton, Norman T. *An Approach to Design.* Boston: Addison-Wesley Press, 1951.

Niece, Robert C. *Art: An Approach.* Dubuque, Iowa: William C. Brown & Co., 1959.

Papanek, Victor. *"Big Character" Poster No. 1: Work Chart for De-*

signers, Charlottenlund, Denmark: Finn Sloth Publications, 1973.

———. *Design For Human Scale*. New York: Van Nostrand Reinhold, 1983.

———. "Die Aussicht von Heute" [The view from today] in *Design ist Unsichtbar (Design is Invisible)*. Vienna, Austria: Löcker Verlag, 1981.

———. "Kymmenen Ympäristöä" [Environments for discovery]. *Ornamo* magazine (bilingual). Helsinki, Finland: February, 1970.

———. "Socio-Environmental Consequences of Design." In *Health & Industrial Growth*. Holland: Associated Scientific Publishers, 1975. (CIBA Symposium XXII).

———. "Areas of Attack for Responsible Design." In *Man-made Futures*. London: Hutchinson, 1974.

———. "Friendship First, Competition Second!" *Casabella* (Milan), December 1974.

———. "Project Batta Köya." *Industrial Design*, July-August 1975.

———. "On Resolving Contradictions Between Theory and Practice." *Mobilia* (Denmark), July-August 1974.

Papanek, Victor, and Hennessey, James. *How Things Don't Work*. New York: Pantheon Books, 1977.

———. *Nomadic Furniture*. New York: Pantheon, 1973.

———. *Nomadic Furniture 2*. New York: Pantheon, 1974.

Pentagram. *Living by Design*. London: Lund Humphries. 1978.

———. *Pentagram*. London: Lund Humphries, 1972.

Pile, John F. *Design*. Amherst: University of Massachusetts Press, 1979.

Potter, Norman. *What is a Designer: Things, Places, Messages*. London: Hyphen Press, 1980.

Pye, David. *The Nature & Aesthetics of Design*. New York: Van Nostrand Reinhold, 1978.

Rand, Paul. *Thoughts on Design*. London: Studio Vista, 1970.

Schumacher, E. F. *Good Work*. New York: Harper & Row, 1979.

Vignelli, Massimo, and Vignelli, Lella. *Design: Vignelli*. New York: Rizzoli, 1981.

INDUSTRIAL AND PRODUCT DESIGN

Aluminum Company of America. *Design Forecast No. 1 & No. 2*. Pittsburgh: Aluminum Company of America, 1959, 1960.

Beresford, Evans J. *Form in Engineering Design*. Oxford: Clarendon Press, 1954.

Black, Misha. *Australian Papers*. Melbourne: Trevor Wilson, 1970.

Braun-Feldweg, Wilhelm. *Industrial Design Heute*. Hamburg, Germany: Rowohlt, 1966.

———. *Normen und Formen Industrieller Produktion*. Ravensburg, Germany: Otto Maier, 1954.

Chase, Herbert. *Handbook on Designing for Quantity Production*. New York: McGraw-Hill, 1950.

The Design Collection: Selected Objects. New York: Museum of Modern Art, 1970.

Doblin, Jay. *One Hundred Great Product Designs*. New York: Reinhold, 1969.

Drexler, Arthur. *Introduction to Twentieth Century Design*. New York: Museum of Modern Art, 1959.

———. *The Package*. New York: Museum of Modern Art, 1959.

Dreyfuss, Henry. *Designing for People*. New York: Simon & Schuster, 1951.

Eksell, Olle. *Design = Ekonomi*. Stockholm: Bonniers, 1964.

Ekuan, Kenji. *Industrial Design Lectures*. Melbourne: Trevor Wilson, 1973.

Farr, Michael. *Design in British Industry*. Cambridge: Cambridge University Press, 1955.

Friedman, William. *Twentieth Century Design: U.S.A.* Buffalo, N.Y.: Albright Art Gallery, 1959.

Functie en Vorm: Industrial Design in the Netherlands. Bussum, Holland: Moussault's Uitgeverij, 1956.

Gestaltende Industrieform in Deutschland. Düsseldorf, Germany: Econ, 1954.

Gloag, John. *Self Training for Industrial Designers*. London: Allen & Unwin, 1947.

Hiesinger, Cathryn B., and Marcus, George H. (eds.). *Design Since 1945*. Philadelphia: Museum of Art, 1983.

Holland, Laurence B. (ed.). *Who Designs America?* New York: Anchor, 1966.

Jacobson, Egbert. *Basic Color*. Chicago: Paul Theobald, 1948.

Johnson, Philip. *Machine Art*. New York: Museum of Modern Art, 1934.

Latham, Richard. *Industrial Design Lectures*. Melbourne: Trevor Wilson, 1972.

Lippincott, J. Gordon. *Design for Business*. Chicago: Paul Theobald, 1947.

Loewy, Raymond. *Never Leave Well Enough Alone*. New York: Simon & Schuster, 1950.

Lucie-Smith, Edward. *A History of Industrial Design*. New York: Van Nostrand Reinhold, 1983.

Noyes, Eliot F. *Organic Design*. New York: Museum of Modern Art,
      1941.
Pevsner, Nikolaus. *An Enquiry into Industrial Art in England*. Cam-
      bridge: Cambridge University Press, 1937.
————. *Pioneers of Modern Design*. Middlesex: Penguin, 1970.
Read, Sir Herbert. *Art in Industry*. London: Faber, 1966.
Teague, Walter Dorwin. *Design this Day*. New York: Harcourt,
      Brace, 1940.
Van Doren, Harold. *Industrial Design*. 2d ed. New York: McGraw-
      Hill, 1954.
Wallance, Don. *Shaping America's Products*. New York: Reinhold,
      1956.
Yran, Knut. . . . *A Joy Forever*. Melbourne: IDIA, 1980.
Zanuso, Marco. *Industrial Design Lectures*. Melbourne: Trevor Wil-
      son, 1971.

The following magazines were also consulted:

Architectura Cuba (Cuba)
Arkkitehti-Lehti (Finland)
Aspen (U.S.A.)
China Life (Peking)
Craft Horizons (U.S.A.)
Der Spiegel (Germany)
Design (England)
Design & Environment (U.S.A.)
Design in Australia (Australia)
Design Quarterly (U.S.A.)
Design Studies (England)
Designcourse (U.S.A.)
Designer (England)
Designscape (New Zealand)
Domus (Italy)
Dot Zero (U.S.A.)
Draken (Sweden)
Environment (U.S.A.)
Form (Sweden)
form (Germany)
Form & Zweck (German Democratic Republic)
Graphis (Switzerland)
IDEA (Japan)
IDSA Journal (U.S.A.)
Industrial Design (U.S.A.)
Journal of Creative Behavior (U.S.A.)

Kaiser Aluminum News (U.S.A.)
Kenchiko Bunko (Japan)
Mimar: Architecture in Development (Singapore)
Mobilia (Denmark)
Modo (Italy)
Newsweek (U.S.A.)
Ornamo (Finland)
Ottagono (Italy)
Start (Yugoslavia)
Stile Industria (Italy)
Sweden NOW (Sweden)
Time (U.S.A.)
Ulm (Germany)
&/*sdo* (Helsinki and Stockholm)

News items from the following sources were also used as references:

All Things Considered (U.S.A.)
BBC (England)
CBC (Canada)
NBC (U.S.A.)
CBS (U.S.A.)
ABC (U.S.A.)
ABC (Australia)
PBS (U.S.A.)
Associated Press
United Press International

Index